Living in Allah's Presence
Aspects of Islamic Spirituality

Living in Allah's Presence

Aspects of Islamic Spirituality

Abdur Rashid Siddiqui

The Islamic Foundation

Published by
THE ISLAMIC FOUNDATION
Markfield Conference Centre, Ratby Lane,
Markfield, Leicestershire LE67 9SY, United Kingdom
E-mail: publications@islamic-foundation.com
Web site: www.islamic-foundation.com

Quran House, P.O. Box 30611, Nairobi, Kenya

P.M.B. 3193, Kano, Nigeria

Distributed by
Kube Publishing Ltd.,
Tel: +44(0)1530 249230, Fax: +44(0)1530 249656
Email: info@kubepublishing.com

A Cataloguing-in-Publication Data record for this Book is available from the British Library

ISBN 978–0–86037–576–0 *paperback*

Typesetting by: N.A. Qaddoura
Cover design by: Nasir Cadir

بسم الله الرحمن الرحيم

Contents

Transliteration Table vii
Foreword (by Khurshid Ahmad) viii
Introduction xiv

1. Friday Prayers (*Ṣalāt al-Jumuʿah*) 1
2. Heart (*Qalb*) 9
3. Intention (*Niyyah*) 17
4. Sincerity (*Ikhlās*) 24
5. God-consciousness (*Taqwā*) 31
6. Perseverance (*Ṣabr*) 39
7. Thankfulness (*Shukr*) 47
8. Wisdom (*Ḥikmah*) 54
9. Reflection (*Tafakkur*) 60
10. Trust (*Amānah*) 67
11. Truthfulness (*Ṣidq*) 74
12. Reliance (*Tawakkul*) 81
13. Certainty (*Yaqīn*) 89
14. Supplication (*Duʿā'*) 95
15. Humility in Prayers (*Khushūʿ fī al-Ṣalāh*) 103
16. Fear (*Khawf*) 110
17. Tranquility and Calmness (*Sakīnah wa Iṭmi'nān*) 118
18. Humility (*Tawāḍuʿ*) 125
19. Morality (*Akhlāq*) 132
20. Good Nature (*Ḥusn al-Khulq*) 138
21. Modesty (*Ḥayā'*) 146

22. Steadfastness (*Istiqāmah*) 153
23. Self-Scrutiny (*Muḥasābah*) 160
24. Asceticism (*Zuhd*) 167
25. Commanding Good and Forbidding Evil (*Al-Amr bi al-Maʿrūf wa al-Nahy ʿan al-Munkar*) 175

Appendix 183
First *Khuṭbah* 183
Second *Khuṭbah* 185

Transliteration Table

Consonants. Arabic

initial, unexpressed, medial and final: ء ’

ا	a	د	d	ض	ḍ	ك	k
ب	b	ذ	dh	ط	ṭ	ل	l
ت	t	ر	r	ظ	ẓ	م	m
ث	th	ز	z	ع	‘	ن	n
ج	j	س	s	غ	gh	هـ	h
ح	ḥ	ش	sh	ف	f	و	w
خ	kh	ص	ṣ	ق	q	ي	y

Vowels, diphthongs, etc.

short:	ـَ	a	ـِ	i	ـُ	u
long:	ـَا	ā	ـُو	ū	ـِي	ī
diphthongs:			ـَوْ	aw		
			ـَيْ	ay		

Foreword

Looking into the long vista of history, one finds two very distinct approaches to life, society, and destiny, without ignoring the fact that within these major streams there are serious and even wide-ranging variations as well as a number of commonalties and overlaps. The dominant characteristic of the first approach is that it is faith-based, rooted in a worldview centered on God, the Creator, the Master, the Sustainer, the Sovereign and the Final Authority. The other looks upon man as self-sufficient, or, at best, as a social animal, engaged in the glorification of self-interest and material and physical fulfillment, seen as the be-all and end-all of existence.

The most powerful and all-embracing expression of this second approach has taken place in the post-Enlightenment era of European and American history and can justifiably be described as the dominant secular paradigm of contemporary Western civilization. The Islamic approach to life, culture and civilization blossoms into an altogether different paradigm. *Tawḥīd* (Oneness of God) is the foundation on which this approach is based. While physical and material dimensions of life are affirmed and acknowledged to the fullest extent, the distinctive character of this approach is its God-centredness and its assigning a higher and decisive role to the spiritual and moral dimensions in understanding the reality of existence, physical and human, and, consequently, the origin, role, mission and destiny of man. Human existence is characterized by an integrated vision of two dimensions, the terrestrial and the metaphysical, the material and the moral and spiritual. The Islamic narrative of the creation of man, his position and role in life and career on earth, and his mission and destiny are clearly and beautifully stated in the Qur'ān, the real and ultimate source of guidance (*hidāyah*):

> *Recall when your Lord said to the angels: 'I will indeed bring into living a human being out of dry ringing clay wrought from black mud. When I have completed shaping him and have breathed into him of My Spirit then fall you down before him in prostration.'*
>
> (al-Ḥijr 15: 28-29)

The purpose was not just one more addition to the rich multitudes of creation, but one who was to be God's representative and vicegerent (*khalīfah*) to fulfill a mission assigned to him to be discharged in the light of the guidance (*hidāyah*) revealed to him concurrently with the beginning of his mission on the Earth:

> *Just think when your Lord said to the angels: 'Lo! I am about to place a vicegerent on earth', they said: 'Will You place on it one who will spread mischief and shed blood while we celebrate Your Glory and extol Your Holiness.' Then Allah taught Adam the names of all things and presented them to the angels and said: 'If you are right (that the appointment of a vicegerent will cause mischief) then tell Me the names of these things.' They said, 'Glory to You! We have no knowledge except what You taught us. You, only You are All-Knowing, All-Wise.' Then Allah said to Adam: 'Tell them the names of these things.' And when he had told them the names of all things, Allah said: 'Did I not say to you that I know everything about the heavens and the earth which are beyond your range of knowledge and I know all that you disclose and also all that you hide.'*
>
> (al-Baqarah 2: 30-32)

Allah not only created man from clay (the material and physical dimension) but also breathed into him from His Spirit (the spiritual and moral dimension) which defines the distinctive character of humans. Man has been endowed with intellect, knowledge and discretion and is also blessed with guidance so as to understand the real meaning and purpose of life and make his choice in the light of the guidance so provided to enable him to successfully perform the mission assigned to all human beings, men and women, from Adam and Eve to eternity. The path to success and the errands and pitfalls that would lead to failure have been clearly identified. The journey on earth did not begin in darkness, but with the light of revealed guidance:

> *And guidance shall come to you from Me: then, whosoever will follow My guidance need have no fear, nor shall they grieve. But those who refuse to accept this (guidance) and reject Our Signs as false are destined for Fire where they shall abide forever.*
>
> (al-Baqarah 2: 38)

Belief in and adherence to the ideals, values, norms, rules and regulations so laid down guarantee for all human beings — individuals, communities, and nations — good life on the earth and success and salvation in the life after death. Moral excellence, establishment of justice at all levels of human life and existence, and living a life in Allah's presence is the goal and the prize of this approach. The ultimate goal is greatest proximity to Allah *Subḥānahu wa Taʿālā* so as to achieve real bliss and happiness in this world and salvation in the Hereafter. This is the path to life fulfillment. A *ḥadīth qudsī* describes this relationship and the way to achieve it in a beautiful and moving way:

> Whoever shows enmity to someone who is devoted to Me (*waliyyun*), I shall be at war with him. My servant draws near to Me with nothing more beloved to Me than the religious duties and obligations I have enjoined (*iftaraḍtuhu*) upon him, and My servant continues to draw near to Me with supererogatory works and voluntary

> services (*nawāfil*) so that I shall love him. When I love him, I am his hearing with which he hears, his seeing with which he sees, his hands with which he works and his foot with which he walks. Were he to ask (something) of Me, I would surely give it to him, and were he to ask Me for refuge, I would surely grant it to him."
>
> (Bukhārī)

The relationship so developed is one of devoted companionship and loving friendship *(wilāyah)* and the result is total harmonization of the will of the believer and the servant with the Will of the Creator, the Master, the Lord and the Sustainer. No prize could be greater than this. The entire gamut of physical and material efforts becomes an investment for the achievement of all that is moral and spiritual. Spiritual excellence is achieved, not by denying the physical and material, but through harmonizing it with the Divine and the sublime.

The highest pinnacle of spirituality is attained through total commitment to Allah, unwavering obedience to His Commands, complete dedication to the mission assigned by Him and by fulfilling His Will on the earth (*istikhlāf*). This is done through harnessing all resources of mind and spirit so as to become a true embodiment of the qualities that Allah wants to see in the lives of His servants: in individuals as moral men and women; and, in society, as a moral community and collective entity, including the state. The path to spiritual elevation comes through harnessing the material and the spiritual in the service of moral norms and ideals as spelled out in the Qur'ān and the *Sunnah*.

The dynamics of spirituality in Islam have four dimensions: *the concept*, *the sources*, *the preparation* and *the manifestations*. The concept is the harmonization of human will and life with the Divine Will and Commands. Islam means submission to Allah and being at peace with (a) one's Creator, (b) one's own self and (c) the entire creation, human and physical, local and global, through the pursuit of this path of submission (Islam).

The sources of spirituality are none other than the Qur'ān and the *Sunnah*, the Guidance that Allah has provided through His Book and the

Sunnah of His Prophet (peace and blessings be upon him). The *divine spark* within responds to the Divine Guidance so graciously provided by the Creator Himself. *Tawḥīd* demands that He Alone be the source and that all guidance in this respect be sought from the channels and means He has prescribed. That is why all acts of worship (*ʿibādah*) have been clearly laid down in the *Sharīʿah* and their legitimacy depends on their being divinely laid down (*mashrūʿ*).

It has to be clearly understood that Allah has been kind enough to clearly lay down all the critically important means, methods, instruments and processes for the cultivation and development of spirituality. Acts of worship (*ʿibādāt*) constitute that bedrock, along with all other expressions and modalities for calling Him in remembrance and supplication i.e. seeking His *help*, *succour* and ability and power to act (*tawfīq*).

Finally, the issue of manifestations of spirituality too has not been left to chance, experimentation and personal whims and preferences. From the highly personal aspects of inner feeling and motivation to the multi-dimensional plethora of expressions and manifestations of spirituality have been described in such a manner that, on the one hand, they act as educating tools and processes of self-purification (*tazkiyah*) and, on the other, define, regulate and influence relationships between human beings as individuals, between individuals and institutions, and also seek articulation as defined forms, processes and operations of societal institutions, from family to community, economy, society, state and world order.

Brother Abdur Rashid Siddiqui has very ably tried to cover all these four dimensions of spirituality in a series of *Friday Khuṭubāt* (sermons) that he has delivered over the last three decades at the University of Leicester and the Islamic Foundation. Fifty-five such presentations have been published in the two volumes of *Lift up Your Hearts!,* published by the Islamic Foundation. The latest series of 25 reflections is now being published as *Living in Allah's Presence: Aspects of Islamic Spirituality.* Looking upon the topics covered, it is not an exaggeration to suggest that all the four dimensions of spirituality identified above have been covered with clarity and compassion. Everything said is based on the Qur'ān and the *Sunnah* and no important dimension has been left out. Form and spirit get equal importance in these presentations, because *'ibādah* is an objective in itself as much as it is instrumental in enabling humans to live as *Khulafā'* in this world.

Taken together they constitute a beautiful bouquet of all that makes life meaningful and Islamic. They cover all the three dimensions of human life and behaviour: vertical relationship with Allah, the Creator; the relationship with one's own soul and self; and, the horizontal relationship with other human beings, institutions, society, and the whole stream of history. Taken together these volumes represent the sum and substance of the dynamics of spirituality in Islam and its recipe to make us good Muslims and good human beings. The appeal is to both the heart and the mind. The message is to discover our Lord, to build a true relationship with Him, to make a resolve to live in His presence, to strive to fulfill His Will on the earth, and to seek His Pleasure in the life-to-come. May Allah open our hearts to this message and enable us to respond to this Divine calling. (*Āmīn*)

Leicester
21st Dhū al-Ḥijjah 1433
6th November 2012

Khurshid Ahmad

Introduction

I thank *Allah Subḥanahu wa Taʿālā* for enabling me to compile the present volume, third in the series of *Khuṭubāt* for Friday Prayers. Those who have seen the two earlier volumes *Lift Up Your Hearts!* of this series know that they contain *khuṭubāt* I gave at the University of Leicester, UK, over the course of many years. After my retirement from the university that activity ceased. However, during the last few years I once again began giving the Friday *Khuṭbah* at the Islamic Foundation Mosque, Markfield, Leicestershire. This present collection includes those given there.

The first volume dealt with basic Islamic beliefs and practices and some fundamental Islamic concepts. In the second volume I tried to tackle many moral and social issues from an Islamic perspective for the Muslim community of the West. Therein, I also covered our relationship with Allah and His Prophet (peace be upon him) as well as with each other. The present volume looks exclusively at self-purification (*tazkiyah*) covering such subjects as intention, sincerity, God-consciousness (*taqwā*), certainty (*yaqīn*), reliance (*tawakkul*), humility (*tawāḍuʿ*), steadfastness (*istiqāmah*) and wisdom (*ḥikmah*). Essentially, it is these Qur'ānic concepts that form the bedrock of the Islamic value system.

In the Qur'ān, Islam is referred to as *al-Dīn al-Fiṭrah*, thereby indicating that man by his very nature is inclined to submit to the Will of Allah like all other creatures. The Qur'ān mentions this in *Sūrah al-Rūm*:

فَأَقِمْ وَجْهَكَ لِلدِّينِ حَنِيفًا ۚ فِطْرَتَ ٱللَّهِ ٱلَّتِى فَطَرَ ٱلنَّاسَ عَلَيْهَا ۚ لَا تَبْدِيلَ
لِخَلْقِ ٱللَّهِ ۚ ذَٰلِكَ ٱلدِّينُ ٱلْقَيِّمُ وَلَٰكِنَّ أَكْثَرَ ٱلنَّاسِ لَا يَعْلَمُونَ ﴿٣٠﴾

So set your face single-mindedly to the true faith and adhere to fiṭrah (nature) on which Allah has created human beings. The mould fashioned by Allah cannot be altered. That is true straight faith, although most people do not know.
(Al-Rūm 30: 30)

There is an inherent harmony and equilibrium in nature and adhering to the Divine Law produces the metaphysical correlation between the cosmos and human beings. There is a well-known *ḥadīth* in which the Prophet (peace be upon him) said: "Every new born child is born in accordance with his true nature and it is his parents who make him into a Christian, a Jew or a fire-worshipper." Thus *fiṭrah* is a crucial factor and an important concept in Islamic teachings. It presupposes that by their nature human beings are inclined towards goodness and that in their true state they are positively predisposed towards submission and obedience to Allah. The subjects chosen in this collection of *khuṭubāt* deal with those natural human characteristics (*fiṭrah*) that are universally considered praiseworthy. These Qur'ānic concepts are the bedrock of the Islamic value system. Thus, in order to understand the message of the Qur'ān one should have a clear grasp of these concepts. It is also hoped that these *khuṭubāt* will inspire and motivate readers to follow the guidance they provide therein.

The second verse of *Sūrah al-Jumuʿah* specifies the functions of the Prophet as:

هُوَ ٱلَّذِى بَعَثَ فِى ٱلْأُمِّيِّـۧنَ رَسُولًا مِّنْهُمْ يَتْلُوا۟ عَلَيْهِمْ ءَايَـٰتِهِۦ وَيُزَكِّيهِمْ
وَيُعَلِّمُهُمُ ٱلْكِتَـٰبَ وَٱلْحِكْمَةَ وَإِن كَانُوا۟ مِن قَبْلُ لَفِى ضَلَـٰلٍ مُّبِينٍ ﴿٢﴾

He it is Who has sent among the unlettered a Messenger from among themselves, one who rehearses to them His verses, and purifies their lives, and imparts to them the Book and wisdom, although before that they were in utter error.
(al-Jumuʿah 62: 2)

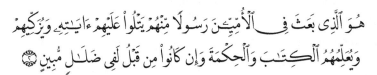

The Prophet (peace be upon him) was assigned to accomplish four important duties: rehearsing the verses of the Qur'ān (*tilāwat āyāt*) self-purification (*tazkiyah*), and teaching of the Book and wisdom, i.e. of the Qur'ān and the example of the Prophet (*ta'līm al-Kitāb wa al-ḥikmah*). If one looks at the purposes of *Jumu'ah* Prayers and the *Khuṭbah*, these were enjoined to achieve the aims described above. Whereas the recitation of the verses is covered by the *Ṣalāt al-Jum'uah*, the rest of the functions are designed to be covered by the Friday *Khuṭbah* itself. One of the important duties of the *khaṭīb* is to provide guidance on how to live according to the dictates of Islam given the current issues and problems faced by the community. However, as the latter are too topical and not of lasting interest, I have not included them in this series of volumes. Although the series is primarily intended for use as a model *khuṭbah*, it can equally adopted for the syllabus of Qur'ānic and Islamic study circles. The references provided will also help in further study of the topics covered.

Those who want to use the model *khuṭubāt* should start with the Arabic part of the first *khuṭbah* given in the Appendix and recite the *āyāh* as given at the start of the *khuṭbah* and then either read the text of the *khuṭbah* or express the contents in his own words. After finishing the first part, the *khaṭīb* should sit down for a while before starting the second *khuṭbah* which is entirely in Arabic and is also given in the Appendix.

Some hints and suggestions as regards the delivery of *khuṭbah* may help those who are not accustomed to public speaking. Note too that almost everyone feels a bit nervous before having to give a *khuṭbah*. In this respect then one should have a positive attitude towards this responsibility, realizing that this is a duty you are performing for the sake of Allah. You should seek His help in accomplishing this task to the best of your ability. The best supplication is the one used by the Prophet Mūsā (peace be upon him) as recorded in *Sūrah Ṭā' Hā'*:

...رَبِّ ٱشْرَحْ لِى صَدْرِى ﴿٢٥﴾ وَيَسِّرْ لِىٓ أَمْرِى ﴿٢٦﴾ وَٱحْلُلْ عُقْدَةً
مِّن لِّسَانِى ﴿٢٧﴾ يَفْقَهُوا۟ قَوْلِى ﴿٢٨﴾

O my Lord! Expand me my breast; ease my task for me; and remove the impediment from my speech. So they may understand what I say.

(Ṭā' Hā' 20: 25-28)

Physical preparation can also help. Two or three deep breaths before you start can relax you. If you are relaxed you will feel happier, and you will behave naturally even if you are tense.

As regards presentation, it is important that what you say comes from deep conviction, from your heart, so that it can touch the hearts of your listeners. For this, it is recommended that you do not to read from the book but rather make a note of important points and try to convey this in your own style. Thus, you will be able to have eye contact with your audience and so maintain their interest. Even if you have to read do not rush instead try to read at a normal speed. Try to make your presentation lively and interesting so that it appeals to your listeners.

I have used many Arabic terms which may be unfamiliar to some listeners, hence always remember to give their English translation and add further explanation if need be. In addition to the references given in the text, I have used the following sources extensively in preparing of these *khuṭubāt*. These may also help readers to gain more familiarity with the issues under discussion. Imām Ghazālī's *Iḥyā' 'Ulūm al-Dīn* is an indispensible work for understanding the topics that I have covered. Various editions of this book, both in full and abridged versions, are available. Other books that I have consulted and found useful are listed below:

- Imām Abū al-Qāsim al-Qushayrī: *al-Risālah al-Qushayrīyah*; translated from the Arabic by B.R. Von Schlegell, entitled *Principles of Sufism*. [Kuala Lumpur: Islamic Book Trust, 2004.]
- M. Fetullah Gülen: *Emeralds Hills of the Heart: Key Concepts in Practice of Sufism*. Izmir: Keynak (Izmir) A.S., [2000?]
- Sayyid Aḥmad 'Urūj Qādrī: *Islāmī Taṣawwuf*. Delhi: Markazī Maktabah Islāmī, 1980 [Urdu].

- Amīn Aḥsan Iṣlāḥī: *Tazkiyah-e-Nafs*. New Delhi: Markazī Maktabah Islāmī, 1999.
- Ṣāliḥ bin ʿAbdullāh: *Khuṭubāt al-Ḥaram*; translated from the Arabic by Saʿīd Aḥmad ʿInāyatullāh. Makkah: al-Maktab al-Imadādiyah, 1427 A.H. [Urdu].
- Muḥammad ʿAbdul Ḥayyi: *Jumuʿah ke Khuṭbe*. Karachi: Fazlee Sons Ltd., 1986 [Urdu].
- Syed Munawwur Hussain Mashhadi: *Rafīq-e-Safar*. Lahore: Maktabah Chirāg-e-Islām, 2001 [Urdu].

I have also used some of my own works, namely:

- *Qur'ānic Keywords: A Reference Guide*. Markfield, Leics.: The Islamic Foundation, 2008.
- *Tazkiyah: the Islamic Path of Self-Development*, edited by Abdur Rashid Siddiqui, Markfield, Leics.: The Islamic Foundation, 2004.
- *Lift Up Your Hearts*! Markfield, Leics.: The Islamic Foundation, 2001-2005, 2 vols.

I have usually relied on Sayyid Mawdūdī's *Towards Understanding the Qur'ān* being the translation of the abridged version of *Tafhīm al-Qur'ān* but I have also used other English translations as well.

I am greatly indebted to my friends and colleagues for their help and guidance provided in improving and embellishing my work. Professor Abdur Raheem Kidwai read the manuscript thoroughly and made corrections and suggestions for its improvement as did Professor Salman Nadvi. Dr Abdullah Sahin has kindly made some useful suggestions which I have included in the text. I am also grateful to Mawlana Iqbal Ahmad Azami for making encouraging comments. I owe a debt of gratitude to my very dear friend, Professor Khurshid Ahmad, who, despite his very busy schedule of duties and ill-health, read the manuscript and graciously agreed to write a foreword. Dr Mohamed Rafeek and Safi Shahada were kind enough to check and trace the Arabic text of the *aḥādīth* and provide the electronic text. I am grateful for their invaluable help. I have greatly benefited with the editorial suggestions of Dr Susanne Thackray. I will be failing in my duty if I do not acknowledge the help of my dear brother Dr Manazir Ahsan for meticulously checking the diacritical markings. Finally I would like to thank the Islamic Foundation and the team at Kube Publishing for undertaking the publication of this book and brother Yahya Birt for proofreading and valuable suggestions for improvement. May Allah reward them all. (*Āmīn*)

I earnestly pray that *Allāh Subḥānahu wa Taʿalā* accept this humble effort of mine and grace it with His Mercy and forgive my errors and shortcomings. I further hope and pray that students in institutions of higher education and others will find this work useful in preparing their own *khuṭubāt*.

Abdur Rashid Siddiqui

Leicester
14th Ṣafar 1433
8th January 2012

I

Friday Prayers (*Ṣalāt al-Jumu'ah*)

يَـٰٓأَيُّهَا ٱلَّذِينَ ءَامَنُوٓا۟ إِذَا نُودِىَ لِلصَّلَوٰةِ مِن يَوْمِ ٱلْجُمُعَةِ فَٱسْعَوْا۟ إِلَىٰ ذِكْرِ
ٱللَّهِ وَذَرُوا۟ ٱلْبَيْعَ ۚ ذَٰلِكُمْ خَيْرٌ لَّكُمْ إِن كُنتُمْ تَعْلَمُونَ ﴿٩﴾

O you who believe! When the call for the prayer is made on Friday, hasten to the remembrance of Allah and give up all trading. That is better for you if you only knew.

(al-Jumu'ah 62: 9)

Friday has a very special significance for Muslims all over the world. The institution of Friday Prayers was established by the Prophet (peace be upon him) after his migration to Madīnah. Migration itself was a decisive event in Islamic history that changed the map of the world. It heralded the founding of the Muslim community as well as the establishing of a society and a state based on Islamic principles and values.

The Prophet (peace be upon him) led the first Jumu'ah Prayer at the habitat of Banī Sālim bin 'Awf on the way from Qubā to Madīnah. Ever since, Jumu'ah has remained a key Islamic institution. It is an occasion for the community of a locality to come together for prayers, exhortation and consolidation.

There are many *aḥādīth* mentioning the importance and blessings of Friday.

عَنْ أَبِي لُبَابَةَ بْنِ عَبْدِ الْـمُنْذِرِ، قَالَ: قَـالَ النَّبِيُّ صَلَّى اللهُ عَلَيْهِ وَسَـلَّمَ: إِنَّ يَوْمَ الْـجُمُعَةِ سَيِّدُ الْأَيَّامِ، وَأَعْظَمُهَا عِنْدَ اللهِ، وَهُوَ أَعْظَمُ عِنْدَ اللهِ مِنْ يَوْمِ الْأَضْحَى وَيَوْمِ الْفِطْرِ، فِيـهِ خَمْسُ خِـلَالٍ، خَلَقَ اللهُ فِيهِ آدَمَ، وَأَهْبَطَ اللهُ فِيهِ آدَمَ إِلَى الْأَرْضِ، وَفِيهِ تَوَفَّى اللهُ آدَمَ، وَفِيهِ سَاعَةٌ لَا يَسْأَلُ اللهَ فِيهَا الْعَبْدُ شَيْئًا إِلَّا أَعْطَاهُ، مَا لَمْ يَسْأَلْ حَرَامًا، وَفِيهِ تَقُومُ السَّاعَةُ.

(ابن ماجه)

It is narrated by Abū Lubābah bin ʿAbd al-Mundher says that the Prophet (peace be upon him) said: Friday is the most excellent and distinguished day among the days of the week in the sight of Allah; so much so that it excels both the day of *ʿĪd al-Fiṭr* and the day of *ʿĪd al-Aḍḥā* on account of the following five merits: Allah created Adam on Friday; He sent him to the Earth on this day as his vicegerent; Adam died on Friday; there is a blessed time on Friday during which a person is granted by Allah anything lawful and good he prays for and Resurrection will take place on Friday.

(Ibn Mājah)

The practice of the Prophet (peace be upon him) was that he would commence his readiness for Friday on the preceding night and would say:

عَنْ أَنَسِ بْنِ مَالِكٍ، رَضِيَ اللهُ عَنْهُ قَالَ: كَانَ رَسُولُ اللهِ صَلَّى اللهُ عَلَيْهِ وَسَلَّمَ يَقُولُ: إِنَّ لَيْلَةَ الْـجُمُعَةِ لَيْلَةٌ غَرَّاءُ، وَيَوْمَهَا يَوْمٌ أَزْهَرُ.

(مسند أحمد وابن السني)

The night before Friday is a white night and Friday is a bright day.

(Narrated by Anas ibn Mālik in Musnad Aḥmad.)

It is also narrated from Jābir that the Prophet (peace be upon him) said:

عَنْ جَابِرٍ أَنَّ رَسُولَ اللهِ صَلَّى اللهُ عَلَيْهِ وَسَلَّمَ قَالَ: مَنْ كَانَ يُؤْمِنُ بِاللهِ وَالْيَوْمِ الآخِرِ، فَعَلَيْهِ الْجُمُعَةُ يَوْمَ الْجُمُعَةِ، فَمَنِ اسْتَغْنَى بِلَهْوٍ أَوْ تِجَارَةٍ اسْتَغْنَى اللهُ عَنْهُ وَاللهُ غَنِيٌّ حَمِيدٌ.

(الدارقطني)

Attending the Friday Prayer is obligatory on every person who believes in Allah and the Last Day – excepting the one who is sick, the traveler, the woman, the child or the slave – the one who ignores it on account of sport or fun, or trade or business, will be ignored by Allah, Who is Self-Sufficient and Most Praiseworthy.

(Dāraquṭnī)

The Prophet (peace be upon him) also gave a dire warning:

رَوَى عَبْدُ اللهِ بْنُ عُمَرَ سَمِعَ رَسُولَ اللهِ صَلَّى اللهُ عَلَيْهِ وَسَلَّمَ يَقُولُ لَيَنْتَهِيَنَّ أَقْوَامٌ عَنْ وَدْعِهِمُ الْجُمُعَاتِ أَوْ لَيَخْتِمَنَّ اللهُ عَلَى قُلُوبِهِمْ ثُمَّ لَيَكُونُنَّ مِنَ الْغَافِلِينَ

(مسلم)

People are warned against neglecting Friday Prayer, otherwise Allah will seal their hearts and they will be condemned to negligence (forever).

(Narrated by ʿAbdullāh ibn ʿUmar in Muslim)

He gave the following advice and guidance for the preparation and offering of Friday Prayers:

عَنْ أَبِي سَعِيدٍ الْخُدْرِيِّ قَالَ: قَالَ رَسُولُ اللهِ صَلَّى اللهُ عَلَيْهِ وَسَلَّمَ مَنِ اغْتَسَلَ يَوْمَ الْجُمُعَةِ وَلَبِسَ مِنْ أَحْسَنِ ثِيَابِهِ، وَمَسَّ مِنْ طِيبٍ إِنْ كَانَ

عِنْدَهُ، ثُمَّ أَتَى الْـجُمُعَةَ فَلَمْ يَتَخَطَّ أَعْنَاقَ النَّاسِ، ثُمَّ صَلَّى مَا كَتَبَ اللهُ لَهُ، ثُمَّ أَنْصَتَ إِذَا خَرَجَ إِمَامُهُ حَتَّى يَفْرُغَ مِنْ صَلَاتِهِ كَانَتْ كَفَّارَةً لِـمَـا بَيْنَهَا وَبَيْنَ جُمُعَتِهِ الَّتِي قَبْلَهَا.

(أبو داوود)

The person who has a bath on Friday, puts on the best available clothes, uses perfume if available, comes for the Prayer, and takes his place quietly without disturbing the people, then offers the Prayer that Allah has destined for him, and sits in perfect silence and peace from the time the Imām takes his place till the completion of the Prayer, he will have all his sins committed since the previous Friday expiated on this account.

(Narrated by Abū Saʿīd al-Khuḍrī in Abū Dāwūd)

The five daily prayers are also required to be offered in congregation (*jamāʿah*) in a mosque but if one misses the congregation, the obligatory prayer can be offered in congregation or individually at home or at some other premises. But not so the Jumuʿah Prayer, as this can only be offered in congregation in a mosque. This establishes it as a permanent institution in its own right. Jumuʿah provides an opportunity for all the people in a wider locality to come together once a week to listen to the *khuṭbah* and pray. After the call for prayer (*adhān*), the Imām addresses the congregation, then leads a two *rakʿah* Prayer. The timings of the prayer is the same as *Ẓuhr* prayers but unlike the four *rakʿah* in *Ẓuhr*, Jumuʿah Prayer has only two obligatory *rakʿah* preceded by the *khuṭbah* given in two parts. These consist of the pronouncement of Allah's Greatness (*ḥamd wa thanā*), peace and blessings on the Prophet (*ṣalawāt wa salām*), the declaration of faith in Allah and His Prophet (*shahādah*), remembrance of Allah, advice to Muslims, sharing the message and meaning of Islam and its obligations, and supplications for the welfare of Muslims. In fact, the *khuṭbah*, delivered in two parts, is the substitute for the two *rakʿah* waived in this prayer. However, if one misses the Jumuʿah Prayer for some reason, then one has to pray the normal *Ẓuhr Ṣalāh*.

Professor Khurshid Ahmad has concisely summed up the uniqueness of Jumu'ah which he identified as having at least three aspects.

Firstly, it represents an in-built arrangement for the education of the Muslims. *Ṣalāh* is preceded by the *khuṭbah*, the purpose of which is to teach and educate the people in Islam, awaken their moral consciousness, increase their understanding of the right way of life (*dīn*), reflect upon the situation in which Muslims find themselves, and share among themselves their concerns, aspirations and obligations towards each other and to humanity at large. There is an integral linkage between the *khuṭbah* and *Ṣalāh*, which sharpens the spiritual experience of the *Ṣalāh* and strengthens one's relationship with Allah and the *ummah*.

Secondly, it provides the members of every community with an opportunity to get together, meet and know each other better, share concerns and become more integrated and solidified. It is a powerful instrument for the socialisation and cultivation of community life. The feeling of brotherhood and of oneness of the *ummah* is strengthened. It also provides a forum for local and wider consultation (*shūrā*).

Thirdly, Jumu'ah represents the ethos of Islam *par excellence*. This is a day for special prayers and remembrance of Allah. The preparations for the prayer are part of the culture of the Jumu'ah. When the call for prayer is made, all business and worldly affairs have to be stopped until the prayer is over. Listening to the *khuṭbah* is obligatory, an inseparable part of the collective prayer and congregation. Any other activity is forbidden until the prayer is concluded. After the prayer, one is free to go back to one's business or continue other activities one is involved in. It is not a designated day of rest as in some other religions. Yet, whatever activity one is engaged in, Allah's remembrance is to be the guiding light. It disciplines the community to respond to the call, fulfil the obligation of collective *dhikr*, re-enter the business of life with full consciousness of what is good and should be pursued as such, and what is wrong and should as such be avoided. Jumu'ah is the symbol of this distinct Islamic approach to life and the way its problems have to be faced.[1]

---

1 Foreword to *Lift up Your Hearts*, 2001, Vol.1, pp. x-xi.

In early Islamic history from the time of the Rightly-guided Caliphs (*al-Khulafā' al-Rāshidūn*) and up to the abolition of the Ottoman caliphate, the Friday *Khuṭbah* was considered a symbol of the authority of the reigning Caliph in which specific mention of his name was made. If this were omitted, then it used to be considered an act of rebellion against the ruling Caliph and his government.

The Prophet's Friday *Khuṭubāt* were informative, conveying the message of Islam, reinforcing their faith (*īmān*) and motivating them to good deeds. His Friday discourses used to be brief, to the point and full of light and guidance. We should remember that the purpose of *khuṭbah* is reminder (*tadhkkur*) and reflection (*tadabbur*). It is essentially an act of worship (*'ibādah*). Thus, people are required to listen attentively and so talking during the *khuṭbah* is not allowed. There are several *aḥādīth* that forbid speaking during the *khuṭbah*.

عَنِ ابْنِ عَبَّاسٍ، قَالَ: قَالَ رَسُولُ اللهِ صَلَّى اللهُ عَلَيْهِ وَسَلَّمَ : مَنْ تَكَلَّمَ يَوْمَ الْجُمُعَةِ وَالْإِمَامُ يَخْطُبُ، فَهُوَ كَمَثَلِ الْحِمَارِ يَحْمِلُ أَسْفَارًا، وَالَّذِي يَقُولُ لَهُ: أَنْصِتْ، لَيْسَ لَهُ جُمُعَةٌ.

(مسند أحمد)

It is reported by Ibn 'Abbās that the Prophet (peace be upon him) said: "Those who talk when the Imām is giving *khuṭbah* on Friday are like a donkey on whom books are laden. Even the one who tells the other person to stop talking loses his Friday Prayers."

(Aḥmad)

It is narrated by Abū Hurayrah that the Prophet (peace be upon him) said:

عَنْ أَبِي هُرَيْرَةَ أَنَّ رَسُولَ اللهِ صَلَّى اللهُ عَلَيْهِ وَسَلَّمَ قَالَ: إِذَا قُلْتَ لِصَاحِبِكَ يَوْمَ الْجُمُعَةِ أَنْصِتْ وَالْإِمَامُ يَخْطُبُ فَقَدْ لَغَوْتَ.

(البخاري ومسلم)

> When the Imām is giving the *khuṭbah* and you tell your friend to be quiet then even this is useless talk.
> (Bukhārī and Muslim)

According to Ḥanafī and Mālikī jurists (*fuqahā'*), even replying to *salām* is not permissible during the *khuṭbah*.

As there are rules of etiquette (*ādāb*) for the congregation, there are also *ādāb* for giving the *khuṭbah*. Hence the one giving the *khuṭbah* should observe the following rules:

- Following the precedent set by the Prophet (peace be upon him) one should be brief and to the point in what one says.
- Recognizing the fact that our congregation is composed of different nationalities, different schools of *fiqh* and followers of different groups actively involved in the revival of Islam, it is essential that we do not raise issues that can be seen to advocate one or another specific point of view.
- Issues on which we disagree are very few and minor. Instead, there is so much to say about those issues on which we do agree.
- Islam is a complete code of life. It covers spiritual, social, economic, political and legal issues. One can talk about any issue without provoking sectarian feelings. Some issues that we may feel are important but which are also controversial require a different forum for discussion and debate where the audience can participate and air their views and ask questions of the speakers. The Friday *Khuṭbah* is not the right forum to raise controversial issues where people may feel uncomfortable, forced to listen but are unable to speak. The creation of such a situation is bad for the Imām as well as for the congregation.
- Such controversial situations have resulted in fights in mosques in both the UK and abroad. Sectarian killings are rife in certain parts of the Muslim world. We should try to create harmony in society. We should create a model of a peaceful Muslim society, one that, despite differences of opinion, works harmoniously in presenting the Islamic way of life.

- As the time for *khuṭbah* is very limited, between 15 and 20 minutes, it is essential that we do not exceed this time. Thus, it is inadvisable to raise complex issues that need extensive explanation. It is also the *Sunnah* of the Prophet (peace be upon him) that he kept the *khuṭbah* very short and relevant to the state of the community.

Finally, on Friday, one should spend as much of one's time as possible in remembrance of Allah, recitation of the Holy Qur'ān (especially *Sūrah al-Kahf* and *Sūrah al-Dukhān* – as they are mentioned by the Prophet), asking Allah's forgiveness and doing other good deeds.

Praise be to Allah, the Lord of the Universe.

اللهُمَّ إِنَّا نَسْأَلُكَ مُوجِبَاتِ رَحْمَتِكَ، وَعَزَائِمَ مَغْفِرَتِكَ، وَالسَّلَامَةَ مِنْ كُلِّ إِثْمٍ، وَالْغَنِيمَةَ مِنْ كُلِّ بِرٍّ، وَالْفَوْزَ بِالْجَنَّةِ، وَالنَّجَاةَ بِعَوْنِكَ مِنَ النَّارِ.

(الحاكم)

O Allah! We seek the means of deserving Your mercy and the means of ascertaining Your forgiveness, protection from all sins, benefit from all virtues, attainment of Paradise and Your help in deliverance from the Hell-fire.

(Ḥākim)

O Allah! Enrich us with the blessings of Friday, accept our prayers and forgive our shortcomings. (*Āmīn*)

2

Heart (*Qalb*)

يَوْمَ لَا يَنفَعُ مَالٌ وَلَا بَنُونَ ﴿٨٨﴾ إِلَّا مَنْ أَتَى ٱللَّهَ بِقَلْبٍ سَلِيمٍ ﴿٨٩﴾

The Day when nothing will avail, neither wealth nor offspring, but only he that brings to Allah a sound heart will (attain success).

(al- Shu'arā' 26: 88-89)

The heart plays a vital role in a person's body. It has both the physical dimension that is essential for existence and it also has the spiritual importance that is indispensible for the continuation of a meaningful life. In medical science, the heart is a piece of flesh that pumps blood through the body. The constant flow of blood through the arteries and veins keeps the body alive. The word *qalb* (pl. *qulūb*) is derived from *qalaba* which means to turn around or to turn about. As the heart is always in motion, turning and beating, it is called *qalb*.

In Qur'ānic terminology, the heart (*qalb*) is the inner self (*nafs*), the faculty of reason (*'aql*) and the soul (*rūḥ*); essentially, whatever motivates a person to do something. It is the source of human reason and emotion. It is the centre of one's personality. It also signifies the spiritual aspect of human beings as it is the centre of all emotions and controls all other faculties such as perception, sensation, reasoning and willpower.

Imām Ghazālī while analyzing the term *qalb* in *Revival of the Religious Sciences* (*Iḥyā' 'Ulūm al-Dīn*) gave its explanation by elaborating on the words "self", "soul" and "reason", as these are all related to the functions of the heart. Each of these terms requires further elucidation as they contain other aspects as well.

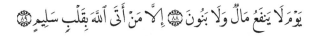

Nafs means ego, spirit, psyche, life, and human being. In Qur'ānic usage, it has a general designation for the self or spiritual reality of living creatures. *Nafas* (pl. *anfās* and *anfus*) also means breath. We can say then that *nafs* is human personality, which by nature (*fiṭrah*) is disposed towards goodness.

Nafs is composed of a complex mixture of opposing forces of good and evil. A person has to choose between the path of righteousness or to go the other way. Thus, one is in a constant struggle against divergent forces. The Qur'ān has identified three aspects of the *nafs*: one, which is called the imperious, carnal self (*al-nafs al-ammārah*) (*Yūsuf* 12: 53). It tempts us to commit evil acts. However, to protect human beings from the treachery of this aspect of *nafs,* there is the reproaching self (*al-nafs al-lawwāmah*), which is called the conscience. When a person commits a sin, his conscience reproaches him for doing such a shameful act. This, in itself, proves that a person has the ability to differentiate between good and bad. Knowing the difference necessitates that there will be a Day of Reckoning. Hence, in *Sūrah al-Qiyāmah*, *al-nafs al-lawwāmah* is cited as a proof of the Day of Resurrection.

لَآ أُقْسِمُ بِيَوْمِ ٱلْقِيَـٰمَةِ ۝١ وَلَآ أُقْسِمُ بِٱلنَّفْسِ ٱللَّوَّامَةِ ۝٢

Nay, I swear by the Day of Resurrection; and nay I swear
by the self-reproaching soul!

(al-Qiyāmah 75: 1-2)

In listening to the voice of one's conscience, if one retracts and repents after committing any wrong act, then one returns to the path of righteousness. This gives one peace of mind. However, ignoring and suppressing it makes conscience's voice dead and one goes down the slippery slope of doom. Resisting temptation, practising self-restraint and acting on the dictates of one's conscience leads one to attain the blessings of the happy, peaceful, satisfied self (*al-nafs al-muṭma'innah*). This is the highest achievement for human beings. This is the stage when one is well-pleased and happy with the Creator and He is also well-pleased with his servant:

يَـٰٓأَيَّتُهَا ٱلنَّفْسُ ٱلْمُطْمَئِنَّةُ ﴿٢٧﴾ ٱرْجِعِىٓ إِلَىٰ رَبِّكِ رَاضِيَةً مَّرْضِيَّةً ﴿٢٨﴾

O serene soul! Return to your Lord well-pleased (with your blissful destination), well-pleasing (to your Lord).

(al-Fajr 89: 27–28)

The word *rūḥ* (soul), which is very subtle and spiritual in nature, is also used in the Qur'ān. It means soul, spirit, and the breath (of life). *Rūḥ* is the ethereal and immortal part of a human being. *Rūḥ* is the spark of Divine origin. When the first human being was created Allah said:

فَإِذَا سَوَّيْتُهُۥ وَنَفَخْتُ فِيهِ مِن رُّوحِى ... ﴿٧٢﴾

I fashioned him (in due proportion) and breathed into him My spirit (Rūḥ)...

(Ṣād 38: 72)

This Divine spark enlightened the human faculties and thus made him the noblest of all creation. The human body is made of dust and after his death becomes part of the earth, but the *rūḥ*, which is of Divine origin, never dies but rather returns to its Creator.

Thus, the *nafs* and the *rūḥ* are two different things. However, sometimes their meanings overlap. The *nafs* refers to human existence and to one's personality and psyche. It is, then, mortal as is mentioned in the Qur'ān:

كُلُّ نَفْسٍ ذَآئِقَةُ ٱلْمَوْتِ ... ﴿١٨٥﴾

Every Nafs shall taste death.

(Āl 'Imrān 3: 185)

The *rūḥ*, however, does not perish for it has been created to abide forever. In other words, it continues to live after death and feels pleasure and pain.

The word *rūḥ* is also used for revelation (*waḥy*):

وَيَسْـَٔلُونَكَ عَنِ ٱلرُّوحِ ۖ قُلِ ٱلرُّوحُ مِنْ أَمْرِ رَبِّى وَمَآ أُوتِيتُم مِّنَ ٱلْعِلْمِ إِلَّا قَلِيلًا ﴿٨٥﴾

They ask you concerning the Rūḥ. Say the Rūḥ (comes) by the command of my Lord: Of knowledge it is only a little that is communicated to you.

(al-Isrā' 17: 85)

Here, *rūḥ* means the nature of revelation (*waḥy*), although some commentators say that *al-Rūḥ* means the Archangel Jibrīl as he is referred to by this title in other places in the Qur'ān.

Finally, reason (*ʿaql*) is yet another very important human faculty. The word *ʿaql* does not appear in the Qur'ān as a noun but rather occurs many times in the verbal form, meaning to understand and grasp fully. The excellence which Allah gave human beings over all other creatures is precisely because man enjoys the faculty of reason. This is what has led to human progress in the arts, sciences and technology. However, there are limitations to *ʿaql* as well. Whilst it has its own sphere of activity in which it can perform, it nevertheless needs Divine guidance to function successfully and submit to the Will of one's Creator. However, whilst it is necessary that we remain guided by our reason, Iqbāl argues that sometimes it is better if we leave decisions to our hearts. The reason for this advice is that *ʿaql* can make one very cautious and reluctant to move towards the dictates of the *Sharīʿah*: for example the hypocrites warned the Muslims during the Battle of Uḥud that they should not to go out and fight and further commented after the battle:

... لَوْ أَطَاعُونَا مَا قُتِلُوا۟ ۗ ... ﴿١٦٨﴾

Had they followed us, they would not have been slain.

(Āl ʿImrān 3: 168)

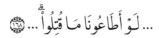

This may look at first sight to be a reasonable statement but such reasoning has to be overruled because if death is destined no one can avert it even if one shuts oneself up in a fortress. However, this should not preclude us from taking reasonable precautions. The Prophet Yaʿqūb (peace be upon him) advised his sons to enter the city from different gates, but he added:

... وَمَآ أُغْنِي عَنكُم مِّنَ ٱللَّهِ مِن شَيْءٍ ۖ إِنِ ٱلْحُكْمُ إِلَّا لِلَّهِ ... ﴿٦٧﴾

I can be of no help to you against Allah. Allah's command alone prevails.

(Yūsuf 12: 67)

This brings us back to the *qalb* which is the locus where *īmān* and conviction resides. It is also the place that is afflicted by disease:

فِي قُلُوبِهِم مَّرَضٌ ... ﴿١٠﴾

In their hearts is a disease…

(al-Baqarah 2: 10)

So what are the diseases of the heart? These are hypocrisy, envy, jealousy, pride, evil desires, corrupt motivations and the like. Then there is weakness of faith. One believes something but yet has no firm conviction. This was the disease of the bedouins who said: "We believe." But Allah says: "You have no faith; but you should say:

قَالَتِ ٱلْأَعْرَابُ ءَامَنَّا ۖ قُل لَّمْ تُؤْمِنُوا۟ وَلَـٰكِن قُولُوٓا۟ أَسْلَمْنَا وَلَمَّا يَدْخُلِ
ٱلْإِيمَـٰنُ فِي قُلُوبِكُمْ ۖ ... ﴿١٤﴾

"*We have submitted our wills to Allah*", *for not yet has Faith entered your hearts.*"

(al-Ḥujurāt 49: 14)

The advice to them here is that if they keep submitting to the requirements of faith, then, by Allah's mercy, their hearts will taste the sweetness of *īmān.* To be successful in the Hereafter, one needs a sound heart. This is the message given by the Prophet (peace be upon him) who said:

قَالَ أَبُو ذَرٍّ: إِنَّ رَسُولَ اللهِ صَلَّى اللهُ عَلَيْهِ وَسَلَّمَ قَالَ: قَدْ أَفْلَحَ مَنْ أَخْلَصَ اللهُ قَلْبَهُ لِلإِيمَانِ، وَجَعَلَ قَلْبَهُ سَلِيمًا.

(البيهقي)

He has succeeded whose heart Allah has purified for *īmān* and made his heart righteous and submissive.

(Narrated by Abū Dharr in Bayhaqī)

The importance of the heart is that it guides human conduct; in other words, it controls all human actions:

فَإِنَّهَا لَا تَعْمَى ٱلْأَبْصَٰرُ وَلَٰكِن تَعْمَى ٱلْقُلُوبُ ٱلَّتِى فِى ٱلصُّدُورِ ﴿٤٦﴾

Thus, it is not the eyes that go blind but it is the heart inside you that goes blind.

(al-Ḥajj 22: 46)

The Prophet (peace be upon him) also explained the importance of the piece of flesh we call the heart:

رَوَى النُّعْمَانَ بْنَ بَشِيرٍ ... إِذَا صَلَحَتْ صَلَحَ الْجَسَدُ كُلُّهُ وَإِذَا فَسَدَتْ فَسَدَ الْجَسَدُ كُلُّهُ ...

(البخاري ومسلم)

... If it is healthy, the whole body is healthy and if it is corrupt the whole body is corrupted.

(Narrated by al-Nuʿmān ibn Bashīr in Bukhārī & Muslim)

Thus, to keep the heart pure we have to safeguard the channels that convey messages to the heart. The Prophet (peace be upon him) explains elsewhere as follows:

قَالَ أَبُو ذَرٍّ: إِنَّ رَسُولَ اللهِ صَلَّى اللهُ عَلَيْهِ وَسَلَّمَ قَالَ: ... فَأَمَّا الأُذُنُ فَقَمِعٌ، وَالْعَيْنُ مُقِرَّةٌ بِمَا يُوعَى الْقَلْبُ ...

(أحمد والبيهقي)

Ears are the filters and eyes are the conveyors of images that reach the heart.

(Narrated by Abū Dharr in Aḥmad and Bayhaqī)

Therefore, we have to safeguard our eyes and ears. Yet there are so many distractions. With the advent of the Internet, access to pornography has become so easy. Then there is vulgar music and obscene literature that tempt people all the time. To resist these temptations, we need very firm *īmān* and strong willpower. We should also seek Allah's help to protect us from these evils. We should remember that we will be asked about our faculties on the Day of Judgement. How have we used them?

إِنَّ ٱلسَّمْعَ وَٱلْبَصَرَ وَٱلْفُؤَادَ كُلُّ أُولَٰٓئِكَ كَانَ عَنْهُ مَسْـُٔولًا ﴿٣٦﴾

Surely every act of hearing or of seeing or of (feeling in) the heart – each of those shall be called to account (*on the Day of Reckoning*).

(al-Isrā' 17: 36)

Thus, it is essential that we try and safeguard our hearts and remain firm on the path of righteousness, despite the many temptations around us. The only source of help for us is the Mercy of Allah, *Subḥānahu wa Ta'ālā*. He has provided us with the means to overcome our difficulties. In this respect, central to the heart is remembrance (*dhikr*). If we remain God-conscious wherever we are and always remember Allah and remind ourselves that we are accountable for all our deeds, we shall be able to protect our hearts from temptation.

The Qur'ān has advised us to pray:

رَبَّنَا لَا تُزِغْ قُلُوبَنَا بَعْدَ إِذْ هَدَيْتَنَا وَهَبْ لَنَا مِن لَّدُنكَ رَحْمَةً ۚ إِنَّكَ أَنتَ ٱلْوَهَّابُ ﴿٨﴾

Our Lord! Do not divert our hearts towards crookedness after You have guided us to the Right Way and bestow upon us Your mercy. Surely it is You Who are the Bestower.

(Āl 'Imrān 3: 8)

Let us pray as the Prophet (peace be upon him) used to pray:

يَا مُقَلِّبَ الْقُلُوبِ ثَبِّتْ قَلْبِي عَلَى دِينِكَ.

(أحمد وابن ماجه)

O Converter of the hearts! Keep my heart firm upon Your *dīn*.

(Aḥmad and Ibn Majāh)

اللهُمَّ مُصَرِّفَ الْقُلُوبِ، اصْرِفْ قُلُوبَنَا إِلَى طَاعَتِكَ.

(مسلم وأحمد)

O Allah Who turns the hearts! Turn our hearts towards Your obedience.

(Muslim and Aḥmad)

اللهُمَّ إِنَّ قُلُوبَنَا وَنَوَاصِينَا بِيَدِكَ لَمْ تُمَلِّكْنَا مِنْهَا شَيْئًا، فَإِذَا فَعَلْتَ ذَلِكَ بِهَا فَكُنْ أَنْتَ وَلِيَّهَا وَاهْدِهَا إِلَى سَوَاءِ السَّبِيلِ.

(أبو نعيم في الحلية)

O Allah! Our hearts and our bodies are in Your Hand so You have not given us any authority over them, but if You do this then You will be their Guardian and guide them towards the Right Path. (*Āmīn*)

(Abū Nu'aym in al-Ḥilyah)

3

Intention (*Niyyah*)

مَن كَانَ يُرِيدُ حَرْثَ ٱلْـَٔاخِرَةِ نَزِدْ لَهُۥ فِى حَرْثِهِۦ ۖ وَمَن كَانَ يُرِيدُ حَرْثَ
ٱلدُّنْيَا نُؤْتِهِۦ مِنْهَا وَمَا لَهُۥ فِى ٱلْـَٔاخِرَةِ مِن نَّصِيبٍ ﴿٢٠﴾

Whoever seeks the harvest of the Hereafter, We shall increase his harvest for him, and whoever seeks the harvest of this world, We shall give him thereof; he will have no share in the Hereafter.

(al-Shūrā 42: 20)

Intention precedes all human action. A person cannot act unless he intends to do so. Hence, intention plays a very important part in our lives. In the verse from *Sūrah al- Shūrā* which I just recited, the word *irādah*, which comes from the root *r-w-d,* has a range of meanings such as to want, to seek, to will, to attempt and to intend. Hence, it could be used in the sense of wish or want as well as determination or will. The word *niyyah* in some way has the same meaning but this word is not used in the Qur'ān. However, there is a famous *ḥadīth* narrated by 'Umar ibn al-Khaṭṭāb that states a very important principle:

عن عُمَرَ بْنَ الْخَطَّاب رَضِيَ اللهُ عَنْهُ قَالَ: سَمِعْتُ رَسُولَ اللهِ صَلَّى اللهُ عَلَيْهِ وَسَلَّمَ، يَقُولُ: إِنَّمَا الْأَعْمَالُ بِالنِّيَّاتِ، وَإِنَّمَا لِكُلِّ امْرِئٍ مَا نَوَى، فَمَنْ كَانَتْ هِجْرَتُهُ إِلَى دُنْيَا يُصِيبُهَا أَوْ إِلَى امْرَأَةٍ يَنْكِحُهَا، فَهِجْرَتُهُ إِلَى مَا هَاجَرَ إِلَيْهِ.

(البخاري ومسلم)

> Surely, all actions are [judged] by intentions and every person shall only have that which he intended. Thus, he whose migration was for Allah and His Messenger, his migration was for Allah and His Messenger, and he whose migration was to achieve some worldly benefit or to take some woman in marriage, his migration was for that which he migrated.
>
> (Bukhārī and Muslim)

The importance of *niyyah* which this *ḥadīth* mentions is such that most collections of *aḥādīth* like *Ṣaḥīḥ al-Bukhārī* and *Riyāḍ al-Ṣāliḥīn* by Imām Nawawī quote this *ḥadīth* first. The background of this *ḥadīth* is that a person migrated from Makkah to Madīnah and his purpose for migration was that he wanted to marry a woman, who insisted that she would marry him on condition that he immigrated to Madīnah. Hence, there is specific mention of this in the *ḥadīth.*

Jamaal al-Din M. Zarabozo, in his commentary on this *ḥadīth,* summarizes its meaning in the following terms:

> Every conscious, intentional act that a rational person performs is driven and brought into being by his intention. Without that intention behind the act, the act would not have been performed. Now this intention must fall into one of three categories: a good, pious intention, a religiously neutral intention [i.e. permissible deeds (*mubāḥāt*)] or an evil intention. In all cases, the person shall get only what he intended.[1]

According to Imām al-Ghazālī in the category of good and pious intentions are all acts of worship (*ʿibādah*) and permissible deeds, while evil includes all unlawful acts. Thus, this *ḥadīth* applies only to the first two categories as an evil deed even done with a good intention cannot become good. Imām Ghazālī who wrote extensively on this topic in *Iḥyā' ʿUlūm al-Dīn* explains this point as follows:

---

1 *Commentary on the Forty Ḥadīth of al-Nawawī*, 1999, Vol. I, p. 137.

No one should imagine from this *ḥadīth* that with good intention sinful acts can become acts of obedience. For example, if someone backbites to please others or robs someone's wealth and distributes it among the poor or builds a mosque, *madrasah* or a lodge for travellers, all these though apparently good deeds are acts of stupidity and ignorance. Acts which are illegal by the *Sharīʿah*, although done with good intention, are still evil deeds.[2]

So what do we mean by a good intention? In simple terms, all good acts are done to seek Allah's pleasure. Thus, migration (*hijrah*), which is mentioned in this *ḥadīth*, is an act of supreme sacrifice. If it is undertaken for the sake of Allah and His Messenger, its reward is guaranteed by Allah. The term "Allah's pleasure" is used in many places in the Qur'ān and its physical manifestation is the reward of forgiveness by Allah (*maghfirah*) and Paradise (*Jannah*). There is even a reward for having good intention. It is narrated by ʿAbdullāh ibn ʿAbbās that the Prophet (peace be upon him) relates from *Allāh Subḥānahu wa Taʿālā*:

عَنِ ابْنِ عَبَّاسٍ رَضِيَ اللهُ عَنْهُمَا، عَنِ النَّبِيِّ صَلَّى اللهُ عَلَيْهِ وَسَلَّمَ فِيمَا
يَرْوِي عَنْ رَبِّهِ عَزَّ وَجَلَّ، قَالَ: قَالَ: ... فَمَنْ هَمَّ بِحَسَنَةٍ فَلَمْ يَعْمَلْهَا،
كَتَبَهَا اللهُ لَهُ عِنْدَهُ حَسَنَةً كَامِلَةً، فَإِنْ هُوَ هَمَّ بِهَا فَعَمِلَهَا كَتَبَهَا اللهُ لَهُ
عِنْدَهُ عَشْرَ حَسَنَاتٍ إِلَى سَبْعِ مِائَةِ ضِعْفٍ إِلَى أَضْعَافٍ كَثِيرَةٍ، وَمَنْ هَمَّ
بِسَيِّئَةٍ فَلَمْ يَعْمَلْهَا، كَتَبَهَا اللهُ لَهُ عِنْدَهُ حَسَنَةً كَامِلَةً، فَإِنْ هُوَ هَمَّ
بِهَا فَعَمِلَهَا كَتَبَهَا اللهُ لَهُ سَيِّئَةً وَاحِدَةً.

(البخاري ومسلم)

Whosoever intended to do some good deed but was unable to perform it, Allah will still reward him for a good deed. However, if he was able to perform that deed then he will get rewards from 10 to 700 or more. If a person

---

[2] *Iḥyā' ʿUlūm al-Dīn*, Vol. 4, Chapter 7.

> intended to do an evil act but did not perform it, Allah will reward him for a good deed. However, if he acted upon it then only one evil act will be recorded.
> (Bukhārī and Muslim)

This shows the generosity of our Creator whereby He does not punish us for having an evil intention until that act is committed.

It is very important that one should always check when doing any good deed that one's intention is pure and that whatever one is intending to do is for Allah's pleasure. If one's intention is to show off, to acquire fame or any other worldly favour then any good deed becomes vitiated and instead of getting a reward one becomes liable for punishment either in this world or in the Hereafter. This is illustrated by the following *ḥadīth qudsī*, narrated on the authority of Abū Hurayrah who heard the Prophet (peace be upon him) say:

عَنْ أَبِي هُرَيرَةَ قَالَ: سَمِعْتُ رَسُولَ اللهِ صَلَّى اللهُ عَلَيْهِ وَسَلَّمَ، يَقُولُ: إِنَّ أَوَّلَ النَّاسِ يُقْضَى يَوْمَ الْقِيَامَةِ عَلَيْهِ رَجُلٌ اسْتُشْهِدَ، فَأُتِيَ بِهِ فَعَرَّفَهُ نِعَمَهُ فَعَرَفَهَا، قَالَ: فَمَا عَمِلْتَ فِيهَا؟، قَالَ: قَاتَلْتُ فِيكَ حَتَّى اسْتُشْهِدْتُ، قَالَ: كَذَبْتَ، وَلَكِنَّكَ قَاتَلْتَ لأَنْ يُقَالَ جَرِيءٌ، فَقَدْ قِيلَ ثُمَّ أُمِرَ بِهِ فَسُحِبَ عَلَى وَجْهِهِ حَتَّى أُلْقِيَ فِي النَّارِ ... .

(مسلم)

> The first people against whom a judgement will be pronounced on the Day of Resurrection will be a man who died as a martyr. Allah will mention the favours he was given and ask him what he did about them. He will say that he fought for Allah's sake until he died as a martyr. Allah will say that he fought because it might be said about him that he was courageous. Then he will be ordered to be dragged along by his face to be cast into the Hell-fire. (Similar will be the cases of a scholar and a philanthropist who although they imparted religious knowledge and gave

large sums of money in charity respectively, their intentions nevertheless were to be recognized for their scholarship and generosity, and as such they had already received their reward in this world. Therefore, they will also be sent into Hell-fire.)

(Muslim)

This is a terrifying *ḥadīth* as those who will be punished were doing good deeds in this world. But as their intention was not to seek Allah's pleasure and gain reward in the Hereafter, they met with a horrifying fate. Hence, although it is essential to do good deeds, it is even more important to be on one's guard and to check whether one's intention is pure. If this is not the case then one's efforts shall be of no avail and one will incur Allah's punishment. May Allah save us from such a horrid calamity. Hence sincerity of intention (*ikhlāṣ al-niyyah*) is required in whatever one does. The following *aḥādīth* elucidate this point further:

عَنْ شَدَّادٌ قَالَ سَمِعْتُ رَسُولَ اللهِ صَلَّى اللهُ عَلَيْهِ وَسَلَّمَ يَقُولُ: مَنْ صَلَّى يُرَائِي فَقَدْ أَشْرَكَ، وَمَنْ صَامَ يُرَائِي فَقَدْ أَشْرَكَ، وَمَنْ تَصَدَّقَ يُرَائِي فَقَدْ أَشْرَكَ

(أحمد)

It is reported by Shaddād ibn Aws who heard the Prophet (peace be upon him) say: "Whoever prayed to show off has committed associated someone or something with the Oneness of Allah (*shirk*). Whoever fasted to show off has committed *shirk* and whoever gave charity to show off has committed *shirk*.

(Aḥmad)

عَنْ مَحْمُودِ بْنِ لَبِيدٍ، أَنَّ رَسُولَ اللهِ صَلَّى اللهُ عَلَيْهِ وَسَلَّمَ قَالَ: إِنَّ أَخْوَفَ مَا أَخَافُ عَلَيْكُمُ الشِّرْكُ الأَصْغَرُ، قَالُوا: وَمَا الشِّرْكُ الأَصْغَرُ يَا رَسُولَ اللهِ؟ قَالَ: الرِّيَاءُ. ...

(أحمد)

Maḥmūd ibn Labīd reported that the Prophet (peace be upon him) said: "I am most fearful about you getting involved in minor *shirk*. People asked him; "O Messenger of Allah! What is minor *shirk*?" He replied: "Showing-off."

(Aḥmad)

As we know, *shirk* is the most heinous of crimes, one which will not be forgiven by Allah. Thus, doing acts to obtain praise from others or to be thought of as pious is sheer hypocrisy, and that is a kind of *shirk*. This means that one should always remain alert and check one's conscience, whenever one does any good deed. Even a small deed done with a good intention is more rewarding as is illustrated by the following incident. During preparations for the Battle of Tabūk, the Prophet (peace be upon him) made a general appeal to collect funds. The Companions responded by bringing large sums of money. ʿAbd al-Raḥmān ibn ʿAwf gave 400,000 dirhams and ʿUthmān ibn ʿAffān donated hundreds of horses and camels, while Abū Bakr al-Ṣiddīq gave everything he possessed. But there was a poor and needy Companion, Abū ʿAqīl al-Anṣarī, who used to work as a labourer on a farm owned by a Jew. He earned a few kilos of dates as his wages and this he brought with a trembling heart and presented the same to the Prophet (peace be upon him) as his contribution, wondering all the while whether these would be of any value. However, the Prophet (peace be upon him) took them and spread them over all the assembled goods and said: "Your reward is more than all that is assembled here." This is reflected in another saying of the Prophet (peace be upon him) that:

عَنْ أَبِي هُرَيْرَةَ ، قَالَ: قَالَ رَسُولُ اللهِ صَلَّى اللهُ عَلَيْهِ وَسَلَّمَ: إِنَّ اللهَ لَا يَنْظُرُ إِلَى صُوَرِكُمْ، وَأَمْوَالِكُمْ، وَلَكِنْ يَنْظُرُ إِلَى قُلُوبِكُمْ وَأَعْمَالِكُمْ.

(مسلم)

Allah does not look at your faces and your wealth but rather He looks at your hearts and your deeds.
(Narrated by Abū Hurayrah in Muslim)

Let us pray to *Allāh Subḥānahu wa Taʿālā* that all our acts and deeds are done with sincere intention. May He save us from showingoff and hypocrisy. As the Prophet (peace be upon him) used to pray:

اللهُمَّ إِنِّي أَعُوذُ بِكَ مِنَ الشِّقَاقِ، وَالنِّفَاقِ، وَسُوءِ الْأَخْلَاقِ.

(أبو داوود)

O Allah! I seek refuge in You from disunity, hypocrisy and bad manners.

(Abū Dāwūd)

اللَّهُمَّ طَهِّرْ قَلْبِي مِنَ النِّفَاقِ، وَعَمَلِي مِنَ الرِّيَاءِ، وَلِسَانِي مِنَ الْكَذِبِ، وَعَيْنِي مِنَ الْخِيَانَةِ، فَإِنَّكَ تَعْلَمُ خَائِنَةَ الْأَعْيُنِ، وَمَا تُخْفِي الصُّدُورُ.

(البيهقي)

O Allah! Purify my heart from hypocrisy and my deeds from showingoff and my tongue from lying and my eyes from treachery as You know the treachery of the eyes and what the hearts conceal. (*Āmīn*)

(Bayhaqī)

4

Sincerity (*Ikhlāṣ*)

وَمَآ أُمِرُوٓا۟ إِلَّا لِيَعْبُدُوا۟ ٱللَّهَ مُخْلِصِينَ لَهُ ٱلدِّينَ حُنَفَآءَ وَيُقِيمُوا۟ ٱلصَّلَوٰةَ
وَيُؤْتُوا۟ ٱلزَّكَوٰةَ ۚ وَذَٰلِكَ دِينُ ٱلْقَيِّمَةِ ﴿٥﴾

Yet all that they had been commanded was that they serve Allah, with utter sincerity, devoting themselves exclusively to Him, and that they establish Prayer and pay Zakāh. That is the right Religion.

(al-Bayyinah 98: 5)

Islam requires that all our acts should be done with purity of intention, clarity of thought, and without pursuing any worldly purpose, seeking only to gain Allah's pleasure. This is the essence of *ikhlāṣ*. The word *ikhlāṣ* comes from the root *khalaṣa*, which literally means the act of purification by the separation of impurities. It means to be pure, unadulterated and unmixed. Hence, *ikhlāṣ* means to be sincere and loyal, one who is pure and of undefiled faith. In Islamic terminology, it means to abstain from ostentation and hypocrisy. Our faith (*īmān*) requires that all good deeds should be done for Allah's sake alone. The Prophet Jesus (peace be upon him) was asked by his Companions: "Who is sincere to Allah?" He said: "Sincere is the one who does everything for Allah's sake and who does not like praise from anyone." (Aḥmad)

The Prophet (peace be upon him) said: "Allah, the Most Exalted, does not accept any act unless it is done exclusively for Him." After saying this, the Prophet (peace be upon him) recited this verse:

أَلَا لِلَّهِ ٱلدِّينُ ٱلْخَالِصُ ... ﴿٣﴾

For most surely it is to Allah alone that the Religion with sincere devotion belongs.

(al-Zumar 39: 3)

In another *ḥadīth qudsī* narrated by Abū Hurayrah, the Prophet (peace be upon him) related that Allah said: "He who has done any deed for Me and associated others with it then I will abandon him with his associating others with God (*shirk*)." In another version it is reported that Allah said: "I am absolved of this deed. It is for the person for whom it is done." (Muslim)

The word *ikhlāṣ* is often used in relation with the word *Dīn* as in the following verses:

هُوَ ٱلْحَىُّ لَآ إِلَـٰهَ إِلَّا هُوَ فَٱدْعُوهُ مُخْلِصِينَ لَهُ ٱلدِّينَ ۗ ٱلْحَمْدُ لِلَّهِ رَبِّ ٱلْعَـٰلَمِينَ ﴿٦٥﴾

He is the Living (*One*)*: There is no God but He; call upon Him, giving sincere devotion. Praise be to Allah, Lord of the Worlds.*

(Ghāfir 40: 65)

قُلْ إِنِّىٓ أُمِرْتُ أَنْ أَعْبُدَ ٱللَّهَ مُخْلِصًا لَّهُ ٱلدِّينَ ﴿١١﴾

Say (*O Prophet*)*: I am commanded to worship Allah, making religion pure for Him* (*only*).

(al-Zumar 39: 11)

قُلِ ٱللَّهَ أَعْبُدُ مُخْلِصًا لَّهُۥ دِينِى ﴿١٤﴾

Say: I worship Allah alone, making my religion pure for Him (*only*).

(al-Zumar 39: 14)

Purifying *dīn* means to avoid showing off (*riyā'*), making a pretence of piety, having sincere faith, and doing all acts exclusively for Allah's pleasure. Thus, the other aspect of *ikhlāṣ* is the purity of one's intention. According to a well-known *ḥadīth*:

إِنَّمَا الأَعْمَالُ بِالنِّيَّاتِ ، وَإِنَّمَا لِكُلِّ امْرِئٍ مَا نَوَى.

(البخاري ومسلم)

All actions are but by intention and one will get the reward for what one has intended.
(Narrated by 'Umar ibn al-Khaṭṭāb in Bukhārī & Muslim)

Thus purity of intention (*ikhlāṣ al-niyyah*) is of paramount importance. This is further elucidated by another *ḥadīth* of the Prophet (peace be upon him) in which he is reported to have said:

قَالَ أَبُو ذَرٍّ: إِنَّ رَسُولَ اللهِ صَلَّى اللهُ عَلَيْهِ وَسَلَّمَ قَالَ: قَدْ أَفْلَحَ مَنْ أَخْلَصَ قَلْبَهُ لِلإِيمَانِ.

(أحمد)

Indeed, the one who has purified his heart for faith has achieved salvation.
(Narrated by Abu Dharr in Aḥmad)

Similarly, the Prophet (peace be upon him) also said:

عَنْ زَيْدِ بْنِ أَرْقَمَ، قَالَ: قَالَ رَسُولُ اللهِ صَلَّى اللهُ عَلَيْهِ وَسَلَّمَ مَنْ قَالَ لا إِلَهَ إِلا اللهُ مُخْلِصًا دَخَلَ الْجَنَّةَ، قِيلَ: وَمَا إِخْلاَصُهَا؟ قَالَ: أَنْ تَحْجُزَهُ عَنْ مَحَارِمِ اللهِ عَزَّ وَجَلَّ.

(الطبراني)

"One who said, 'there is no god except Allah' (*Lā ilāha illa Allāh*) with *ikhlāṣ* shall enter Paradise." When asked: "What does it means to recite this declaration of faith (*kalimah*) with *ikhlāṣ*?" He replied: "If this *kalimah* stops him from doing unlawful acts then this is what is meant by *ikhlāṣ*."

(Narrated by Zayd bin Arqam in Ṭabarānī)

Both *ikhlāṣ* of intention (*niyyah*) and deeds (*'amal*) are necessary for the acceptance of deeds by Allah. This is very graphically and eloquently illustrated in a *ḥadīth qudsī*, in which it is narrated how Allah will deal with a martyr, and a scholar and a wealthy man – all of whom will be hoping that on the Day of Resurrection they will be rewarded for their good deeds. However, Allah will decree that they be cast down into Hell-fire as they were not sincere in their deeds. Each was seeking recognition for their courage, knowledge and generosity in this world and they had already received their reward there.

However, it may be said that even the most sincere of people may sometimes desire that their good efforts are recognized as such. Since this is a natural human weakness, how can one avoid such a tendency? We accept that there should be recognition and praise but who is best qualified to confer such recognition and praise? In essence, none but *Allāh Subḥānahu wa Ta'ālā*. Thus, if we have firm faith in Him and we believe that He sees everything, hears everything and knows everything, then surely He will recognize our sincere efforts. According to a *ḥadīth*, He will praise us in the company of far superior beings – the angels. Thus, whenever we feel the need for recognition and reward, we should channel our thoughts and desires in this direction and, *Inshā'Allāh*, this will help to drive away any germ of ostentation and we will be able to devote our efforts sincerely and wholeheartedly for Allah's sake alone.

The word *ikhlāṣ* in the Qur'ān is used as antonym of hypocrisy (*nifāq*) as well as of associating someone or something with the Oneness of Allah (*shirk*).The Prophet (peace be upon him) indicated the signs of *ikhlāṣ* as well as those of *nifāq*. The signs of *ikhlāṣ*, as listed by Shāh Walīullāh in his book *Ḥujjatullāh al-Bālighah*, are:

1. To love Allah and His Prophet more than anyone else;
2. One's love for others should only be for Allah's sake; and
3. One should hate unbelief (*kufr*) just as one avoids danger from fire.

It is narrated by Shaddād ibn Aws that the Prophet (peace be upon him) said:

عَنْ شَدَّادٌ قَالَ سَمِعْتُ رَسُولَ اللهِ صَلَّى اللهُ عَلَيْهِ وَسَلَّمَ يَقُولُ :مَنْ صَلَّى يُرَائِي فَقَدْ أَشْرَكَ، وَمَنْ صَامَ يُرَائِي فَقَدْ أَشْرَكَ، وَمَنْ تَصَدَّقَ يُرَائِي فَقَدْ أَشْرَكَ.

(أحمد)

He who has prayed to show off has associated someone or something with the Oneness of God (*shirk*) and he who has fasted to show off has committed *shirk* and he who has given charity to show off has committed *shirk*.

(Aḥmad)

The Qur'ān also castigates those whose deeds are done to show off:

فَوَيْلٌ لِّلْمُصَلِّينَ ۝ ٱلَّذِينَ هُمْ عَن صَلَاتِهِمْ سَاهُونَ ۝ ٱلَّذِينَ هُمْ يُرَآءُونَ ۝

Woe, then, to those who pray, but are heedless in their Prayers, those who do good (in order) to be seen, and they deny people the articles of common necessity.

(al-Mā'ūn 107: 4-6)

The highest level of *ikhlāṣ* is portrayed in the following verse of *Sūrah al-Dahr*:

وَيُطْعِمُونَ ٱلطَّعَامَ عَلَىٰ حُبِّهِۦ مِسْكِينًا وَيَتِيمًا وَأَسِيرًا ۝ إِنَّمَا نُطْعِمُكُمْ لِوَجْهِ ٱللَّهِ لَا نُرِيدُ مِنكُمْ جَزَآءً وَلَا شُكُورًا ۝

Those who, for the love of Him, feed the needy, and the orphan, and the captive (saying) "We feed you only for Allah's sake; we do not seek of you any recompense or thanks."

(al-Insān 76: 9-10)

Coincidentally, the word "sincere" can shed some light on the true meaning of *ikhlāṣ*. The root of this English word is from the Latin *sin* and *cere*, which means without wax. Dishonest tradesmen in ancient Rome used to disguise their defective earthen pots by covering over the cracks with wax before selling them. From the outside, the pot would look perfect but as soon as hot water was poured into it the wax would melt and the pot would leak. To reassure their customers, honest tradesmen started labeling their good quality pots with the words *sin cere*, literally meaning without wax. Thus sincerity (*ikhlāṣ*) involves being the same in actual character as in outward appearance. It means being solid the whole way through just as genuine clay pots were perfect throughout – both inside and out.

The word *mukhliṣ* is used several times in the Qur'ān. It means one who is sincere, devoted, virtuous, and righteous. We are required to be *mukhliṣ* in our faith, but this may become dimmed by forgetfulness. Usually, it is only in time of real crisis that we call upon Allah with sincerity. Even non-believers, when stranded at sea in stormy weather, and losing all hope of survival, are thus overwhelmed by fear and cry out for Allah's help. It is then that they sincerely offer their devotion to Him. This scene is depicted in many places in the Qur'ān, (*Yūnus* 10: 22; *al-ʿAnkabūt* 29: 65 and *Luqmān* 31: 32).

As sincerity of intention and deeds should be the basis of all our worship (*ʿibādah*), we should constantly scrutinize our intentions and see if they really reflect the state of our faith (*īmān*). This is so we can hope to be rewarded by our Lord and not be like those who, having done good deeds, will still be empty handed on the Day of Resurrection and who will incur severe punishment as well. May Allah save us from such a dreadful calamity.

Let us pray that Allah helps us to make our intentions pure, our thoughts clean, and our striving only for His sake. May Allah save us from showing off (*riyāʾ*) and hypocrisy (*nifāq*).

اللَّهُمَّ إِنِّي أَعُوذُ بِكَ مِنْ شَرِّ سَمْعِي، وَمِنْ شَرِّ بَصَرِي، وَمِنْ شَرِّ لِسَانِي، وَمِنْ شَرِّ قَلْبِي، وَمِنْ شَرِّ مَنِيِّي يَعْنِي فَرْجَهُ.

(أبو داوود والترمذي)

O Lord! We seek refuge in You from the mischief of our ears and the mischief of our eyes and the mischief of our tongues and the mischief of our hearts and the mischief of our sexual desires. (*Āmīn*)

(Abu Dāwūd and Tirmidhī)

5

God-Consciousness (*Taqwā*)

... إِنَّ أَكْرَمَكُمْ عِندَ ٱللَّهِ أَتْقَىٰكُمْ ... ﴿١٣﴾

Verily the noblest of you in the sight of Allah is the most-God-conscious of you.

(al-Ḥujurāt 49: 13)

The word *taqwā* is extensively used in the Qur'ān and *Sunnah*. It is derived from *wiqāyah*, which means to guard, to protect, to preserve, to shield, and to keep one safe from some harm. In Qur'ānic terminology, it is that state of the heart which gives certainty of Allah's presence at all times, thus differentiating between good and evil and disposing one towards good and creating hatred of evil. This consciousness requires that one should constantly be aware that one is not committing any act that makes one liable of incurring Allah's anger and punishment and this comes from fear of Him. Thus, *taqwā* is often translated as "fear of Allah", but "God-consciousness" is a better translation. However, in some contexts, "fear" is a more appropriate translation.

Taqwā is a comprehensive term that covers all good deeds and acts. As Bāyazīd Busṭāmī, a famous Sufi master said: a God-conscious person is one who whatever he says he says for Allah's sake and whatever he does he does for Allah's sake. This all-embracing meaning is enunciated right at the start of *Sūrah al-Baqarah*, the second *sūrah* of the Qur'ān:

ذَٰلِكَ ٱلْكِتَـٰبُ لَا رَيْبَ ۛ فِيهِ ۛ هُدًى لِّلْمُتَّقِينَ ﴿٢﴾ ٱلَّذِينَ يُؤْمِنُونَ بِٱلْغَيْبِ
وَيُقِيمُونَ ٱلصَّلَوٰةَ وَمِمَّا رَزَقْنَـٰهُمْ يُنفِقُونَ ﴿٣﴾ وَٱلَّذِينَ يُؤْمِنُونَ بِمَآ أُنزِلَ إِلَيْكَ
وَمَآ أُنزِلَ مِن قَبْلِكَ وَبِٱلْـَٔاخِرَةِ هُمْ يُوقِنُونَ ﴿٤﴾

This is the book of Allah, there is no doubt in it; it is guidance for God-conscious people, who believe in the existence of that which is beyond the reach of perception, who establish Prayer and spend out of what We have provided them, who believe in what has been revealed to you and what was revealed before you, and have faith in the Hereafter.
(al-Baqarah 2: 2-3)

According to these verses, the basis of *taqwā* is firm faith in God, His Books and Messengers (who bring this guidance) and the Day of Judgement. These articles of faith are the foundation of Religion (*Dīn*). This is followed by two essential pillars of Islam: one dealing with the rights of the Creator – namely His worship and obedience in the form of Prayer – and the other is *infāq*, spending on the needs of human beings for Allah's sake.

The same message is repeated yet more comprehensively later in *Sūrah al-Baqarah* in the verse known as *Āyah al-Birr* (Verse of Piety):

لَّيْسَ ٱلْبِرَّ أَن تُوَلُّوا۟ وُجُوهَكُمْ قِبَلَ ٱلْمَشْرِقِ وَٱلْمَغْرِبِ وَلَـٰكِنَّ ٱلْبِرَّ مَنْ ءَامَنَ
بِٱللَّهِ وَٱلْيَوْمِ ٱلْـَٔاخِرِ وَٱلْمَلَـٰٓئِكَةِ وَٱلْكِتَـٰبِ وَٱلنَّبِيِّـۧنَ وَءَاتَى ٱلْمَالَ عَلَىٰ
حُبِّهِۦ ذَوِى ٱلْقُرْبَىٰ وَٱلْيَتَـٰمَىٰ وَٱلْمَسَـٰكِينَ وَٱبْنَ ٱلسَّبِيلِ وَٱلسَّآئِلِينَ وَفِى
ٱلرِّقَابِ وَأَقَامَ ٱلصَّلَوٰةَ وَءَاتَى ٱلزَّكَوٰةَ وَٱلْمُوفُونَ بِعَهْدِهِمْ إِذَا عَـٰهَدُوا۟ ۖ
وَٱلصَّـٰبِرِينَ فِى ٱلْبَأْسَآءِ وَٱلضَّرَّآءِ وَحِينَ ٱلْبَأْسِ ۗ أُو۟لَـٰٓئِكَ ٱلَّذِينَ
صَدَقُوا۟ ۖ وَأُو۟لَـٰٓئِكَ هُمُ ٱلْمُتَّقُونَ ﴿١٧٧﴾

Righteousness does not consist in turning your faces towards the east or towards the west; true righteousness consists in believing in Allah and the Last Day, the angels, the Book and the Prophets, and in giving away one's property in love of Him to one's kinsmen, the orphans, the poor and the wayfarer, and to those who ask for help, and in freeing the necks of slaves, and in establishing Prayer and dispensing the Zakāh. True righteousness is attained by those who are faithful to their promise once they have made it and by those who remain steadfast in adversity and affliction and at the time of battle (between Truth and falsehood). Such are the truthful ones; such are the God-fearing.

(al-Baqarah 2: 177)

It is significant to note that in this verse the basic beliefs (*ʿaqā'id*) are followed by the rights of fellow human beings followed by Prayer and *Zakāh*. Thus, truthful and God-conscious are those who are the embodiment of all these virtues and who dedicate all their activities towards what is good. Most importantly, they remain steadfast and firm in the face of adversity.

Deeper study of the Qur'ān shows that *taqwā* is the purpose of all worship (*ʿibādah*) not only in the performance of Prayer and *Zakāh*, but in all of our acts, whether fasting, *Ḥajj*, the sacrifice of animals as well as in the wearing of dress or in the administration of justice. Thus, the first call of all prophets was:

إِنِّي لَكُمْ رَسُولٌ أَمِينٌ ﴿١٢٥﴾ فَاتَّقُوا اللَّهَ وَأَطِيعُونِ ﴿١٢٦﴾

I am to you a Messenger worthy of trust. So fear Allah and obey me.

(al-Shuʿarā' 26: 125-126)

In *Sūrah Āl ʿImrān* it is said:

يَا أَيُّهَا الَّذِينَ آمَنُوا اتَّقُوا اللَّهَ حَقَّ تُقَاتِهِ ... ﴿١٠٢﴾

O you who believe! Be ever God-fearing, with a fear justly due Him.

(Āl ʿImrān 3: 102)

What, then, is the fear of Allah? This is explained in a *ḥadīth*:

عَنْ عَبْدِ اللهِ بْنِ مَسْعُودٍ رَضِيَ اللهُ عَنْهُ، قَالَ: قَالَ رَسُولُ اللهِ صَلَّى اللهُ عَلَيْهِ وَسَلَّمَ: أَنْ يُطَاعَ فَلا يُعْصَى، وَأَنْ يُذْكَرَ فَلا يُنْسَى، وَأَنْ يُشْكَرَ فَلا يُكْفَرَ.

(الحاكم)

Narrated by ʿAbdullāh ibn Masʿūd, who related that the Prophet (peace be upon him) said: "To obey and not disobey; to remember and not to forget; to be thankful and not be ungrateful."

(Ḥākim)

The other verse in *Sūrah al-Taghābun* states:

فَٱتَّقُوا۟ ٱللَّهَ مَا ٱسْتَطَعْتُمْ ... ﴿١٦﴾

Have taqwā of Allah as much as you can.

(al-Taghābun 64: 16)

According to the Companion ʿAbdullāh ibn ʿAbbās, this is the explanation of the verse in *Sūrah Āl ʿImrān* as narrated above. When asked, he said: "O Messenger of Allah! Who has the strength to accomplish this?" Then the Prophet (peace be upon him) recited the verse of *Sūrah al-Taghābun* as cited above. (Al-Bayhaqī) It means one should have *taqwā* of Allah as much as is humanly possible. This is what is meant by His right of *taqwā*.

So far we have discussed the importance of *taqwā* and the attributes of God-fearing people. The benefits and bounties of Allah that are bestowed on those who fulfill the obligations of *taqwā* are immense, both in this world and in the Hereafter. Let us see what one can gain from *taqwā* in this world. I have already recited the verse at the start of the *khuṭbah* that Allah considers a God-fearing person the most noble of people. Other bounties that Allah bestows on him are:

- One gains the companionship of Allah, as stated in *Sūrah al-Naḥl*:

إِنَّ ٱللَّهَ مَعَ ٱلَّذِينَ ٱتَّقَوا۟ وَّٱلَّذِينَ هُم مُّحْسِنُونَ ﴿١٢٨﴾

Surely Allah is with those who hold Him in fear and do good.
(al-Naḥl 16:128)

- One receives *barakah*, blessings and untold rewards as Allah promises:

وَلَوْ أَنَّهُمْ ءَامَنُوا۟ وَٱتَّقَوْا۟ لَمَثُوبَةٌ مِّنْ عِندِ ٱللَّهِ خَيْرٌ ۖ لَّوْ كَانُوا۟ يَعْلَمُونَ ﴿١٠٣﴾

Had they believed and been God-fearing Allah's reward would have been better. Had they but known!
(al-Baqarah 2: 103)

- One will receive provisions and one's needs will be fulfilled as mentioned in *Sūrah al-Ṭalāq:*

... وَمَن يَتَّقِ ٱللَّهَ يَجْعَل لَّهُۥ مَخْرَجًا ﴿٢﴾ وَيَرْزُقْهُ مِنْ حَيْثُ لَا يَحْتَسِبُ ۚ ... ﴿٣﴾

Allah will find a way out for him who fears Allah and will provide him sustenance from whence he never even imagined.
(al-Ṭalāq 65: 2-3)

- One's affairs will be accomplished with ease and comfort. As mentioned in the following verse of the same *sūrah*:

... وَمَن يَتَّقِ ٱللَّهَ يَجْعَل لَّهُۥ مِنْ أَمْرِهِۦ يُسْرًا ﴿٤﴾

Allah will create ease for him who is God-conscious.
(al-Ṭalāq 65: 4)

- One will be free of fear and anxiety or sorrow. As *Sūrah al-Aʿrāf* says:

... فَمَنِ ٱتَّقَىٰ وَأَصْلَحَ فَلَا خَوْفٌ عَلَيْهِمْ وَلَا هُمْ يَحْزَنُونَ ﴿٣٥﴾

Whoever shall fear Allah and act righteously, on them shall be no fear, nor shall they grieve.

(al-Aʿrāf 7: 35)

- One will attain the status of *Walī Allāh* (Friend of Allah) and receive tidings from the angels both in this world and the Hereafter. *Sūrah Yūnus* provides a vivid description of the same:

أَلَآ إِنَّ أَوْلِيَآءَ ٱللَّهِ لَا خَوْفٌ عَلَيْهِمْ وَلَا هُمْ يَحْزَنُونَ ﴿٦٢﴾ ٱلَّذِينَ ءَامَنُوا۟
وَكَانُوا۟ يَتَّقُونَ ﴿٦٣﴾ لَهُمُ ٱلْبُشْرَىٰ فِى ٱلْحَيَوٰةِ ٱلدُّنْيَا وَفِى ٱلْءَاخِرَةِ ... ﴿٦٤﴾

Surely the friends of Allah have nothing to fear, nor shall they grieve – the ones who believe and are God-fearing. For them are glad tidings in this world and the Hereafter.

(Yūnus 10: 62-64)

As regards the rewards promised to the God-fearing in the Hereafter, these are enumerated extensively both in the Qur'ān and *aḥādīth*. Some of the relevant verses are:

- Lofty abodes in Paradise (*Jannah*) as promised by Allah:

لَٰكِنِ ٱلَّذِينَ ٱتَّقَوْا۟ رَبَّهُمْ لَهُمْ غُرَفٌ مِّن فَوْقِهَا غُرَفٌ مَّبْنِيَّةٌ تَجْرِى
مِن تَحْتِهَا ٱلْأَنْهَٰرُ ۖ وَعْدَ ٱللَّهِ ۖ لَا يُخْلِفُ ٱللَّهُ ٱلْمِيعَادَ ﴿٢٠﴾

But those who fear their Lord shall have lofty mansions built over one another beneath which rivers flow. This is Allah's promise and never does Allah fail to fulfill His promise.

(al-Zumar 39: 20)

- They will be seated near the Throne of Allah as described in *Sūrah al-Qamar*:

إِنَّ ٱلْمُتَّقِينَ فِى جَنَّـٰتٍ وَنَهَرٍ ﴿٥٤﴾ فِى مَقْعَدِ صِدْقٍ عِندَ مَلِيكٍ مُّقْتَدِرٍۭ ﴿٥٥﴾

Surely the God-fearing will dwell amidst Gardens and running streams where they will be seated in the presence of a King, Mighty in Power.

(al-Qamar 54: 54-55)

- They will be in shades of Paradise and have an enjoyable life as depicted in *Sūrah al-Mursalāt*:

إِنَّ ٱلْمُتَّقِينَ فِى ظِلَـٰلٍ وَعُيُونٍ ﴿٤١﴾ وَفَوَٰكِهَ مِمَّا يَشْتَهُونَ ﴿٤٢﴾ كُلُوا۟ وَٱشْرَبُوا۟ هَنِيٓـًٔۢا بِمَا كُنتُمْ تَعْمَلُونَ ﴿٤٣﴾

Behold, the God-fearing will enjoy cool shade, and springs and the fruits that they desire. Eat and drink and may every joy attend you as a reward for your good deeds.

(al-Mursalāt 77: 41-43)

One may get the impression from the preceding discussion that God-fearing people are so pious and virtuous that their lives are blameless and that they hardly commit any sin. We know all human beings commit mistakes and sin as do the God-fearing (*muttaqīn*). As the Qur'ān says:

وَٱلَّذِينَ إِذَا فَعَلُوا۟ فَـٰحِشَةً أَوْ ظَلَمُوٓا۟ أَنفُسَهُمْ ذَكَرُوا۟ ٱللَّهَ فَٱسْتَغْفَرُوا۟ لِذُنُوبِهِمْ وَمَن يَغْفِرُ ٱلذُّنُوبَ إِلَّا ٱللَّهُ وَلَمْ يُصِرُّوا۟ عَلَىٰ مَا فَعَلُوا۟ وَهُمْ يَعْلَمُونَ ﴿١٣٥﴾ أُو۟لَـٰٓئِكَ جَزَآؤُهُم مَّغْفِرَةٌ مِّن رَّبِّهِمْ وَجَنَّـٰتٌ تَجْرِى مِن تَحْتِهَا ٱلْأَنْهَـٰرُ خَـٰلِدِينَ فِيهَا ۚ وَنِعْمَ أَجْرُ ٱلْعَـٰمِلِينَ ﴿١٣٦﴾

These [the God-fearing] are the ones who, when they commit any indecency or wrong themselves, instantly remember Allah and implore forgiveness for their sins – for who will forgive sins save Allah? – and do not willfully persist in the wrong they had committed. They shall be recompensed by forgiveness from their Lord and by Gardens beneath which rivers flow; there they shall abide. How good is the reward of those who earnestly labour!

(Āl ʿImrān 3: 135-136)

The quality of a *muttaqī* is to remain alert and if he slips and commits a sin he instantly repents and does not persist in wrongdoing.

Our all worthy predecessors always counselled each other about incorporating *taqwā* into their lives. So in following their footsteps, I remind myself and you about cultivating *taqwā* by repeating the words of the Prophet (peace be upon him) who told Muʿādh ibn Jabal: "Acquire *taqwā* wherever you are."

O Merciful One! Our hearts are between Your compassionate Fingers and you change them as You wish. Keep our hearts firm on our *Dīn*. Make our hearts satisfied with Your remembrance and bestow tranquility (*sakīnah*) upon our hearts. Bind us to the words of *taqwā* and make us capable of acquiring it. O Allah, grant us *taqwā* and help us to remain steadfast upon Your way. (*Āmīn*)

6

Perseverance (*Ṣabr*)

يَـٰٓأَيُّهَا ٱلَّذِينَ ءَامَنُوا۟ ٱسْتَعِينُوا۟ بِٱلصَّبْرِ وَٱلصَّلَوٰةِ ۚ إِنَّ ٱللَّهَ مَعَ ٱلصَّـٰبِرِينَ ﴿١٥٣﴾

O you who believe! Seek help in patience and in prayer; Allah is with those who patiently persevere.

(al-Baqarah 2: 153)

We all encounter many problems in our lives. These may range from difficulties we may face with regard to illness in our family and friends or losing our loved ones. It could be unemployment or financial loss in business. It could be a natural disaster that has devastated our homes, workplaces and possessions. In addition to these problems, those who have committed themselves to travel the path of truth and righteousness often have to face persecution. To remain firm and bear these calamities with patience and perseverance is called *ṣabr* in Islamic terminology. It comes from the root *ṣabara* which means to bind, to tie, to fetter or to shackle. It also means to be patient, forbearing or to persevere. The essence of *ṣabr* is endurance or bearing pain, suffering and difficulty and showing perseverance and fortitude against them and dealing with these problems calmly without losing hope. Thus, *ṣabr* is to control oneself from anxiety, despondency and dejection whilst managing to remain firm on one's standpoint. It also includes controlling oneself and refraining from all that the *Sharīʿah* has declared unlawful. *Ṣabr* requires one to persevere with satisfaction of heart and to never veer from the path of righteousness.

According to Imām Ghazālī, *ṣabr* is one of the foundational stones of the *Dīn* (Religion). Because of its importance, *ṣabr* is regarded as half of *Dīn*, the other half being thankfulness (*shukr*). In this respect, the following saying of the Prophet (peace be upon him) is very pertinent:

عَنْ صُهَيْب، قَـالَ: قَالَ رَسُـولُ اللهِ صَلَّى اللهُ عَلَيْهِ وَسَلَّمَ: عَجَبًـا لأَمْرِ الْـمُؤْمِنِ، إِنَّ أَمْـرَهُ كُلَّهُ خَيْرٌ، وَلَيْسَ ذَاكَ لأَحَدٍ إِلَّا لِلْمُؤْمِنِ إِنْ أَصَابَتْهُ سَرَّاءُ شَكَرَ، فَكَانَ خَيْرًا لَهُ، وَإِنْ أَصَابَتْهُ ضَرَّاءُ صَبَرَ، فَكَانَ خَيْرًا لَهُ.

(مسلم)

How remarkable a believer's affair is! For it is always to his advantage, and this is peculiar to none other than a believer. If some good happens to him, he gives thanks to Allah and this is to his advantage; and if something harmful happens to him, he endures it patiently, and this is to his advantage also.

(Narrated by Ṣuhayb in Muslim)

It is also to be noted that *al-Ṣabūr* and *al-Shakūr* are both among the Most Beautiful Names (*al-Asmā' al-Ḥusnā*) of Allah. When *Shakūr* is used for Allah, it means that He recognizes and appreciates the efforts of His servants and gives suitable rewards for the smallest service performed by them, however defective. *Ṣabūr* indicates Allah's immense patience in dealing with His servants.

Usually people regard *ṣabr* as submission, weakness and wretchedness. This is the attitude one adopts when one feels helpless and destitute, but *ṣabr* actually means to overcome difficulties with courage and determination. *Ṣabr* is also the name of a bitter plant, the aloe. Symbolically, this indicates that practising patience (*ṣabr*) is not agreeable to human nature; indeed, it is a bitter pill to swallow.

There are many occasions where *ṣabr* is required and some of these are:

1. Enduring difficulties while fulfilling the obligations required of a believer. For example, Ramaḍān is called the month of *ṣabr* as fasting requires perseverance and patience. Similarly, fulfilling other commandments also need *ṣabr*.
2. There is perseverance in adversity as indicated in the Qur'ān:

... وَٱلصَّٰبِرِينَ فِى ٱلْبَأْسَآءِ وَٱلضَّرَّآءِ وَحِينَ ٱلْبَأْسِ ... ﴿١٧٧﴾

...And to be firm and patient, in pain (or suffering) and adversity and throughout all periods of panic...

(al-Baqarah 2: 177)

3. *Ṣabr* is required in safeguarding oneself from the temptations of the carnal self (*al-nafs al-ammārah*). One should always keep one's desires under control and remain firm when facing temptation as the Prophet Yūsuf (peace be upon him) said:

... إِنَّ ٱلنَّفْسَ لَأَمَّارَةٌۢ بِٱلسُّوٓءِ... ﴿٥٣﴾

Surely one's carnal self prompts one to evil...

(Yūsuf 12: 53)

One has to refrain from all evil acts such as the accumulation of wealth by illegal means, i.e. by cheating or defrauding. There are also many other situations that require self-control.

4. Conveying the message of Islam to others also requires much patience. For example, one may have to bear constant ridicule and opposition. Initially, this might only be verbal abuse but it could be physical persecution as well. The Prophet (peace be upon him) was constantly advised to be patient with those who argued with him and rejected Islam's message. We know that he was not an impatient person. Yet in the Makkan *Sūrah*s he was reminded on no less than 18 occasions to be patient. Thus, during that period, the Prophet (peace be upon him) instructed believers to remain patient against all oppression,

to bear it with dignity and never to retaliate. This was the same advice that Luqmān gave his son:

... وَٱصْبِرْ عَلَىٰ مَآ أَصَابَكَ ۖ إِنَّ ذَٰلِكَ مِنْ عَزْمِ ٱلْأُمُورِ ﴿١٧﴾

And endure with patience whatever affliction befalls you.
Surely this is a thing requiring great resolve.
(Luqmān 31: 17)

During the Madīnan period, the believers were also included in this instruction to practise *ṣabr*, for example, in the verse I recited at the start of the *khuṭbah* that advises believers to seek help from prayer and *ṣabr*. The same message is also delivered in *Sūrah Āl ʿImrān* as:

يَٰٓأَيُّهَا ٱلَّذِينَ ءَامَنُوا۟ ٱصْبِرُوا۟ وَصَابِرُوا۟ وَرَابِطُوا۟ وَٱتَّقُوا۟ ٱللَّهَ
لَعَلَّكُمْ تُفْلِحُونَ ﴿٢٠٠﴾

O you who believe! Be steadfast, and vie in steadfastness,
stand firm in your faith, and remain God-conscious
that you may attain success.
(Āl ʿImrān 3: 200)

Here, the instruction is for collective *ṣabr*. As we know, *Sūrah Āl ʿImrān* was revealed after the Battle of Uḥud. The instructions given are clear that there should be patience (*ṣabr*) and firmness against all odds. The believers should struggle hard, remain firm and steadfast, not succumb to temptation, and never listen to the defeatists or those who create discord. It is essential that as believers they should resist their desires, ambitions, weaknesses and failings. They should persevere when faced by the weaknesses, perversions and deceits of others. They should be ready to face stiff opposition and falsehood. They will overcome if they remain patient and firm. The verse then asks the believers to excel in perseverance (*muṣābarah*) with regard to their enemies and opponents. They should overcome their enemies who try to exhaust their patience.

In a prolonged struggle they should not fail but rather be firmer and more patient than their adversaries, whether these be external enemies or from within their own ranks. If they want to succeed against their enemies they should excel in their resolve and determination. The message is the same for us today. We have to learn to be patient when dealing with provocation and opposition. Unfortunately, as a nation, our response is often an emotional outburst.

Ṣabr is one of greatest virtues that believers are asked to make part of their lives. In more than 70 places it is praised in the Qur'ān. Some of the verses are as follows:

أُوْلَـٰٓئِكَ يُجْزَوْنَ ٱلْغُرْفَةَ بِمَا صَبَرُواْ وَيُلَقَّوْنَ فِيهَا تَحِيَّةً وَسَلَـٰمًا ﴿٧٥﴾

They are the ones who will be rewarded for their patience: lofty palaces will be granted to them, and they will be received with greeting and salutation.

(al-Furqān 25: 75)

إِنِّى جَزَيْتُهُمُ ٱلْيَوْمَ بِمَا صَبَرُوٓاْ أَنَّهُمْ هُمُ ٱلْفَآئِزُونَ ﴿١١١﴾

I have rewarded them this day for their steadfastness, so that they alone are triumphant.

(*al-Mu'minūn* 23: 111)

... إِنَّمَا يُوَفَّى ٱلصَّـٰبِرُونَ أَجْرَهُم بِغَيْرِ حِسَابٍ ﴿١٠﴾

Verily those who persevere shall be granted their reward beyond all reckoning.

(al-Zumar 39: 10)

This last verse indicates that the reward of *ṣabr* is an exception to the general rule according to which each good deed receives its proportionate reward. But for *ṣabr*, like fasting, it is said that the reward will be without reckoning. As fasting is a kind of *ṣabr*, about which Allah has said: "Fasting is for Me and I will give reward for it," it is worth noting that although all acts of worship (*ʿibādah*) are for Allah, fasting alone is singled out for this honour.

There are many *aḥādīth* that extol the virtues of *ṣabr*. It is related by Abū Saʿīd al-Khudrī that the Prophet (peace be upon him) said:

عَنْ أَبِي سَعِيدٍ الْـخُدْرِيِّ رَضِيَ اللهُ عَنْهُ قَالَ: قَالَ رَسُولُ اللهِ صَلَّى اللهُ عَلَيْهِ وَسَلَّمَ: وَمَنْ يَتَصَبَّرْ يُصَبِّرْهُ اللهُ، وَمَا أُعْطِيَ أَحَدٌ عَطَاءً خَيْرًا وَأَوْسَعَ مِنَ الصَّبْرِ.

(البخاري ومسلم)

One who tries to be patient Allah will give him patience.
There is no better gift than the patience given to someone.
(Bukhārī and Muslim)

عَنْ عَمْرِو بْنِ عَبَسَةَ، قَالَ: أَتَيْتُ رَسُولَ اللهِ صَلَّى اللهُ عَلَيْهِ وَسَلَّمَ، فَقُلْتُ: مَا الْإِيمَـانُ؟ قَالَ: الصَّبْرُ وَالسَّمَـاحَةُ.

(أحمد والبيهقي في الزهد الكبير)

It narrated by ʿAmr ibn ʿAbasa that when a person asked the Prophet (peace be upon him): "What is Faith (*Īmān*)?" He replied: "Faith is perseverance (*ṣabr*) and generosity."
(Aḥmad and Bayhaqī)

عَنْ سُفْيَانَ بْنِ عَبْدِ اللهِ الثَّقَفِيِّ، قَالَ: قُلْتُ: يَا رَسُولَ اللهِ، قُلْ لِي فِي الْإِسْلَامِ قَوْلًا لَا أَسْـأَلُ عَنْهُ أَحَدًا بَعْدَكَ، قَـالَ: قُلْ: آمَنْتُ بِاللهِ، فَاسْتَقِمْ.

(مسلم)

It is narrated by Sufyān ibn ʿAbdullāh that he once asked: "O Messenger of Allah! Tell me something about Islam which I can ask no one but you." The Prophet (peace be upon him) said: "Say: I believe in Allah and remain steadfast."
(Muslim)

As we know, Allah's help is needed to perform any good deed, the performance of which relies partly upon one's own determination. Yet it is said about *ṣabr* that it can only be acquired with Allah's help:

وَٱصْبِرْ وَمَا صَبْرُكَ إِلَّا بِٱللَّهِ ... ﴿١٢٧﴾

And bear with patience, and your patience is only because of the help of Allah.

(al-Naḥl 16: 127)

To cultivate *ṣabr*, one needs absolute devotion to Allah and making one's wish and desire subservient to His will. One should realize that this life is transitory and enduring any and all difficulties here is only shortlived whereas the pleasures of the Next Life are forever. Hence, it is prudent to bear all problems, discomforts and difficulties without complaint and to hope for reward in the Hereafter, *Inshā' Allāh*.

We should also know that it is the Practice (*Sunnah*) of Allah to test people of faith (*īmān*). Without this testing, it is not possible to ascertain those who are truthful in their commitment and those who are fraudulent. Thus, by this test, all cheats and hypocrites are identified and are removed from the organization (*Jamā'ah*) of true believers. By the process of going through a baptism of fire, Allah purifies the character of the believers. As it is said in *Sūrah Āl 'Imrān*:

... وَلِيَبْتَلِيَ ٱللَّهُ مَا فِي صُدُورِكُمْ وَلِيُمَحِّصَ مَا فِي قُلُوبِكُمْ ... ﴿١٥٤﴾

All this has happened so that Allah might test the thoughts you entertained in your hearts, and purge your hearts of impurities.

(Āl 'Imrān 3: 154)

So how should one cultivate *ṣabr*? Surely the most important source is *Ṣalāh*. We see that in many places in the Qur'ān both *ṣabr* and *Ṣalāh* are mentioned together. Of course, fasting is the best training for acquiring *ṣabr*. And finally our constant prayer to *Allāh Subḥānahu wa Taʿālā* should be to bestow *ṣabr* upon us.

So let us pray that Allah may bless us with steadfastness, perseverance and commitment to continue to seek His pleasure and nearness. May Allah make us remain firm in performing our duties and help us endure whatever displeasing things happen to us. Let us maintain our Love of Allah and desire to meet Him and bear all afflictions and difficulties and remain steadfast on the Right Path. (*Āmīn*)

7

Thankfulness (*Shukr*)

وَإِذْ تَأَذَّنَ رَبُّكُمْ لَئِن شَكَرْتُمْ لَأَزِيدَنَّكُمْ ۖ وَلَئِن كَفَرْتُمْ إِنَّ عَذَابِي لَشَدِيدٌ ﴿٧﴾

And recall when your Lord proclaimed: "If you are grateful, I will add more (favours) unto you. But if you show ingratitude, truly My punishment is terrible indeed."

(Ibrāhīm 14: 7)

In our day-to-day dealings with people, we are usually polite and give thanks for any little favour received. Similarly, it is incumbent upon us that we should, as recipients of Allah's innumerable blessing (*niʿmah*), be grateful to Him. His bounties are indeed innumerable as the Qur'ān says:

وَإِن تَعُدُّوا نِعْمَةَ اللَّهِ لَا تُحْصُوهَا ۗ إِنَّ اللَّهَ لَغَفُورٌ رَّحِيمٌ ﴿١٨﴾

For, were you to count the favours of Allah, you will not be able to count them. Surely Allah is Ever Forgiving, Most Merciful.

(al-Naḥl 16: 18)

Yet very few of us are as thankful for Allah's bounties as we ought to be. It says in *Sūrah Saba'*:

... وَقَلِيلٌ مِّنْ عِبَادِيَ الشَّكُورُ ﴿١٣﴾

Few of My servants are truly thankful.

(Saba' 34: 13)

The word *shukr* comes from *shakara* meaning to give thanks, to be thankful, to be grateful. Hence, *shukr* from this root means thankfulness, gratefulness or gratitude. *Shukr* is the opposite of *kufr* which means to be ungrateful and it also contains the meaning of denying something. Hence, *kufr* is used for disbelief: that is, hiding the truth or denying its recognition. The other word used is *shakūr* which is the superlative of *shākir* (grateful) thus implying that there are indeed very few who thank Allah enough, which is well within their capacity. *Shākir* and *Shakūr* are among the Most Beautiful Names (*al-Asmā' al-Ḥusnā*) of Allah as well. They can also be used for other people. Both words, when applied to human beings, have in them the idea of appreciation, recognition, gratitude as shown in deeds of goodness and righteousness. When Allah is described as *Shākir* and *Shakūr*, it means that He recognizes and appreciates the efforts of His servants and gives suitable rewards for the smallest service performed by them, however defective.

...وَمَن تَطَوَّعَ خَيْرًا فَإِنَّ ٱللَّهَ شَاكِرٌ عَلِيمٌ ﴿١٥٨﴾

And whoever does a good deed voluntarily should know that Allah is Appreciative, All-Knowing.

(al-Baqarah 2: 158)

إِن تُقْرِضُوا۟ ٱللَّهَ قَرْضًا حَسَنًا يُضَٰعِفْهُ لَكُمْ وَيَغْفِرْ لَكُمْ ۚ
وَٱللَّهُ شَكُورٌ حَلِيمٌ ﴿١٧﴾

If you give Allah a goodly loan, He will double it for you and will forgive you. Allah is most Appreciative, Most Forbearing.

(al-Taghābun 64: 17)

So why do we not thank Allah as much as we should? The reason is that we do not realize what bounties He has bestowed upon us. Sheikh Sa'dī in the Introduction to his famous book *Gulistān* writes: "When we breathe in it helps in promoting our lives and when we breathe out it gives us satisfaction. Thus in each breath there are two bounties and for each bounty we should give thanks." We only become aware of Allah's bounties when we are deprived of them. We are ungrateful for our health, wealth and time. It is only when we are ill, poor and dying that we know what bounties we have lost.

Again, Sheikh Sa'dī relating a story about himself said that while travelling he became so destitute that he could not even afford a pair of shoes and he was very sad and upset about this situation. Then, when he entered a mosque in Damascus and saw a man without any legs, he prostrated, instantly thanking Allah that by His grace he at least had legs even though he had no shoes.

We should realize, as the Qur'ān says:

... وَمَن يَشْكُرْ فَإِنَّمَا يَشْكُرُ لِنَفْسِهِۦ ۖ وَمَن كَفَرَ فَإِنَّ ٱللَّهَ غَنِىٌّ حَمِيدٌ ﴿١٢﴾

Whosoever is grateful to Allah it is for his own profit as [it does not give any benefit to His Creator] but if anyone is ungrateful, of course Allah is free of all wants, Immensely Praiseworthy.

(Luqmān 31: 12)

Thus, by thanking Allah, one is fulfilling one's duty. Yet Allah in His infinite mercy has also decreed:

... لَئِن شَكَرْتُمْ لَأَزِيدَنَّكُمْ ۖ ... ﴿٧﴾

If you are grateful, I will add more (favours) unto you.

(Ibrāhīm 14: 7)

Imām Ghazālī pointed out that the granting of all other bounties like giving provision, accepting repentance, offering forgiveness (*maghfirah*), accepting supplication and bestowing contentment are all conditional on Allah's will. There is, however, no such condition attached to increasing the favours for him who gives thanks.

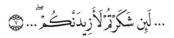

As for our worldly livelihoods:

... وَٱللَّهُ يَرۡزُقُ مَن يَشَآءُ بِغَيۡرِ حِسَابٖ ﴿٢١٢﴾

Allah grants it to whomsoever He wills without measure.
(al-Baqarah 2: 212)

Regarding repentance:

... وَيَتُوبُ ٱللَّهُ عَلَىٰ مَن يَشَآءُۗ ... ﴿١٥﴾

And [He] will enable whomsoever He wills to repent.
(al-Tawbah 9: 15)

Regarding forgiveness:

... وَيَغۡفِرُ مَا دُونَ ذَٰلِكَ لِمَن يَشَآءُۚ ... ﴿٤٨﴾

He forgives any other sins for whomever He wills.
(al-Nisāʾ 4: 48)

For removing distress:

... فَيَكۡشِفُ مَا تَدۡعُونَ إِلَيۡهِ إِن شَآءَ ... ﴿٤١﴾

If He so wills, He removes the distress for which you had cried to Him.
(al-Anʿām 6: 41)

As for providing for us:

... وَإِنۡ خِفۡتُمۡ عَيۡلَةٗ فَسَوۡفَ يُغۡنِيكُمُ ٱللَّهُ مِن فَضۡلِهِۦٓ إِن شَآءَۚ ... ﴿٢٨﴾

And should you fear poverty, Allah will enrich you out of His bounty, if He wills.
(al-Tawbah 9: 28)

So what should our attitude be when we receive Allah's bounties? Firstly, we should acknowledge His favour gracefully. We should recognize it in our conscience and our hearts. Hence it should be a heartfelt gratitude with which we offer our thanks both physically and verbally and not just a customary gesture of saying "*Alḥamdulillāh*". Secondly, we should show this gratitude by our attitude of real affection towards our Generous Benefactor. It is also a demand of our faith (*īmān*) that
... وَٱلَّذِينَ ءَامَنُوٓا۟ أَشَدُّ حُبًّا لِّلَّهِ ... ﴿١٦٥﴾ *we love Allah more than all else.* (al-Baqarah 2: 165)

Thirdly, we should recompense this by our actions, in other words, by not misusing the favours received. Hence, if Allah has given us wealth we should not squander it but use it as prescribed by the *Sharīʿah*. Fourthly, we should realize that even the favours we receive from others are really given by Allah. As to whatever others give, they can only give with Allah's will and His command. Finally and most importantly, as we are thanking Allah for the favours we receive from Him, how can we then dare disobey His commands at the same time? If we keep acknowledging His bounties, gifts and favours, we are honour bound to live a life of obedience and not to willfully do things that we know will displease our Benefactor.

Ṣabr is usually associated with enduring hardship and affliction, whereas *shukr* relates to having blessings and comfort. However, one should always be thankful to Allah whatever comes one's way. We should cultivate the habit of saying "*Alḥamdulillāh*" in all circumstances. It is to be noted that the word *ḥamd* is usually translated as praise but gratitude is also an integral part of its meaning. The more accurate translation, then, would be grateful praise. The word *Ḥamd* is exclusively used for Allah and *Ḥamd* is more expansive than *shukr*. *Ḥamd* is an acknowledgement that someone embodies the excellent qualities of beneficence and radiates blessings and benedictions.

Imām Ghazālī narrated this saying of ʿUmar ibn al-Khaṭṭāb: "Whatever hardship I faced, it brought four rewards from Allah. Firstly, this hardship was related to worldly affairs and not my Religion (*Dīn*). Secondly, it might have been a much greater calamity, but by the grace of Allah I only suffered a lesser affliction. Thirdly, I remained content with whatever was destined for me, and, finally, I hope I will be rewarded for this affliction."

Imām Ghazālī relates a similar story about a learned person upon whom someone threw a handful of ashes as he was passing by. He instantly bowed down and thanked Allah. When people asked him why he was thanking Allah, he replied: "Maybe someone could have thrown burning cinders on me. It is Allah's mercy that saved me from a greater calamity."

Of course, this is the highest status of *shukr* that is only attained by those whose hearts and souls are overawed with Allah's greatness and they remain forever grateful to Him. It is narrated from Allah's Messenger (peace be upon him) that the Prophet Dāwūd (peace be upon him) said to God Almighty:

عَنِ الْمُغِيرَةِ بْنِ عُتَيْبَةَ، قَالَ: قَالَ دَاوُدُ عَلَيْهِ السَّلَامُ: يَا رَبِّ، كَيْفَ أُطِيقُ شُكْرَكَ وَأَنْتَ الَّذِي تُنْعِمُ عَلَيَّ، ثُمَّ تَرْزُقُنِي عَلَى النِّعْمَةِ الشُّكْرَ، ثُمَّ تَزِيدُنِي فِي نِعْمَةٍ بَعْدَ نِعْمَةٍ، فَالنِّعْمَةُ مِنْكَ يَا رَبِّ، وَالشُّكْرُ مِنْكَ، وَكَيْفَ أُطِيقُ شُكْرَكَ؟ قَالَ: الْآنَ عَرَفْتَنِي يَا دَاوُدُ حَقَّ مَعْرِفَتِي.

(البيهقي)

"O Lord! How shall I be able to perform the duty of thankfulness to You? When thanking You is yet another favour of Yours that requires thanks, You keep bestowing upon favour after favour, so how can I thank you?" The Almighty responded to him: "Just now, O Dāwūd, you have performed the obligation of knowing Me."

(Narrated by al-Mughīrah ibn ʿUtaybah in Bayhaqī)

Looking at the life of the Prophet (peace be upon him), we see that he was constantly full of gratitude towards Allah. On one occasion when *Umm al-Mu'minīn* ʿĀ'ishah noticed his feet had swollen due to his long night vigils, she questioned him: "Since Allah has forgiven all your sins that you might have committed and may commit in future, why do you tire yourself with so much night prayer?" As the Prophet (peace be upon him) was always aware of his duty of thankfulness, he replied:

... أَفَلَا أُحِبُّ أَنْ أَكُونَ عَبْدًا شَكُورًا.

(البخاري ومسلم)

Should I not then be a grateful servant of my Lord?

(Bukhārī and Muslim)

So let us pray as the Prophet (peace be upon him) taught us:

... اللهُمَّ أَعِنِّي عَلَى شُكْرِكَ، وَذِكْرِكَ، وَحُسْنِ عِبَادَتِكَ.

(أحمد)

O Allah! Help me (and us) in thanking You and remembering You and worshipping You in the best of ways.

(Aḥmad)

May *Allāh Subḥānahu wa Taʿālā* give us the ability to do (*tawfīq*) that we may realize the value of His bounties and be always grateful and express our thanks by remaining faithful to Him. O Allah! Include us among Your servants whom You love and who always remain grateful to You. O Allah! Keep us constant in Your remembrance, Your thankfulness and Your worship. (*Āmīn*)

8

Wisdom (*Ḥikmah*)

يُؤۡتِى ٱلۡحِكۡمَةَ مَن يَشَآءُۚ وَمَن يُؤۡتَ ٱلۡحِكۡمَةَ فَقَدۡ أُوتِىَ خَيۡرًا كَثِيرًاۗ
وَمَا يَذَّكَّرُ إِلَّآ أُوْلُواْ ٱلۡأَلۡبَٰبِ ﴿٢٦٩﴾

He grants wisdom to those whom He wills; and whoever is granted wisdom has indeed been granted a bounty overflowing. Yet none except people of understanding take heed.
(al-Baqarah 2: 269)

Allāh Subḥānahu wa Taʿālā has bestowed many bounties on human beings. Of them, the most valuable and precious is the faculty of reason that gives them superiority over many of Allah's creation. Reason's pinnacle is the gift of wisdom (*ḥikmah*). The word *ḥikmah* comes from *ḥakama* which means to pass judgement or to express an opinion, and *al-ḥukm* is to give a decision about something. Thus, *ḥikmah* means such knowledge as provides profound insight and the ability to give an accurate judgement.

The verse of *Sūrah al-Baqarah* which I just recited tells us that *al-ḥikmah* is indeed an overflowing bounty. It is interesting to note that this verse occurs in the course of a passage encouraging believers to spend in Allah's way and not to be deceived by Satan's trick of threatening poverty if one gives away money in charity. In this context, *al-ḥikmah* is that gift which safeguards a person from following Satan's path and so, instead of miserliness, one spends wealth generously in good causes.

Imām Ḥamīd al-Dīn al-Farāhī in his book *Ḥikmat-e-Qur'ān* discussed this topic comprehensively. The following passage from his Introduction is worth quoting:

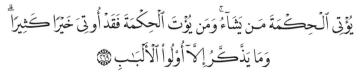

> The words of wisdom are very clear and apparent and thus they penetrate one's heart without any need of proof. *Ḥikmah* is a light which illuminates all surroundings. Thus, it enlightens the knowledge one possesses. Just as fire creates heat that is felt by everyone so does wisdom. The acquisition of wisdom leads one to recognize the truth. Hence his speech becomes truthful and so also his actions. A wise person (*ḥakīm*) notices the lifting up of his heart and his speech becoming effective. His actions are based on goodness and he becomes the epitome of the highest moral standards.[1]

This gives us some idea that the quality of wisdom is indeed very valuable. We read in the Qur'ān that one of the important tasks that was assigned to the Prophet (peace be upon him) was the teaching of *ḥikmah*.

لَقَدْ مَنَّ ٱللَّهُ عَلَى ٱلْمُؤْمِنِينَ إِذْ بَعَثَ فِيهِمْ رَسُولًا مِّنْ أَنفُسِهِمْ يَتْلُوا۟ عَلَيْهِمْ
ءَايَٰتِهِۦ وَيُزَكِّيهِمْ وَيُعَلِّمُهُمُ ٱلْكِتَٰبَ وَٱلْحِكْمَةَ وَإِن كَانُوا۟ مِن
قَبْلُ لَفِى ضَلَٰلٍ مُّبِينٍ ﴿١٦٤﴾

Allah did confer a great favour on the believers when He sent a Messenger among themselves, rehearsing unto them the signs of Allah, purifying them and instructing them in Scripture and wisdom, while before that they were in manifest error."

(Āl ʿImrān 3: 164; al-Baqarah 2: 129 and 151; al-Jumuʿah 62: 2)

The importance of this verse is such that it is repeated four times in the Qur'ān: twice in *Sūrah al-Baqarah*, and once each in *Sūrah*s *Āl ʿImrān* and *al-Jumuʿah* with some slight variations. The teaching of *ḥikmah* has two aspects: on the one hand, giving people the gems of wisdom and, on

---

[1] *Ḥikmat-e-Qur'ān*, 1995, pp. 16-17.

the other hand, creating in them the ability to cultivate *ḥikmah* in their thinking. According to Imām Shāfiʿī and many other commentators, *ḥikmah* here and in some other verses refers to the *aḥādīth* of the Prophet (peace be upon him). Of course his speech was full of pearls of wisdom.

The prime recipients of *ḥikmah* were Allah's messengers and prophets as well as those on whom Allah wished to bestow this blessing. The Prophet Dāwūd (peace be upon him) is specifically mentioned in the Qur'ān as the one who was blessed with this virtue.

وَشَدَدْنَا مُلْكَهُۥ وَءَاتَيْنَٰهُ ٱلْحِكْمَةَ وَفَصْلَ ٱلْخِطَابِ ۝٢٠

And We strengthened his kingdom and endowed him with wisdom and sound judgement in speech and decision.
(Ṣād 38: 20)

So also was his son the Prophet Sulaymān (peace be upon him) endowed with great wisdom. There is a legal case mentioned in the Qur'ān which came for decision before the Prophet Dāwūd (peace be upon him). The incident concerned a shepherd's flock of sheep that had inadvertently entered another person's field, causing damage, perhaps destroying a whole year's crop. The Prophet Dāwūd (peace be upon him) decided that the entire flock of sheep should be given to the aggrieved party as compensation. However, the Prophet Sulaymān (peace be upon him) disagreed with this judgement and suggested that the owner of the field should only retain the sheep for a year and use their milk, wool and young lambs as compensation and then return the sheep to their owner. This seemed to be a more equitable judgement and, to the Prophet Dāwūd's merit, he accepted this decision although it came from his son (*al-Anbiyā'* 21: 78-79). In the Old Testament, there is the *Book of Proverbs*, part of which is attributed to the Prophet Sulaymān, and which contains many gems of wisdom.

Of course, all other prophets were given *ḥikmah*. This wisdom is only acquired through revelation, and the prophets transmitted it to others. In this respect, the name of Luqmān is specifically mentioned in the Qur'ān:

وَلَقَدْ ءَاتَيْنَا لُقْمَٰنَ ٱلْحِكْمَةَ أَنِ ٱشْكُرْ لِلَّهِ ۚ ... ﴿١٢﴾

We bestowed wisdom upon Luqmān, (commanding): "Give thanks to Allah."

(Luqmān 31: 12)

Luqmān was well known in Arabia for his wisdom and sagacity. Although details about him are scanty, we do know that he epitomized perfect wisdom. Indeed, some of the sayings that are quoted in *Sūrah Luqmān* testify to this immense enlightenment and sagacity. It is not certain whether he was a prophet or not.

It is worth noting that it is incumbent upon the recipients of *ḥikmah* to be thankful to Allah and to acknowledge His grace. We see that the Prophet Dāwūd's progeny as well as Luqmān's were reminded that they should be thankful to Allah for His bounty. And Allah has promised that:

... لَئِن شَكَرْتُمْ لَأَزِيدَنَّكُمْ ۖ ... ﴿٧﴾

If you give thanks, He will certainly grant you more.

(Ibrāhīm 14: 7)

The question one can ask is how to acquire *ḥikmah*? As I have said before this is an exclusive gift from Allah. There is no other way of acquiring it. Thus, one should sincerely humble oneself before Allah and seek His help, and immerse oneself in the Qur'ān and the *aḥādīth* of the Prophet (peace be upon him) to discover such *ḥikmah*. Of course, this requires complete dedication and the utmost patience. We see this in the story of the Prophet Mūsā (peace be upon him) and Khiḍr to whom he was sent to acquire hidden knowledge. The basic condition agreed to by the Prophet Mūsā before the start of the journey was that he would bear patiently with everything he saw and could not comprehend, and without question. On their journey, when some events took place, the Prophet Mūsā could not refrain from objecting to each event and, hence, the journey ended. Then, he was told of Allah's *ḥikmah* behind each event.

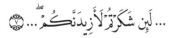

This journey convinced the Prophet Mūsā (peace be upon him) about how things that seem apparently unjust and oppressive actually have a greater purpose behind them.

The lessons we can learn from this episode are many. It is our duty to remain convinced that if the righteous are suffering then there must be Allah's *ḥikmah* in this. There must be some goodness that has been intended by Allah. If those who are tyrants and oppressors are just left alone to do what they want, then again there must be some *ḥikmah*. We have to remain patient and this will save us from the promptings of our arch enemy Satan, who tries to depress and make us lose hope in Allah.

There is no doubt that *ḥikmah* is required in conducting all affairs in our lives. As we have seen before, it is of the utmost importance for those who have to solve legal problems and preside over the judiciary. The other area where the Qur'ān has emphasized *ḥikmah* is in presenting *da'wah*. In *Sūrah al-Naḥl*, the believers are instructed to:

ٱدْعُ إِلَىٰ سَبِيلِ رَبِّكَ بِٱلْحِكْمَةِ وَٱلْمَوْعِظَةِ ٱلْحَسَنَةِ ۖ وَجَٰدِلْهُم
بِٱلَّتِى هِىَ أَحْسَنُ ۚ ... ﴿١٢٥﴾

Invite all to the way of your Lord with wisdom and beautiful preaching and argue with them in ways that are best and gracious...

(al-Naḥl 16: 125)

Here, *al-ḥikmah* means that our preaching must not be dogmatic and offensive, but rather gentle and considerate. Our manner and mode of argument must not be acrimonious but rather courteous and most gracious based on logic and convincing proof. It should be noted that here Allah has mentioned the word *ḥikmah* first and *maw'iẓah* second. Calling to Allah's path requires gaining the knowledge, experience and sensitivity to judge the receptiveness of the person you are inviting; it also needs all the resources of eloquent and persuasive language to convey the call to Allah in the best manner.

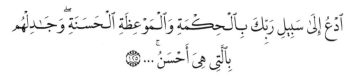

One of the blessings of *ḥikmah* is the ability to arrive at a balanced and correct judgement. Its other benefits enable one to live a chaste moral life and adopt a civilized approach in personal and social affairs. It is for this reason that the word *ḥikmah* is used to indicate maturity in reason and moral virtue. A person who is wise and cultured is called a *ḥakīm*. When he looks at the universe and notices its balance, order and harmony, he realizes that it is not created without purpose. Thus, when we study the Qur'ān, it constantly reminds us to think, reflect and use our faculties of sight, hearing and reason to understand our surroundings. This is the key to acquiring *ḥikmah*.

Let us conclude with this *du'ā'* taught by our beloved Prophet (peace be upon him):

... اللهُمَّ إِنِّي أَعُوذُ بِكَ مِنْ عِلْمٍ لَا يَنْفَعُ، وَمِنْ قَلْبٍ لَا يَخْشَعُ، وَمِنْ نَفْسٍ لَا تَشْبَعُ، وَمِنْ دَعْوَةٍ لَا يُسْتَجَابُ لَهَا.

(مسلم)

O Lord! I seek refuge in You from knowledge that is not beneficial; I seek refuge in You from the heart that has no humility; I seek refuge in You from the soul that is restless; I seek refuge in You from the prayer that is not accepted.

(Narrated by Zayd ibn Arqam in Muslim)

O Lord! Increase our knowledge and endow us with *ḥikmah*. (*Āmīn*)

9

Reflection (*Tafakkur*)

إِنَّ فِي خَلْقِ ٱلسَّمَٰوَٰتِ وَٱلْأَرْضِ وَٱخْتِلَٰفِ ٱلَّيْلِ وَٱلنَّهَارِ لَءَايَٰتٍ
لِّأُو۟لِى ٱلْأَلْبَٰبِ ﴿١٩٠﴾ ٱلَّذِينَ يَذْكُرُونَ ٱللَّهَ قِيَٰمًا وَقُعُودًا وَعَلَىٰ جُنُوبِهِمْ
وَيَتَفَكَّرُونَ فِي خَلْقِ ٱلسَّمَٰوَٰتِ وَٱلْأَرْضِ رَبَّنَا مَا خَلَقْتَ هَٰذَا بَٰطِلًا
سُبْحَٰنَكَ فَقِنَا عَذَابَ ٱلنَّارِ ﴿١٩١﴾

Surely in the creation of the heavens and the earth, and in the alternation of night and day, are signs for people of understanding, those who remember Allah while standing, sitting or reclining, and reflect in the creation of the heavens and the earth, (saying): "Our Lord! You have not created this in vain. Glory to You! Save us, then, from the chastisement of Fire."
(Āl 'Imrān 3: 190-191)

Allāh, Subḥānahu wa Ta'ālā has endowed human beings with the faculties of reasoning and thinking so that they can think and reflect. This gives humanity superiority over all creation; this is what distinguishes us from animals. This is an essential bounty from Allah such that we can live and survive in this world. Without this, we cannot make any progress in this world nor can we achieve salvation in the Hereafter. This is the essential key that leads us to Allah. Hence, the Qur'ān has repeatedly instructed us to reflect, think and ponder upon the universe all around us. The verses from *Sūrah Āl 'Imrān* I recited at the start of this *khuṭbah* specifically mention the attribute of people of understanding that, when they reflect on the creation of the heavens and the earth, the result of their reflection leads them to discover the reality of His Divine presence. When they see order, symmetry, balance and harmony in the universe they reach the logical conclusion that there is a Creator of this universe, Who has not created this in vain and, hence, there will be a Day of Accounting.

Even now those scientists who study and reflect on the creation of the Universe also arrive at the same conclusion. Sir James Jeans (1877-1946) after studying the universe wrote this in his fascinating book:

> The stream of human knowledge is heading towards a non-mechanical reality. The universe begins to look more like a great thought than a great machine. Mind no longer appears to be an accidental intruder into the realm of matter. We are beginning to suspect that we ought rather to hail it as the creator and governor of this realm.[1]

More recently the most celebrated physicist of modern times, Stephen Hawking, in his book *A Brief History of Time* that has sold millions of copies worldwide, concludes by speculating about the existence of God:

> If we find the answer to that [a complete theory], it would be the ultimate triumph of human reason – for then we would know the mind of God.[2]

However, in his latest book *The Grand Design* (2010) he retracted from this opinion, saying that there is no place for God in theories about the creation of the universe.[3]

Even after acknowledging the presence of God, these scientists did not reach the ultimate conclusion that there should be a Day of Accounting.

---

1 *The Mysterious Universe*, 1930, p. 137.

2 *A Brief History of Time*, 1988, p. 175.

3 *The Times*, 2nd September 2010

The outcome of reflection should be that when one reaches the ultimate reality of knowing the purpose of creation, the Oneness of God, the need for guidance and being accountable to Him should become apparent. However, instead, they still continue to look for a "God Particle" and search for Darwin's missing link, whereas those with true wisdom surrender themselves before the Almighty and acknowledge His bounties and tremble with fear at their accountability. This is illustrated by the conduct of our beloved Prophet (peace be upon him). When 'Aṭā' and 'Ubayd ibn 'Umayr visited *Umm al-Mu'minīn* 'Ā'ishah, Ibn 'Umayr asked her to narrate some unusual event from the life of the Prophet (peace be upon him), so she spoke about one night when the Prophet left her in bed and performed *wuḍū'* and started praying and cried so much that his beard became wet and so did the spot where he prostrated. Then he rested in bed until Bilāl came to tell him about *Fajr* Prayer. When he was asked why was he crying when all of his former and future shortcomings were forgiven, he replied: "Tonight the following verses (the last ten verses of *Sūrah Āl 'Imrān* starting with "Surely in the creation of the heavens and the earth...") were revealed to me. Should I not be a grateful servant?" (Ibn Ḥibbān) Then he added: "Doom for him who reads them and does not reflect upon them." Imām al-Awzā'ī was asked what the limit of reflection (*tafakkur*) over these verses is. He replied: "One should read them and thoroughly understand them." On this basis, by Imām Ḥasan al-Baṣrī said that "An hour's reflection is better than observing the Night Vigil (*Qiyām al-Layl*) through the whole night." Al-Fuḍayl ibn 'Iyāḍ used to say: "*Tafakkur* is a mirror that reveals a person's good and evil deeds."

I have quoted all these from Imām Ghazālī's monumental work *Iḥyā' 'Ulūm al-Dīn*, Volume 4, Chapter 9 on *Fikr* and *'Ibrah* (*Reflection and Admonition*).

So what should one reflect upon and how should one undertake this process? There are of course many avenues open to us for reflection. One is encouraged to reflect upon the Names of *Allāh Subḥānahu wa Ta'āla*. According to a *ḥadīth* narrated by Abū Hurayrah, the Holy Prophet (peace be upon him) said:

عَنْ أَبِي هُرَيْرَةَ، رِوَايَةً قَالَ: لِلّٰهِ تِسْعَةٌ وَتِسْعُونَ اسْمًا، مِائَةٌ إِلَّا وَاحِدًا
لَا يَحْفَظُهَا أَحَدٌ إِلَّا دَخَلَ الْجَنَّةَ.

(البخاري ومسلم)

Verily, there are ninety-nine Names of Allah; whosoever recites them shall enter Paradise.

(Bukhārī and Muslim)

These names are collectively known as the Most Beautiful Names (*al-Asmā' al-Ḥusnā*) and some are mentioned in the Qur'ān in the following verses: *al-Baqarah* 2: 255; *al-Ḥadīd* 57: 1–6 and *al-Ḥashr* 59: 22–24. They also appear as a pair of Names at the end of many verses, being appropriate to the subject of these discourses. These Names express the Attributes of Allah. They lead us to the proper understanding of our relationship with our Creator. They also provide a focal point for us to contemplate and, thus, fashion our lives according to them. However, one should not contemplate the person of Allah but rather only reflect upon His attributes.

The other area for reflection is Allah's creation. As mentioned in the verses of *Sūrah Āl 'Imrān*, the entire universe that surrounds us invites us to reflect upon its creation in order to understand the purpose of creation and to recognize that there is a Creator Who is Almighty and Powerful. As the following verses of *Sūrah al-Ghāshiyah* ask us:

أَفَلَا يَنظُرُونَ إِلَى ٱلْإِبِلِ كَيْفَ خُلِقَتْ ﴿١٧﴾ وَإِلَى ٱلسَّمَآءِ كَيْفَ رُفِعَتْ ﴿١٨﴾
وَإِلَى ٱلْجِبَالِ كَيْفَ نُصِبَتْ ﴿١٩﴾ وَإِلَى ٱلْأَرْضِ كَيْفَ سُطِحَتْ ﴿٢٠﴾

Do they not observe the camels: how they were created? And the sky: how it was raised high? And the mountains: how they were fixed? And the earth, how it was spread out?

(al-Ghāshiyah 88: 17-20)

These and similar verses of the Qur'ān remind us again and again that we should keep our faculties of sight, hearing and understanding open to reflect upon the creation around us. One should not lead life like a blind or deaf person. Indeed, one of the qualities of Allah's servants mentioned in *Sūrah al- Furqān* is:

وَٱلَّذِينَ إِذَا ذُكِّرُواْ بِـَٔايَٰتِ رَبِّهِمۡ لَمۡ يَخِرُّواْ عَلَيۡهَا صُمّٗا وَعُمۡيَانٗا ﴿٧٣﴾

When they are reminded of the signs of their Lord, do not turn a deaf ear and a blind eye to them.

(al-Furqān 25: 73)

And instructive too is the conversation that will take place on the Day of Judgement:

... وَنَحۡشُرُهُۥ يَوۡمَ ٱلۡقِيَٰمَةِ أَعۡمَىٰ ﴿١٢٤﴾ قَالَ رَبِّ لِمَ حَشَرۡتَنِيٓ أَعۡمَىٰ وَقَدۡ كُنتُ
بَصِيرٗا ﴿١٢٥﴾ قَالَ كَذَٰلِكَ أَتَتۡكَ ءَايَٰتُنَا فَنَسِيتَهَاۖ وَكَذَٰلِكَ ٱلۡيَوۡمَ تُنسَىٰ ﴿١٢٦﴾

We will raise him blind on the Day of Resurrection, whereupon he shall say: "Lord! Why have you raised me blind when I had sight in the world?" He will say: "Even so, it is. Our signs came to you and you ignored them. So, shall you be ignored on this Day."

(*Ṭā' Hā'* 20: 124-126)

The same message is given in *Sūrah al-Isrā'*:

وَمَن كَانَ فِي هَٰذِهِۦٓ أَعۡمَىٰ فَهُوَ فِي ٱلۡأٓخِرَةِ أَعۡمَىٰ... ﴿٧٢﴾

Those who were blind in this life will be blind in the Hereafter.

(al-Isrā' 17: 72)

We should also reflect on human history, and specifically on how powerful and mighty empires collapsed, the only signs they left behind being ruins. The Qur'ān repeatedly encourages us to visit these sites and take a lesson from their annihilation.

... أَفَلَمْ يَسِيرُوا۟ فِى ٱلْأَرْضِ فَيَنظُرُوا۟ كَيْفَ كَانَ عَـٰقِبَةُ ٱلَّذِينَ مِن قَبْلِهِمْ ۗ وَلَدَارُ
ٱلْـَٔاخِرَةِ خَيْرٌ لِّلَّذِينَ ٱتَّقَوْا۟ ۗ أَفَلَا تَعْقِلُونَ ﴿١٠٩﴾

Have they not travelled in the land that they may observe the end of those who were before them? Certainly the abode of the Hereafter is much better for the God-fearing. Do you not then reflect?

(Yūsuf 12: 109)

قُلْ سِيرُوا۟ فِى ٱلْأَرْضِ فَٱنظُرُوا۟ كَيْفَ كَانَ عَـٰقِبَةُ ٱلَّذِينَ مِن قَبْلُ ۚ كَانَ
أَكْثَرُهُم مُّشْرِكِينَ ﴿٤٢﴾

Say: Traverse in the land, and see what was the end of those who were before you? Most of them associated others with Allah in His Divinity.

(al-Rūm 30: 42)

Even if we were to reflect upon the events of the last 30 years we can see that our recent history saw the graveyard of so-called superpowers.

The other area that we are also encouraged to reflect upon is our own selves and our society.

أَوَلَمْ يَتَفَكَّرُوا۟ فِىٓ أَنفُسِهِم ۗ ... ﴿٨﴾

Do they not reflect upon themselves?

(al-Rūm 30: 8)

وَمِنْ ءَايَـٰتِهِۦٓ أَنْ خَلَقَ لَكُم مِّنْ أَنفُسِكُمْ أَزْوَٰجًا لِّتَسْكُنُوٓا۟ إِلَيْهَا وَجَعَلَ
بَيْنَكُم مَّوَدَّةً وَرَحْمَةً ۚ إِنَّ فِى ذَٰلِكَ لَـَٔايَـٰتٍ لِّقَوْمٍ يَتَفَكَّرُونَ ﴿٢١﴾

And of His signs is that: He has created mates for you from your own kind that you may find peace in them and He has set between you love and mercy. Surely there are signs in this for those who reflect.

(al-Rūm 30: 21)

Finally, one should always reflect upon death, which we see all around us, and remind ourselves that we have to meet it eventually. In other words, what preparations have we made for this eventuality? The Prophet (peace be upon him) advised us always to remember death, which obliterates all pleasures.

Let us pray to *Allāh, Subḥānahu wa Taʿālā* that He gives us the wisdom to reflect upon His creation and bounties and that we take heed from the events that unfold before us every day. We should realize that our duration of stay on this earth is short-lived and that eventually we are accountable to Allah for all our acts. Hence, we make a start here by doing good deeds, *Inshā' Allāh.*

اللَّهُمَّ انْفَعْنِي بِمَا عَلَّمْتَنِي، وَعَلِّمْنِي مَا يَنْفَعُنِي، وَزِدْنِي عِلْمًا، الْحَمْدُ لِلَّهِ عَلَى كُلِّ حَالٍ، وَأَعُوذُ بِاللهِ مِنْ حَالِ أَهْلِ النَّارِ.

(الترمذي)

O Allah! Whatever knowledge You have bestowed on us make it useful for us and increase our knowledge. All thankful praise is for Allah in all circumstances and we seek Allah's protection from the affairs of the people of the Fire. (*Āmīn*)

(Tirmidhī)

10

Trust (*Amānah*)

إِنَّ ٱللَّهَ يَأْمُرُكُمْ أَن تُؤَدُّوا۟ ٱلْأَمَـٰنَـٰتِ إِلَىٰٓ أَهْلِهَا وَإِذَا حَكَمْتُم بَيْنَ
ٱلنَّاسِ أَن تَحْكُمُوا۟ بِٱلْعَدْلِ ... ﴿٥٨﴾

Allah commands you to deliver trusts to those worthy of them; and when you judge between people, judge with justice.
(al-Nisā' 4: 58)

Allah's command in this verse imposes a serious responsibility on us. A Muslim's entire life is a trust (*amānah*) from Allah. All of us are appointed as trustees (*khulufā'*) of this world. We are required to use our talents and our energies to follow the guidance given by Allah. If we fulfill this obligation properly, we will be carrying out the duty of *amānah* in a befitting manner. However, if we are negligent, then we are betraying the trust reposed in us.

The root of the Arabic word *amānah* stems from *a-m-n,* meaning to be faithful, reliable and trustworthy. It is normally used in the course of transactions and dealings with people and *amānah* implies delivering to them whatever they have entrusted to others. It means honesty in everyday transactions and fulfilling one's obligations. This noble quality is one of the characteristics of true believers.

وَٱلَّذِينَ هُمْ لِأَمَـٰنَـٰتِهِمْ وَعَهْدِهِمْ رَٰعُونَ ﴿٨﴾

Those are true to their trusts and their covenants.
(al-Mu'minūn 23: 8 and al-Ma'ārij 70: 32)

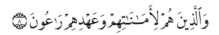

Amānah as a keyword is not just limited to mutual dealings but covers a very wide spectrum. The instruction is: "*Allah commands you to deliver trusts to those worthy of them*" (al-Nisā' 4: 58). Here, *amānah* implies an office of trust (i.e. religious, community and political leadership). This responsibility should not be given to immoral, incompetent or corrupt people. Such important or responsible offices should only be entrusted to those who are capable of undertaking the burdens of such positions. The use of the word *amānah* for official responsibilities conveys the concept that these are given in trust by Allah and it is to Him that people will be held accountable. The word *amānah* is again used in the same sense in *Sūrah al-Anfāl*:

يَـٰٓأَيُّهَا ٱلَّذِينَ ءَامَنُوا۟ لَا تَخُونُوا۟ ٱللَّهَ وَٱلرَّسُولَ وَتَخُونُوٓا۟ أَمَـٰنَـٰتِكُمْ
وَأَنتُمْ تَعْلَمُونَ ﴿٢٧﴾

O you who believe! Do not be unfaithful to Allah and the Messenger, or knowingly betray [other people's] trust in you.
(al-Anfāl 8: 27)

Here "trust" means an obligation arising out of an agreement or as part of any responsibility that is given to a person. The word *amānah* for positions of responsibility is also used in many *aḥādīth*. Once the Prophet (peace be up on him) was asked when the Day of Judgement will be? He replied:

عَنْ أَبِي هُرَيْرَةَ رَضِيَ اللهُ عَنْهُ، قَالَ: قَالَ رَسُولُ اللهِ صَلى
اللهُ عَلَيْهِ وَسَلَّمَ إِذَا ضُيِّعَتِ الْأَمَانَةُ، فَانْتَظِرِ السَّاعَةَ، قَالَ:
كَيْفَ إِضَاعَتُهَا يَا رَسُولَ اللهِ؟ قَالَ: إِذَا أُسْنِدَ الْأَمْرُ
إِلَى غَيْرِ أَهْلِهِ فَانْتَظِرِ السَّاعَةَ.

(البخاري)

"When *amānah* is destroyed." Then he was asked
"What is meant by the destruction of *amānah*?"

He said: "When affairs [of government] are entrusted to incompetent people."
(Narrated by Abū Hurayrah in Bukhārī)

This means that giving political leadership and authority to incapable, immoral, untrustworthy and impious people leads to the downfall and destruction of civil society. Similar is the use of the word *amānah* in *Sūrah al-Aḥzāb*:

إِنَّا عَرَضْنَا ٱلْأَمَانَةَ عَلَى ٱلسَّمَـٰوَٰتِ وَٱلْأَرْضِ وَٱلْجِبَالِ فَأَبَيْنَ أَن يَحْمِلْنَهَا
وَأَشْفَقْنَ مِنْهَا وَحَمَلَهَا ٱلْإِنسَـٰنُ ۖ إِنَّهُۥ كَانَ ظَلُومًا جَهُولًا ﴿٧٢﴾

We indeed offer the trust to the Heavens and the Earth and the mountains but they refused to undertake it being afraid thereof. But man undertook it; he was indeed unjust and foolish.
(al-Aḥzāb 33: 72)

Here, the concept of *amānah* conveys the role of being a trustee or vicegerent of Allah, which requires free will and the ability to obey or disobey. This undertaking given to human beings is an *amānah* and it requires that they fulfill their obligations and be accountable to Allah in the Hereafter. To emphasize the gravity of such an undertaking, Allah has mentioned that the heavens and earth as well as the mountains declined to accept this challenge because it was a trial that they found themselves incapable of doing justice to. Of course, one cannot understand the mode of their refusal so perhaps this is narrated in the form of a parable. Man, having accepted this role of *khilāfah*, should be mindful of this *amānah*, otherwise it will be foolhardy for us to neglect it.

The verse recited at the beginning of this *khuṭbah* gave us the basic guidance about conferring responsibility on someone or appointing someone to an important post. It implies that, for example, casting a vote is an *amānah* and that it is our duty to vote for one who is in our view the most capable. But who is the most capable person? The Qur'ān provides some fundamental guidance. When one of the Prophets of the tribe of Israel appointed Ṭālūt as their king, they objected asking by what right should he rule over them when they were more worthy given he was not very wealthy? Their Prophet replied:

... إِنَّ ٱللَّهَ ٱصْطَفَىٰهُ عَلَيْكُمْ وَزَادَهُۥ بَسْطَةً فِى ٱلْعِلْمِ وَٱلْجِسْمِ ۖ ... ﴿٢٤٧﴾

Allah has chosen him over you and has given him great knowledge and stature.

(al-Baqarah 2: 247)

Thus, the person you chose to vote for should be intelligent as well as physically capable of undertaking the stress and arduous tasks that a politician is required to do. Being wealthy or a person of high status should not be the criteria for electing someone.

The other quality mentioned in *Sūrah al-Nisā'* is competence in solving intricate problems. Hence, the instruction given is that if any important issue arises it should be referred to the Prophet (peace be upon him) or to those in authority who are competent.

وَإِذَا جَآءَهُمْ أَمْرٌ مِّنَ ٱلْأَمْنِ أَوِ ٱلْخَوْفِ أَذَاعُوا۟ بِهِۦ ۖ وَلَوْ رَدُّوهُ إِلَى ٱلرَّسُولِ
وَإِلَىٰٓ أُو۟لِى ٱلْأَمْرِ مِنْهُمْ لَعَلِمَهُ ٱلَّذِينَ يَسْتَنۢبِطُونَهُۥ مِنْهُمْ ۗ ... ﴿٨٣﴾

When there comes to them a matter – be it of general security or alarm – they broadcast it. But if they referred it to the Messenger, and to those in authority among them, those of them who could discover its veracity would know of it and act accordingly.

(al-Nisā' 4: 83)

The ability of arriving at results by logical deduction (*istinbāṭ*) requires a higher degree of competency and of intellect. This is what is required of leadership.

Other qualities of course include being trustworthy, reliable or being capable of managing affairs properly. This is the reason why the Prophet Yūsuf (peace be upon him) was put in charge of the treasury by the King. The conversation between them is recorded in the Qur'ān. The Prophet Yūsuf (peace be upon him) said:

قَالَ ٱجْعَلْنِى عَلَىٰ خَزَآئِنِ ٱلْأَرْضِ ۖ إِنِّى حَفِيظٌ عَلِيمٌ ﴿٥٥﴾

Place me in charge of the treasures of the land. I am a good guardian and know my task well.

(Yūsuf 12: 55)

When we employ someone, we look for trustworthiness and the physical and mental capabilities of the person. This is what one of the daughters of the old man of Median emphasized when she recommended that the Prophet Mūsā (peace be upon him) be employed by her father. She said:

...يَـٰٓأَبَتِ ٱسْتَـْٔجِرْهُ ۖ إِنَّ خَيْرَ مَنِ ٱسْتَـْٔجَرْتَ ٱلْقَوِىُّ ٱلْأَمِينُ ﴿٢٦﴾

Father! Employ this man in your service. The best whom you might employ is he who is strong and trustworthy.

(al-Qaṣaṣ 28: 26)

Thus, we see that the Qur'ān provides enough guidance for us to select or elect the right person.

However, there are certain people who are against Muslims taking part in elections as Britain is not an Islamic country. Their argument is that, for Muslims, sovereignty belongs to Allah and as our parliament also claims to be sovereign in enacting legislation, so our participation as Muslims in this process is unlawful. On the face of it, this looks a valid argument. However, one has to distinguish between living under Islamic rule and living in a non-Muslim country. Muslims living in a non-Muslim land have no control over the national parliament and legislature, yet they live there under an agreement with the state and are bound by its laws. In such a case, Muslims are obliged to participate in the workings of the state and to safeguard themselves as much as possible by taking part in elections. By not electing good and honest people, they will be helping those parties which are anti-Muslim and whose agenda is to create problems. Our task in this country should be the welfare of this society, which also means electing those whom we know are capable and honest and whom will also be helpful to our cause. Millions of Muslims are now living in non-Muslim countries across the world. In order to provide them with guidance in their day-to-day affairs, there has recently developed a type of *fiqh* called *Fiqh al-Aqallīyāt* – laws for Muslims living as a minority in non-Muslim countries. According to the *fuqahā'*, Muslims living in such countries should take part in the processes of elections which can safeguard their interests and provide concessions that will allow them to practise their religion freely and without hindrance.

This is illustrated by the *Sīrah* of the Prophet (peace be upon him). He sought alliances with non-Muslims both in the Makkan and Madīnan periods. After the death of Abū Ṭālib when Abū Lahab became the chief of the tribe of Hāshim, the Prophet (peace be upon him) lost the protection of his clan. Thus, when he went to Ṭā'if, he found himself in difficulty when returning to Makkah. He tried to seek the protection of Suhayl ibn ʿAmr but he refused. Then the Prophet asked for the protection of Muṭʿim ibn ʿAdī who was related to the tribe of ʿAbd Manāf and he readily provided his protection. The Prophet spent the night in his house. The next day, he and his sons took the Prophet to the Kaʿbah where he announced that he had given the Prophet his protection and so, no one should harm him. In such a tribal society, individuals needed the support of their own tribe or protection from some other tribe to survive. The Prophet (peace be upon him) asked his Companions to migrate to Abyssinia to escape the persecution they were facing in Makkah. There Muslims lived under the protection of a Christian King and they also actively defended the state when an enemy army attacked Abyssinia.

I have given these details to assure Muslims that they are not doing anything unlawful, but, on the contrary, they are performing their civic duties to this society.

Some people ask what is the point of voting? All the candidates are the same. They make promises and then break them. We know that there are politicians who have misused their positions and who have been involved in corrupt practices. But then there are others as well who have not done so. Our efforts should be directed to trying to elect honest and trustworthy people. This is even more important in those constituencies where the Muslim vote can be decisive. Thus we can exert our voting power to elect those who are sympathetic to our cause. One of the *du'ā'* narrated by Ibn 'Umar from the Prophet (peace upon him) is:

عَنِ ابْنَ عُمَرَ قَالَ: ... وَلَا تُسَلِّطْ عَلَيْنَا مَنْ لَا يَرْحَمُنَا.

(الترمذي)

[O Lord!] Do not impose those upon us who are not merciful to us.

(Tirmidhī)

... اللَّهُمَّ أَلْهِمْنِي رُشْدِي وَأَعِذْنِي مِنْ شَرِّ نَفْسِي.

(الترمذي)

O Lord! Infuse guidance (in our hearts) and save us from the mischief of our carnal self.

(Tirmidhī)

O Lord! Forgive our sins done in secret or in public, whether in ignorance or wilfully. May *Allāh Subḥānahu wa Ta'ālā* guide us to the right path. Give us the courage and wisdom to act in the best interests of our society by fulfilling the responsibility entrusted to us. (*Āmīn*)

11

Truth (*Ṣidq*)

يَـٰٓأَيُّهَا ٱلَّذِينَ ءَامَنُوا۟ ٱتَّقُوا۟ ٱللَّهَ وَكُونُوا۟ مَعَ ٱلصَّـٰدِقِينَ ﴿١١٩﴾

O you who believe! Fear God and be with the truthful ones.
(al-Tawbah 9: 119)

In this verse *Allāh Subḥānahu wa Taʿālā* gives us two specific commands. The first is to remain mindful and conscious of Him. The word *ittaqū* that is used is a verb from which the word *taqwā* comes. *Taqwā* is very difficult to translate into only one word. It is often translated as "fear", that is to refrain from doing wrong because of fear of punishment. Yet *taqwā* is much more than just fear, hence God-consciousness is a better term, one that conveys its more comprehensive meaning.

A study of the Holy Qur'ān shows that the acquisition of *taqwā* is the purpose of all worship (*ʿibādah*), be it Prayers, Fasting, *Zakāh*, *Ḥajj* or even sacrifice. Similarly, in all our activities, *taqwā* is required. Even guidance from the Qur'ān is for those who are God-conscious (*Muttaqūn*) هُدًى لِّلْمُتَّقِينَ ﴿٢﴾ *guidance for the God-conscious* (al-Baqarah 2: 2)

Taqwā helps one to remain conscious of one's responsibility for one's own actions and one's accountability to Allah on the Day of Judgement. Hence this God-consciousness restrains one from deviating from the path of righteousness.

The second command is to remain in the company of those who are truthful. The word *ṣādiqīn* is the plural of the word *ṣādiq* which comes from *ṣidq* meaning truth. *Ṣidq* itself comes from *ṣadaqa*, meaning to speak the truth or to be sincere. *Ṣidq* from this root means truth or sincerity. Truthfulness should be reflected both in creed (*ʿaqāʾid*) and deeds (*ʿamal*). The essence of *ṣidq* is that a thing should reflect its true nature. When what is being said reflects what is in one's heart then it is *ṣidq*. There should be harmony between the tongue and heart. Otherwise, it may be that what is being said is true yet if the speaker does not believe in it, then he will not be considered as truthful. This is why the hypocrites were branded as liars.

إِذَا جَآءَكَ ٱلْمُنَـٰفِقُونَ قَالُوا۟ نَشْهَدُ إِنَّكَ لَرَسُولُ ٱللَّهِ ۗ وَٱللَّهُ يَعْلَمُ إِنَّكَ لَرَسُولُهُۥ
وَٱللَّهُ يَشْهَدُ إِنَّ ٱلْمُنَـٰفِقِينَ لَكَـٰذِبُونَ ۝١

When the hypocrites come to you, they say "We bear witness that you are indeed the Messenger of Allah." And Allah knows that you are indeed His Messenger, and Allah bears witness that the hypocrites are indeed liars.

(al-Manāfiqūn 63: 1)

Thus, saying something that one does not believe amounts to lying.

Ṣidq is considered a cornerstone of faith and "the mother of all virtues". *Ṣidq* as reflecting one's inner conviction and outward action is the hallmark of a true believer. Imām Ghazālī, in *Iḥyā' ʿUlūm al-Dīn*, has a special chapter on *ṣidq*. He pairs it with intention (*niyyah*) and sincerity (*ikhlāṣ*) and enumerates upon six different aspects of truthfulness:

Firstly, one should be truthful in speech. This means that one should safeguard one's tongue from saying anything that is untrue and that one should try to fulfill all the promises one has made. Secondly, one should have true intention and volition. This means that one's *niyyah* should always be to seek Allah's pleasure when performing any act. Thirdly, one should have full determination in undertaking any task. This means that one should have firm resolve to act on that which one believes in. Fourthly, one should be faithful to one's determination. This means that one should do what one has promised oneself to do. Fifthly, one should be sincere in one's actions or deeds. This means that one's outward behaviour should not convey an impression that does not correspond with the reality of one's inner self. In other words, one should safeguard oneself from a display of outward piety. Finally, one should strive in attaining the status of real *īmān* as described in *Sūrah al-Ḥujurāt*:

إِنَّمَا ٱلْمُؤْمِنُونَ ٱلَّذِينَ ءَامَنُوا۟ بِٱللَّهِ وَرَسُولِهِۦ ثُمَّ لَمْ يَرْتَابُوا۟ وَجَٰهَدُوا۟ بِأَمْوَٰلِهِمْ
وَأَنفُسِهِمْ فِى سَبِيلِ ٱللَّهِ ۚ أُو۟لَٰٓئِكَ هُمُ ٱلصَّٰدِقُونَ ﴿١٥﴾

Only those are believers who have believed in Allah and His Messenger, and have never doubted, but have striven with their possessions and their lives in the cause of Allah: such are the truthful ones.

(al-Ḥujurāt 49: 15)

In many verses of the Qur'ān, the attitude and qualities of a true believer are portrayed as integrity and truthfulness in speech, action, feeling and innermost inclination. The Qur'ān also regards such a degree of integrity and truthfulness as the basis of happiness both in this world and the Hereafter. The following are just a few verses that exemplify this.

وَقُل رَّبِّ أَدْخِلْنِى مُدْخَلَ صِدْقٍ وَأَخْرِجْنِى مُخْرَجَ صِدْقٍ وَٱجْعَل لِّى
مِن لَّدُنكَ سُلْطَٰنًا نَّصِيرًا ﴿٨٠﴾

And say: My Lord! Cause me to enter, wherever it be, with Truth, and cause me to leave, wherever it be, with Truth, and support me with authority from Yourself.

(al-Isrā' 17: 80)

The word *ṣidq* here signifies honour, influence and strength. This verse was revealed just before the Prophet's migration to Madīnah and, although it is in the form of a prayer, it conveys great tidings that his leaving of Makkah and entry into Madīnah is with truth, sincerity and honour. This verse from *Sūrah al-Shu'arā'*:

وَٱجْعَل لِّى لِسَانَ صِدْقٍ فِى ٱلْءَاخِرِينَ ﴿٨٤﴾

And grant me an honourable reputation
among later generations.
(al-Shuʿarāʾ 26: 84)

Thus, in this prayer of the Prophet Ibrāhīm (peace be upon him), he asks Allah that he might be remembered and praised by truthful tongues in later generations. Ordinary praise may mean nothing if it is due to flattery or manipulation. Truthful and sincere praise is indeed real praise. And, indeed, he and his progeny are remembered with reverence and honour even after many centuries.

Finally, this depiction of the believers resting in Paradise in Allah's presence is the highest understanding of spiritual truth gained through intellect and social interaction.

إِنَّ ٱلْمُتَّقِينَ فِى جَنَّـٰتٍ وَنَهَرٍ ﴿٥٤﴾ فِى مَقْعَدِ صِدْقٍ عِندَ مَلِيكٍ مُّقْتَدِرٍۭ ﴿٥٥﴾

Surely the righteous will dwell amidst gardens and rivers, in an assembly of truth in the presence of a Mighty King.
(al-Qamar 54: 54-55)

Entering and departing with truth, sincerity and honour and being remembered for truthfulness throughout the ages and being presented to the Lord near the seat of truthfulness is indeed a long road – extending from this world to the Hereafter.

There are many *aḥādīth* extolling the virtue of truthfulness. One *ḥadīth*, related by ʿAbdullāh ibn Masʿūd says:

عَن ابْنِ مَسْعُودٍ رضي الله عنه عن النَّبيِّ صَلّى اللهُ عَلَيْهِ وسَلَّم قَالَ:
إِنَّ الصِّدْقَ يَهْدِي إِلَى الْبِرِّ وَإِنَّ الْبِرَّ يَهْدِي إِلَى الجَنَّة، وَإِنَّ الرَّجُلَ
لِيَصْدُقُ حَتَّى يُكتَبَ عِنْدَ اللهِ صِدِّيقاً، وإِنَّ الْكَذِبَ يَهْدِي إِلَى
الفجُورِ وَإِنَّ الفجُورَ يَهْدِي إِلَى النَّارِ، وَإِنَّ الرَّجُلَ لَيَكْذِبُ
حَتَّى يُكتَبَ عِنْدَ اللهِ كَذَّاباً.

(البخاري ومسلم)

Truth leads to piety and piety leads to *Jannah.* A person speaks the truth and makes it his habit until he is written as *ṣiddīq* before Allah. Falsehood leads to sin and sin leads to the Fire. A person starts telling lies and makes this his habit and thus he is written as a liar before Allah.

(Bukhārī and Muslim)

The word *ṣiddīq* is the intensive form of *ṣādiq*. It means one who is strictly veracious, honest, righteous and upright. *Ṣiddīq* is one who is truthful in his speech and his beliefs and this he testifies (*taṣdīq*) to with his actions; because of their sincerity and truth, *ṣiddīqūn* are ranked after the Prophets (*al-Nisā'* 4: 69). This was the rank held by some special Companions and the first among them was Abū Bakr on whom the Prophet (peace be upon him) bestowed the honour of *al-Ṣiddīq* for his unflinching love and support for him. He unhesitantly confirmed the event of *Miʿrāj* when accosted by the Quraysh and this without ascertaining it from the Prophet (peace be upon him).

Kidhb is the antonym of *ṣidq*. It comes from *kadhaba* which means to lie, to deceive, to delude or to mislead. Thus, *kidhb* means lie, deceit or falsehood and *kādhib* is a liar and so also is *kadhdhāb*, which is an intensive form. The Qur'ān portrays the contrasting personalities of a truthful and a lying person in the following terms:

فَأَمَّا مَنْ أَعْطَىٰ وَاتَّقَىٰ ﴿٥﴾ وَصَدَّقَ بِالْحُسْنَىٰ ﴿٦﴾ فَسَنُيَسِّرُهُ لِلْيُسْرَىٰ ﴿٧﴾
وَأَمَّا مَنْ بَخِلَ وَاسْتَغْنَىٰ ﴿٨﴾ وَكَذَّبَ بِالْحُسْنَىٰ ﴿٩﴾ فَسَنُيَسِّرُهُ لِلْعُسْرَىٰ ﴿١٠﴾

So he who gives (in charity) and fears (Allah) and (in all sincerity) testifies to the best – We will indeed make smooth for him the path to bliss. But he who is a greedy miser and thinks himself self-sufficient, and gives the lie to the best – We will indeed make smooth for him the path of misery.

(al-Layl 92: 5-10)

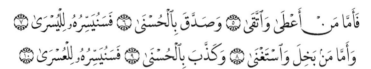

Finally, it is worth considering that there is an emphasis on one not just being truthful but that one should also remain in the company of others who are truthful.

We know that in Islam all acts of worship (*ʿibādah*) are communal. Thus, brotherhood and community life is essential for achieving self-purification. It is vital for us to develop a strong bond of brotherhood to sustain the seed of *īmān*. Brotherhood reinforces human potentiality and commitment. Thus, the Holy Qur'ān instructs the Prophet (peace be upon him):

وَٱصْبِرْ نَفْسَكَ مَعَ ٱلَّذِينَ يَدْعُونَ رَبَّهُم بِٱلْغَدَوٰةِ وَٱلْعَشِيِّ يُرِيدُونَ وَجْهَهُۥ... ﴿٢٨﴾

Keep yourself content with those who call upon their Lord morning and evening, seeking His pleasure.

(al-Kahf 18: 28)

An eminent scholar of the Indo-Pak Subcontinent, Sheikh ʿUthmān ibn ʿAlī Hujwirī in his famous book *Kashf al-Maḥjūb* related a story about a person performing *ṭawāf* in the Kaʿbah and praying: "O Lord! Make my friends pious." He was asked why at this blessed place he was not praying for himself but rather only for his friends. He replied: "I will return to my friends from here, if they are pious I will become pious in their company. If they are evil then I will be the same with them."

Modern psychological research also confirms that peer influence is a very powerful agent in human behaviour. Group life is a most powerful way to stimulate and inspire people. Thus, it is essential that we keep the company of those who are our fellow travellers. This is what a great Persian poet, Shaikh Saʿdī has said: the company of the pious will make you pious and the company of the wicked will make you wicked.

... رَبِّ تَقَبَّلْ تَوْبَتِي وَاغْسِلْ حَوْبَتِي وَأَجِبْ دَعْوَتِي وَثَبِّتْ حُجَّتِي
وَاهْدِ قَلْبِي وَسَدِّدْ لِسَانِي وَاسْلُلْ سَخِيمَةَ قَلْبِي.

(أحمد)

O Allah! Accept my repentance. Wash away my sins.
Accept my prayers. Give permanence to my pleading.
Guide my heart and make my tongue truthful.
Remove all aliments from my heart.

(Aḥmad)

May *Allāh Subḥānahu wa Ta'ālā* make us truthful and make us persevere in the path of truthfulness in the company of the pious. (*Āmīn*)

12

Reliance (*Tawakkul*)

...وَعَلَى ٱللَّهِ فَلْيَتَوَكَّلِ ٱلْمُتَوَكِّلُونَ ﴿١٢﴾

Let anyone who trusts, trust in Allah.

(Ibrāhīm 14: 12)

In this age of uncertainty, people have lost faith in everything. They have often been betrayed by those whom they trusted. They have even lost faith as well in the established institutions due to rampant greed and corruption. So, in this situation, the verse I recited aptly reminds us that it is only Allah Who truly deserves our trust. He will never fail us.

The word *tawakkul* comes from *wakala*, meaning to entrust to someone, to authorize, to empower or to appoint someone as representative. Hence, the word *wakīl*, meaning an attorney or lawyer, comes from this root, as does *tawakkul* meaning trust or confidence. However, this word is exclusively used for trust in Allah.

The essence of this reliance on Allah means that one should have complete faith in His guidance. One should take all necessary measures and fulfill all the conditions in order to achieve the desired result, but then rely on Allah that He, the All-Powerful and Almighty, will make it happen. *Tawakkul* also requires that one should not rely solely on one's own abilities and endeavours but exclusively put one's faith in Allah's help and support. One should have absolute conviction and confidence that whatever promises Allah has made to believers will definitely be fulfilled. In this way, after making all the necessary efforts, one should leave the result to Allah and have faith in Him that the outcome will be favourable.

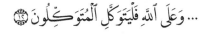

Imām Abū al-Qāsim al-Qushayrī, the author of a famous book on Sufism, *al-Risālah al-Qushayrīyah*, relates from his teacher, the equally eminent Imām Abū ʿAlī al-Daqqāq, that there are three degrees of trust in God: first trust, then surrender, and finally assigning all one's affairs to God. The one who has trust in God is at peace with His promise, the one who surrenders to Him is content with His knowledge, and one who assigns one's affairs to God is satisfied with His wisdom. This is the promise that Allah has given us:

... وَمَن يَتَوَكَّلْ عَلَى ٱللَّهِ فَهُوَ حَسْبُهُۥٓ ۚ إِنَّ ٱللَّهَ بَٰلِغُ أَمْرِهِۦ ۚ قَدْ جَعَلَ
ٱللَّهُ لِكُلِّ شَىْءٍ قَدْرًا ﴿٣﴾

Whoever puts his trust in Allah, He shall suffice him. Surely Allah brings about what He decrees. Allah has set a measure for everything.

(al-Ṭalāq 65: 3)

One of Allah's attributes is *Al-Wakīl.* This means that if one relies on Allah and leaves one's affairs to Him then "Allah suffices and He is the best Disposer of Affairs (*Wakīl*)." (*Āl ʿImrān* 3: 173; *al-Nisā'* 4: 81; *al-Ṭalāq* 65: 3).

Such complete reliance on Allah is exemplified from the lives of many Prophets. They totally submitted themselves to His Will and relied solely on Him in whichever adverse situations they faced. Whenever they faced persecution from unbelievers, they always said:

وَمَا لَنَآ أَلَّا نَتَوَكَّلَ عَلَى ٱللَّهِ وَقَدْ هَدَىٰنَا سُبُلَنَا ۚ وَلَنَصْبِرَنَّ عَلَىٰ مَآ ءَاذَيْتُمُونَا ۚ
وَعَلَى ٱللَّهِ فَلْيَتَوَكَّلِ ٱلْمُتَوَكِّلُونَ ﴿١٢﴾

Why should we not put our trust in Allah when it is indeed He Who guided us to the ways of our lives? We shall surely continue to remain steadfast in face of your persecution. Let anyone who trusts, trust in Allah.

(Ibrāhīm 14: 12)

The same message was given by our beloved Prophet (peace be upon him) when he told the unbelievers:

... إِنْ أَرَادَنِيَ ٱللَّهُ بِضُرٍّ هَلْ هُنَّ كَـٰشِفَـٰتُ ضُرِّهِۦٓ أَوْ أَرَادَنِي بِرَحْمَةٍ هَلْ هُنَّ
مُمْسِكَـٰتُ رَحْمَتِهِۦ ۚ قُلْ حَسْبِيَ ٱللَّهُ ۖ عَلَيْهِ يَتَوَكَّلُ ٱلْمُتَوَكِّلُونَ ﴿٣٨﴾

If Allah should will that an affliction befall me, will those deities remove the harm inflicted by Him? Or if Allah should will that I receive (His) Mercy, will they be able to withhold His Mercy from me? Tell them: "Allah is sufficient for me; those who trust should put their trust in Him."

(al-Zumar 39: 38)

As a practical way of demonstrating that the idols which people worship are helpless, the Prophet Ibrāhīm (peace be upon him) smashed them all, sparing only the supreme one among them. When his people came and saw their idols in this state they suspected that it must be the work of the young man named Ibrāhīm. So when he was asked about this incident, he innocently pointed to their supreme idol. As soon as they realized their folly in worshipping idols that would neither hear nor speak, yet, in their disgust, they wanted to take revenge. Thus, they prepared a pit of fire into which they intended to throw Ibrāhīm. The Prophet Ibrāhīm (peace be upon him) is reported to have said:

عَنِ ابْنِ عَبَّاسٍ قال: حَسْبُنَا اللهُ وَنِعْمَ الوَكِيلُ... .

(البخاري)

Allah is sufficient for me and what an excellent Guardian He is.

(Related by 'Abdullāh ibn 'Abbās in Bukhārī)

As we know, by the command of Allah, the fire became cool and safe for Ibrāhīm (peace be upon him).

Similarly, when the Prophet Mūsā (peace be upon him) and the tribe of Israel were pursued by Pharaoh's army, the open sea was in front of them and there was no escape route. They were in a quandary:

...قَالَ أَصۡحَٰبُ مُوسَىٰٓ إِنَّا لَمُدۡرَكُونَ ۝٦١ قَالَ كَلَّآۖ إِنَّ مَعِيَ رَبِّي سَيَهۡدِينِ ۝٦٢

The companions of Mūsā cried out: "We are overtaken." Mūsā said: "Certainly not. My Lord is with me; He will direct me."

(al-Shu'arā' 26: 61-62)

Facing such a precarious situation, the Prophet Mūsā (peace be upon him) had unshaken faith in His Lord that He would guide him and save both him and his companions.

During his migration to Madīnah, the Prophet (peace be upon him), together with Abū Bakr al-Ṣiddīq, secluded themselves in a cave known as Thawr while they were hotly pursued by the unbelievers. It so happened that the pursuers nearly reached the cave and Abū Bakr was very anxious that they would be captured. But the Prophet (peace be upon him) peacefully and calmly reassured him saying:

...لَا تَحۡزَنۡ إِنَّ ٱللَّهَ مَعَنَاۖ... ۝٤٠

Do not grieve, Allah is with us.

(al-Tawbah 9: 40)

This unshaken faith of the Prophet (peace be upon him) inspired his Companions as well. Thus, after the Battle of Uḥud, the retreating Makkans for a while considered making another attack and the Prophet (peace be upon) once again called his Companions, who had already suffered injuries, to reassemble. The hypocrites warned them:

إِيمَٰنٗا وَقَالُواْ حَسۡبُنَا ٱللَّهُ وَنِعۡمَ ٱلۡوَكِيلُ ۝١٧٣

"Behold, a host has gathered around you and you should fear them." It only increased their faith and they answered: "Allah is Sufficient for us; and what an excellent Guardian He is."

(Āl 'Imrān 3: 173)

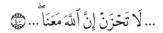

How beautiful is the following saying of the Prophet (peace be upon him), narrated by 'Umar ibn al-Khaṭṭāb, which combines exerting effort and *tawakkul*:

عَنْ عُمَرَ بْنِ الْـخَطَّاب رَضِيَ اللهُ عَنْهُ، أَنّ رَسُولَ اللهِ صَلَّى اللهُ عَلَيْهِ وَسَلَّمَ، قَالَ: لَوْ أَنَّكُمْ تَوَكَّلْتُمْ عَلَى اللهِ حَقَّ تَوَكُّلِه، لَرَزَقَكُمْ كَمَا يَرْزُقُ الطَّيْرَ، تَغْدُو خِمَاصًا، وَتَرُوحُ بِطَانًا.

(الحاكم وابن ماجه)

If you were able to rely on Allah as true reliance on Him
requires He would provide you as He provides birds
that leave their nests hungry in the morning
and return full in the evenings.
(Ḥākim and Ibn Mājah)

This means that birds fly out in the morning with the hope of finding food and through their effort and the grace of Allah return satiated in the evening. So, *tawakkul* requires that one rely on Allah. This does not mean, however, that one should not make any effort to achieve the desired result. It is incumbent upon human beings to make all possible efforts yet not to rely solely on them but instead to have *tawakkul* in Allah that their efforts will be fruitful. This is illustrated by the advice the Prophet (peace be upon him) gave to a man who asked him:

يَقُولُ أَنَسَ بْنَ مَالِكٍ قَالَ رَجُلٌ: يَا رَسُولَ اللهِ، أَعْقِلُهَا وَأَتَوَكَّلُ أَوْ أُطْلِقُهَا وَأَتَوَكَّلُ قَالَ: اعْقِلْهَا وَتَوَكَّلْ.

(الترمذي)

"O Messenger of Allah, should I tie the rope of the camel
or leave it alone and have *tawakkul* in Allah (that the
camel will be safe)?" The Prophet (peace be upon him)
said: "Tie the camel and have *tawakkul* in Allah."
(Narrated by Anas ibn Mālik in Tirmidhī)

This means that one should take all precautionary measures and then leave it to Allah and one should accept whatever the outcome is gracefully. As it is said: "Effort is on my part and the end result is in Allah's Hand."

The same was the case when the Prophet Ya'qūb (peace be upon him) sent his sons to Egypt and, as a precautionary measure, advised them to enter through the city's different gates. However, he realized that his own precaution would only work if that was what Allah willed. So he added:

... وَمَآ أُغْنِي عَنكُم مِّنَ ٱللَّهِ مِن شَيْءٍ إِنِ ٱلْحُكْمُ إِلَّا لِلَّهِ عَلَيْهِ تَوَكَّلْتُ وَعَلَيْهِ فَلْيَتَوَكَّلِ ٱلْمُتَوَكِّلُونَ ﴿٦٧﴾

I can be of no help to you against Allah. Allah's command alone prevails. I put my trust in Him and so should all who have faith put their trust in Him.

(Yūsuf 12: 67).

The Qur'ānic advice in this respect is that, in all affairs, believers should make mutual consultation (*shūrā*) and then:

... وَشَاوِرْهُمْ فِي ٱلْأَمْرِ فَإِذَا عَزَمْتَ فَتَوَكَّلْ عَلَى ٱللَّهِ إِنَّ ٱللَّهَ يُحِبُّ ٱلْمُتَوَكِّلِينَ ﴿١٥٩﴾

Take counsel from them in matters of importance. And when a decision has been taken, put your trust in Allah for Allah loves those who put their trust in Him.

(Āl 'Imrān 3: 159)

It is related by 'Abdullāh ibn Mas'ūd that the Messenger of Allah (peace be upon him) is reported to have said:

قَالَ عَبْدُ اللهِ ابْنُ مَسْعُودٍ: قَالَ النَّبِيُّ صَلَّى اللهُ عَلَيْهِ وَسَلَّمَ: عُرِضَتْ عَلَيَّ الأُمَمُ فَأَخَذَ النَّبِيُّ يَمُرُّ مَعَهُ الأُمَّةُ، وَالنَّبِيُّ يَمُرُّ مَعَهُ النَّفَرُ،

وَالنَّبِيُّ يَمُرُّ مَعَهُ الْعَشَرَةُ، وَالنَّبِيُّ يَمُرُّ مَعَهُ الْخَمْسَةُ، وَالنَّبِيُّ يَمُرُّ وَحْدَهُ، فَنَظَرْتُ فَإِذَا سَوَادٌ كَثِيرٌ قُلْتُ: يَا جِبْرِيلُ: هَؤُلَاءِ أُمَّتِي، قَالَ: لَا، وَلَكِنْ انْظُرْ إِلَى الْأُفُقِ، فَنَظَرْتُ: فَإِذَا سَوَادٌ كَثِيرٌ، قَالَ: هَؤُلَاءِ أُمَّتُكَ، وَهَؤُلَاءِ سَبْعُونَ أَلْفًا قُدَّامَهُمْ لَا حِسَابَ عَلَيْهِمْ وَلَا عَذَابَ، قُلْتُ: وَلِمَ، قَالَ: كَانُوا لَا يَكْتَوُونَ وَلَا يَسْتَرْقُونَ، وَلَا يَتَطَيَّرُونَ، وَعَلَى رَبِّهِمْ يَتَوَكَّلُونَ، فَقَامَ إِلَيْهِ عُكَّاشَةُ بْنُ مِحْصَنٍ، فَقَالَ: ادْعُ اللهَ أَنْ يَجْعَلَنِي مِنْهُمْ، قَالَ: اللَّهُمَّ اجْعَلْهُ مِنْهُمْ، ثُمَّ قَامَ إِلَيْهِ رَجُلٌ آخَرُ، قَالَ: ادْعُ اللهَ أَنْ يَجْعَلَنِي مِنْهُمْ، قَالَ: سَبَقَكَ بِهَا عُكَّاشَةُ.

(البخاري ومسلم)

I was shown all the communities. Then I was shown one that filled the entire horizon and [Jibrīl] said it is your *ummah*. Then I was told that among them will be seventy thousand who will enter Paradise without reckoning and punishment. They neither cast spells, nor cauterized themselves, nor sought omens but rather they trusted in Allah. Then ʿUkkāshah ibn Muḥṣin al-Asadī stood up and requested: "O Messenger of Allah! Pray to Allah to make me one of them." The Prophet (peace be upon him) replied: "You will be one of them." Then another person stood up and said: "Pray to Allah to make me one of them." The Prophet (peace be upon him) replied: "ʿUkkāshah came ahead of you."

(Bukhārī and Muslim)

Let me finish by quoting a few couplets from Ibrāhīm Ḥaqqī's *Tafwīḍ Nāmah* (*Description of Self-surrendering*):

Put your trust in God, Who is the Truth
And commit to Him your affairs
So that you may find peace

Be patient and agree (with whatever He does)
Let us see what our Master does
He does well whatever He does.

It is narrated by ʿAbdullāh ibn ʿAbbās that when the Prophet (peace be upon him) used to wake up during the night for prayers, he used to recite a *duʿā'*, part of which is as follows:

... اللَّهُمَّ لَكَ أَسْلَمْتُ، وَبِكَ آمَنْتُ، وَعَلَيْكَ تَوَكَّلْتُ، وَإِلَيْكَ أَنَبْتُ، وَبِكَ خَاصَمْتُ، وَإِلَيْكَ حَاكَمْتُ، فَاغْفِرْ لِي مَا قَدَّمْتُ وَأَخَّرْتُ، وَأَسْرَرْتُ وَأَعْلَنْتُ، أَنْتَ إِلَـهِي، لَا إِلَـهَ إِلَّا أَنْتَ.

(أحمد)

O Allah! I submit to You, I believe in You, I rely on You, I turn to You, I fight with Your help, and I leave all my affairs to You so forgive my sins whenever I commit them, those I have done and those I have yet to do, those done in secret and those done openly. You are my Lord: there is no god except You.

(Aḥmad)

So let us pray that *Allāh Subḥānahu wa Taʿālā* makes ourhearts subservient to His Will and that we completely rely upon Him. (*Āmīn*)

13

Certainty (*Yaqīn*)

الٓمٓ ۞ ذَٰلِكَ ٱلْكِتَٰبُ لَا رَيْبَ ۛ فِيهِ ۛ هُدًى لِّلْمُتَّقِينَ ۞ ٱلَّذِينَ يُؤْمِنُونَ
بِٱلْغَيْبِ وَيُقِيمُونَ ٱلصَّلَوٰةَ وَمِمَّا رَزَقْنَٰهُمْ يُنفِقُونَ ۞ وَٱلَّذِينَ يُؤْمِنُونَ
بِمَآ أُنزِلَ إِلَيْكَ وَمَآ أُنزِلَ مِن قَبْلِكَ وَبِٱلْءَاخِرَةِ هُمْ يُوقِنُونَ ۞

Alif Lām Mīm. This is the Book of Allah, there is no doubt in it, and it is guidance for all the God-conscious, who believe in [the existence of] that which is beyond the reach of human perception, who establish prayers and spend out of what We have provided them, who believe in what has been revealed to you and in what has been revealed before you, and who are certain of the Hereafter.

(al-Baqarah 2: 1-4)

Skepticism is a disease that is widespread in our society. Although we know and are convinced about our faith, yet we still often suffer from some lingering doubts that prevent us from committing ourselves wholeheartedly to the cause in which we believe. As there are things which we are required to believe but which cannot be perceived by our senses, we become doubtful of their existence. It is for this reason that at the very beginning of the Qur'ān, it is emphatically stated that there is no doubt what is being revealed in this Divine Book. Thus, one is required to believe in things that are beyond one's perception. This conviction and certainty is called *yaqīn*. It comes from *yaqina* which means to be sure, to be certain or to be convinced. *Yaqīn* means certainty, certitude or conviction and having no doubt about the truth of something. Its opposite is *ẓann* and *rayb* (doubt, suspicion, uncertainty). As death is the most certain event in our life, it is referred to as *yaqīn*.

وَٱعْبُدْ رَبَّكَ حَتَّىٰ يَأْتِيَكَ ٱلْيَقِينُ ﴿٩٩﴾

And serve your Lord until there come unto you the hour that is certain (death).
(al-Ḥijr 15: 99; and a similar reference in al-Muddaththir 74: 47)

There are three levels of certainty of knowledge. The first is certainty of mind. Human beings use their knowledge and experience and infer from something they know to something of which they are not quite certain. For example by looking at smoke one infers that there must be fire somewhere; in other words, we know by experience that there is no smoke without fire. In Qur'ānic terminology this is called *ʿIlm al-Yaqīn*.

كَلَّا لَوْ تَعْلَمُونَ عِلْمَ ٱلْيَقِينِ ﴿٥﴾

Nay, would that you knew with the certainty of knowledge.
(al-Takāthur 102: 5)

This means if you knew with certainty of knowledge what your attitude would lead to, you would not have acted the way you did. The Qur'ānic assertion is that if one uses one's reason one can be certain of the Day of Judgement, otherwise when one sees the retribution of one's sins and the reality of the Hell-fire on that day with one's own eyes, one has to believe it. As it is said: seeing is believing. In Qur'ānic terminology, this is called *ʿAyn al-Yaqīn*:

ثُمَّ لَتَرَوُنَّهَا عَيْنَ ٱلْيَقِينِ ﴿٧﴾

You will see it with certainty of sight.
(al-Takāthur 102: 7)

Yet there is a further degree of certainty with neither error of judgement nor error of sight. Sometimes, for example, it happens that one can be deluded by one's sight: we might see a rope at night and think it is a snake or we are mesmerized by visual tricks performed by magicians. Absolute truth, however, without any possibility of doubt, is called *Ḥaqq al-Yaqīn*:

إِنَّ هَٰذَا لَهُوَ حَقُّ ٱلْيَقِينِ ﴿٩٥﴾

Verily, this is the very Truth and assured certainty.
(al-Wāqiʿah 56: 95; and a similar reference in al-Ḥaqqah 69: 51)

Going back to the example of smoke leading to the assumption of fire, this is certainty of knowledge (*ʿIlm al-Yaqīn*). However, seeing the fire with one's own eyes is certainty of sight (*ʿAyn al-Yaqīn*), and assured certainty and truth (*Ḥaqq al-Yaqīn*) is when one puts one's hand in the fire and it burns. This is the last degree of certainty required of us if we are to have true faith. We should believe in Allah and the Day of Judgment and all matters that are beyond our perception as if we have physically experienced them.

However, there is some difference between *yaqīn* and *īmān* (faith). *Īmān* means to believe or to testify and to accept, which is the opposite of to deny or to reject; whereas, *yaqīn* is certainty of belief which is the opposite of doubt. Believing in something is not conditional on certainty. So to persist in acts of submission could lead to *īmān*, as these verses of *Sūrah al-Ḥujurāt* advise the desert Arabs:

قَالَتِ ٱلْأَعْرَابُ ءَامَنَّا ۖ قُل لَّمْ تُؤْمِنُوا۟ وَلَٰكِن قُولُوٓا۟ أَسْلَمْنَا وَلَمَّا يَدْخُلِ
ٱلْإِيمَٰنُ فِى قُلُوبِكُمْ ۖ وَإِن تُطِيعُوا۟ ٱللَّهَ وَرَسُولَهُۥ لَا يَلِتْكُم مِّنْ أَعْمَٰلِكُمْ شَيْـًٔا ۚ
إِنَّ ٱللَّهَ غَفُورٌ رَّحِيمٌ ﴿١٤﴾ إِنَّمَا ٱلْمُؤْمِنُونَ ٱلَّذِينَ ءَامَنُوا۟ بِٱللَّهِ وَرَسُولِهِۦ ثُمَّ لَمْ يَرْتَابُوا۟
وَجَٰهَدُوا۟ بِأَمْوَٰلِهِمْ وَأَنفُسِهِمْ فِى سَبِيلِ ٱللَّهِ ۚ أُو۟لَٰٓئِكَ هُمُ ٱلصَّٰدِقُونَ ﴿١٥﴾

The desert Arabs say: "We believe." Say (O Prophet): "You have no faith, you should rather say: 'We have submitted our wills to Allah'"; for faith has not yet entered your hearts. But if you obey Allah and His Messenger, He will not diminish any of your deeds: for Allah is Oft-Forgiving, Most Compassionate. Indeed the ones possessed of true faith are those who believed in Allah and His Messenger and they did not entertain any doubt and strove hard in the Way of Allah with their lives and their possessions. These are the truthful ones.

(al-Ḥujurāt 49: 14-15)

Thus, true faith (*īmān*) requires unflinching belief without any shadow of a doubt in one's heart and mind.

However, we should also know that to have certainty may not always lead one to *īmān*. The Jews of Madīnah knew in their hearts and were certain that the Prophet (peace be upon him) was the true Messenger of Allah, yet their pride and jealousy prevented them from accepting *īmān*.

ٱلَّذِينَ ءَاتَيْنَٰهُمُ ٱلْكِتَٰبَ يَعْرِفُونَهُۥ كَمَا يَعْرِفُونَ أَبْنَآءَهُمُ ٱلَّذِينَ
خَسِرُوٓا۟ أَنفُسَهُمْ فَهُمْ لَا يُؤْمِنُونَ ﴿٢٠﴾

Those to whom We have given the Book recognize him as they recognize their own sons; yet those who have lost their own souls will not believe.

(al-An'ām 6: 20 and al-Baqarah 2: 146)

Thus, in order to gain certainty, one should try to acquire true knowledge. Seeking true knowledge means starting with purity of intention to study the Signs of Allah's existence and His Oneness in this universe. One should reflect upon how Allah dealt with those who transgressed and how they faced destruction. One should ponder upon the manifestations of Allah's Names and Attributes surrounding us. By persisting in acts of worship (*'ibādah*) and utterly depending on Allah's Will and Mercy, satisfaction in our hearts and certainty in our souls will be created. Once one is convinced of fundamental truths, then prejudices and other considerations should not keep one from these convictions.

Certainty is the key to achieving ultimate success in this life and the Hereafter. Certainty gives one the courage and confidence to overcome seemingly invincible obstacles. One such tale of certainty is the legendary success achieved by Ṭāriq ibn Ziyād. He was so convinced that he would be successful in conquering Andalusia that after reaching the shores of Spain, he ordered his army to burn their boats. Thus, he made it clear to his armed forces that there was no way back. There was the enemy in front and the sea at their backs. They fought with astounding courage and defeated the enemy. The place where Ṭāriq ibn Ziyād landed his forces was called Lion's Rock but after his conquest it was re-named Jabal al-Ṭāriq, better known as Gibraltar.

Even today, for the revival of the Muslim *ummah*, we need this conviction that we can overcome the difficulties we face. This was the message of poet-philosopher 'Allāmah Iqbāl. Seeing the utter despair engulfing Muslims at the turn of the 20th century when almost all Muslim nations were under colonial rule, he preached the concept of *khūdī*, meaning self- recognition, self-reliance, self-respect and self-confidence. So, in his poetry, Iqbāl consistently urged Muslims to acquire *yaqīn*.

> Firm certainty, constant struggle and love are the conquerors of the world
> In the struggle of life these are the real weapons for men
> O Ignorant! Acquire *yaqīn*, as *yaqīn*
> Provides that strength in poverty that overpowers monarchy.

> *Yaqīn* is sitting in a fire like Ibrāhīm
> *Yaqīn* is devotion to Allah and self-realization
> Listen, O prisoner of modernism!
> Uncertainty is worse than slavery.

On the authority of 'Abdullāh ibn Mas'ūd, the Prophet (peace be upon him) said:

عَنِ ابْنِ مَسْعُودٍ، عَنِ النَّبِيِّ صَلَّى اللهُ عَلَيْهِ وَسَلَّمَ، قَالَ: لا تُرْضِيَنَّ أَحَدًا بِسَخَطِ اللهِ، وَلا تَحْمَدَنَّ أَحَدًا عَلَى فَضْلِ اللهِ، وَلا تَذُمَّنَّ أَحَدًا عَلَى مَا لَمْ يُؤْتِكَ اللهُ، فَإِنَّ رِزْقَ اللهِ لا يَسُوقُهُ إِلَيْكَ حِرْصُ حَرِيصٍ، وَلا يَرُدُّهُ عَنْكَ كَرَاهِيَةُ كَارِهٍ، وَإِنَّ اللهَ تَعَالَى بِقِسْطِهِ وَعَدْلِهِ جَعَلَ الرَّوْحَ وَالْفَرَحَ فِي الرِّضَا وَالْيَقِينِ، وَجَعَلَ الْهَمَّ وَالْحَزَنَ فِي السَّخَطِ.

(الطبراني في الكبير)

Do not seek to please anyone at the price of Allah's wrath, do not offer thanks to anyone for the bounty of Allah, do not find fault with anyone for something Allah has withheld from you, for the sustenance of Allah is not brought to you by the greed of the greedy nor is it driven away from you by the hatred of the one who hates you. By means of justice and fairness, *Allāh Subḥānahu wa Taʿālā* has placed repose and delights in contentment and certainty, and distress and sorrow in suspicion and anger.

(Ṭabarānī)

O Allah! Give us that certainty and conviction that renders our worldly loss worthless.

(Tirmidhī)

O Allah! Give us the contentment and certainty that we should acquire Your pleasure as well as real happiness and tranquility in this world and the Hereafter.

... اللَّهُمَّ أَحْسِنْ عَاقِبَتَنَا فِي الْأُمُورِ كُلِّهَا، وَأَجِرْنَا مِنْ خِزْيِ الدُّنْيَا وَعَذَابِ الْآخِرَةِ.

(أحمد)

O Allah! Conclude all our affairs with a better end and save us from disgrace in the world and punishment in the *Ākhirah*. (*Āmīn*)

(Aḥmad)

14

Supplication (*Du'ā'*)

ٱدْعُوا۟ رَبَّكُمْ تَضَرُّعًا وَخُفْيَةً ۚ إِنَّهُۥ لَا يُحِبُّ ٱلْمُعْتَدِينَ ﴿٥٥﴾ وَلَا تُفْسِدُوا۟ فِى
ٱلْأَرْضِ بَعْدَ إِصْلَـٰحِهَا وَٱدْعُوهُ خَوْفًا وَطَمَعًا ۚ إِنَّ رَحْمَتَ ٱللَّهِ قَرِيبٌ
مِّنَ ٱلْمُحْسِنِينَ ﴿٥٦﴾

Call on your Lord with humility and in secret for Allah loves not those who trespass beyond the bounds. Do no mischief on the earth after it has been set in order, but call on Him with fear and longing (in your hearts). For the mercy of Allah is (always) near to those who do good.

(al-A'rāf 7: 55-6)

We are all entirely dependent upon Allah's grace and mercy. There are many ways of invoking His help and seeking His pleasure and nearness. However, as mentioned in a *ḥadīth* narrated by Anas ibn Mālik:

عَنْ أَنَسِ بْنِ مَالِك، عَنِ النَّبِيِّ صَلَّى اللهُ عَلَيْهِ وَسَلَّمَ
قَالَ: الدُّعَاءُ مُخُّ الْعِبَادَةِ.

(الترمذي)

"*Du'ā'* is the essence of all worship (*'ibādah*)."

(Tirmidhī)

Du'ā' occupies a pivotal position in religion (*dīn*), as it is stated in another *ḥadīth*, narrated by Nu'mān ibn Bashīr:

عَنِ النُّعْمَـانِ بْنِ بَشِيرٍ ، قَالَ: سَمِعْتُ النَّبِيَّ صَلَّى اللهُ عَلَيْهِ وَسَلَّمَ، يَقُولُ: الدُّعَاءُ هُوَ الْعِبَادَةُ.

(الترمذي)

"*Du'ā'* is worship (*'ibādah*) itself."

(Tirmidhī)

The word *du'ā'* is derived from *da'ā*, which means to call or to summon. There are many verses in which the word *da'ā* is used in its dictionary sense. For example:

وَمَنْ أَحْسَنُ قَوْلًا مِّمَّن دَعَآ إِلَى ٱللَّهِ وَعَمِلَ صَـٰلِحًا وَقَالَ إِنَّنِى مِنَ ٱلْمُسْلِمِينَ ﴿٣٣﴾

Who is better in speech than one who calls (people) to Allah, works righteousness, and says, "I am of those who bow in Islam"?

(Fuṣṣilat 41: 33)

However, *du'ā'* in common parlance means invocation, supplication, a request or plea to Allah. The Qur'ān explains the attributes and character, as well as etiquette (*adab*), of making *du'ā'* in a number of places. I have already recited a couple of verses from *Sūrah al-A'rāf* instructing us to make *du'ā'* with humility, in private, with fear as well as longing for Allah's mercy. In *Sūrah al-Isrā'* it is said:

... وَلَا تَجْهَرْ بِصَلَاتِكَ وَلَا تُخَافِتْ بِهَا وَٱبْتَغِ بَيْنَ ذَٰلِكَ سَبِيلًا ﴿١١٠﴾

Neither offer your prayer aloud nor in too low a tone, but follow a middle course.

(al-Isrā' 17: 110)

Du'ā' is the embodiment of one's humility before one's Lord and one's trust and hopes in Divine Help and Mercy. In this state of complete submission and humility, whatever words come from one's heart is *du'ā'*. When this *du'ā'* is accompanied by good deeds (*'amal ṣāliḥ*) and is expressed with utter helplessness and humility then Allah's mercy and forgiveness is to be expected in response to it. On the other hand, making *duʿā'* causally or as a ritual without real commitment is of no avail. We are required to make *duʿā'* only to Allah to seek His help and to call upon Him. Most of the rites performed in all our *ʿibādah* consist of *duʿā'*. We should always seek Allah's help, His guidance and mercy to traverse through life, and success facilitated by Him (*tawfīq*).

There is a general misconception about *duʿā'* among common people. They think that certain specific words uttered are magical in themselves and, after repeating them a certain number of times on certain days or on specific auspicious times, this will in itself bring about the desired results. The other common misconception is that if a *duʿā'* does not seem to be accepted in the precise manner required then it is rejected by Allah, and, consequently, one becomes disheartened and despairs. However, this is a reflection of a business mentality. As related by Abū Saʿīd, the Prophet (peace be upon him) gave the following pertinent guidance in this respect:

عَنْ أَبِي سَعِيدٍ، أَنَّ النَّبِيَّ صَلَّى اللهُ عَلَيْهِ وَسَلَّمَ قَالَ: مَا مِنْ مُسْلِم يَدْعُو بِدَعْوَةٍ لَيْسَ فِيهَا إِثْمٌ وَلَا قَطِيعَةُ رَحِمٍ، إِلَّا أَعْطَاهُ اللهُ بِهَا إِحْدَى ثَلَاثٍ: إِمَّا أَنْ تُعَجَّلَ لَهُ دَعْوَتُهُ، وَإِمَّا أَنْ يَدَّخِرَهَا لَهُ فِي الْآخِرَةِ، وَإِمَّا أَنْ يَصْرِفَ عَنْهُ مِنَ السُّوءِ مِثْلَهَا ....

(أحمد)

Whoever asks Allah, his prayer is always accepted, provided he has not asked for some sinful thing or to sever relationships. Allah will give him one of three outcomes: he either receives the benefit in this world or it is saved for him in the Hereafter or some of his sins equal to the prayer are forgiven.

(Aḥmad)

The reason is that Allah knows best whether what we have asked for is really suitable for us: so either He accepts what is being asked for, or gives something better than what was requested, or instead grants us a reward in the Hereafter. Allah Himself has asked us to make *duʿā'* and He promised to answer all who call upon Him.

وَإِذَا سَأَلَكَ عِبَادِى عَنِّى فَإِنِّى قَرِيبٌ أُجِيبُ دَعْوَةَ ٱلدَّاعِ إِذَا دَعَانِ فَلْيَسْتَجِيبُوا۟
لِى وَلْيُؤْمِنُوا۟ بِى لَعَلَّهُمْ يَرْشُدُونَ ﴿١٨٦﴾

(*O Muḥammad*), *When my servants ask you about Me, tell them I am indeed close* (*to them*): *I listen to the prayer of every suppliant when he calls upon Me. Let them also listen to My call and believe in Me; perhaps they will be guided aright.*
(al-Baqarah 2: 186)

It is our duty to remain hopeful and keep faith in Allah's promise and His mercy.

However, if one's prayers are not answered, then one should also scrutinize one's lifestyle. If one does not fulfill one's obligations imposed by the *Sharīʿah* and does not care whether one's earnings are lawful or unlawful, then uttering a few words of prayer will not fulfill the aims of *duʿā'*. This is well illustrated by a *ḥadīth* in which the Prophet (peace be up on him) narrated the following:

عَنْ أَبِي هُرَيْرَةَ قَالَ: ذَكَرَ النَّبِيُّ صَلَّى اللهُ عَلَيْهِ وَسَلَّمَ الرَّجُلَ
يُطِيلُ السَّفَرَ أَشْعَثَ أَغْبَرَ يَمُدُّ يَدَيْهِ إِلَى اللهِ عَزَّ وَجَلَّ يَارَبِّ
يَارَبِّ، وَمَطْعَمُهُ حَرَامٌ، وَمَشْرَبُهُ حَرَامٌ، وَمَلْبَسُهُ حَرَامٌ،
وَغُذِّيَ بِالْحَرَامِ، فَأَنَّى يُسْتَجَابُ لِذَلِكَ.

(البخاري)

A person who was on a long journey in a dishevelled state, covered in dust and stretching both his hands towards the sky, calling: "O My Lord! O My Lord!", while his condition was that his food was unlawful, his drink was unlawful and his dress was unlawful. He was

being nourished by unlawful (*ḥarām*) means.
So how could his prayer be granted?
(Narrated by Abū Hurayah in Bukhārī.)

There are certain things that one should avoid while making supplication as they are against the etiquette (*adab*) of *du'ā'*. First, one should not make *du'ā'* conditional on Allah's will. Whatever one has to ask, one should categorically request Allah for its fulfillment.

It is narrated by Abū Hurayrah that the Prophet (peace be upon him) said:

عَنْ أَبِي هُرَيْرَةَ رَضِيَ اللهُ عَنْهُ، أَنَّ رَسُولَ اللهِ صَلَّى اللهُ عَلَيْهِ وَسَلَّمَ، قَالَ: لَا يَقُولَنَّ أَحَدَكُمُ اللَّهُمَّ اغْفِرْ لِي إِنْ شِئْتَ، اللَّهُمَّ ارْحَمْنِي إِنْ شِئْتَ لِيَعْزِمْ الْمَسْأَلَةَ، فَإِنَّهُ لَا مُكْرِهَ لَهُ.

(البخاري ومسلم)

One should not say: "O Allah! Forgive my sins if You wish or O Allah! Have mercy on me if You wish." One should pray with firm conviction as there is no one who can coerce Allah.
(Bukhārī and Muslim)

Secondly, *du'ā'* should be made without ostentation and affectation. One should not use rhymed and flowery language as this makes it soulless and deprives it of presence of heart and mind as well as the feeling of humility. If we attempt to do this, then our mind is engaged in searching for suitable rhyming words.

عَنْ عِكْرِمَةَ، أَنَّ ابْنَ عَبَّاسٍ، قَالَ: فَانْظُرِ السَّجْعَ مِنَ الدُّعَاءِ فَاجْتَنِبْهُ، فَإِنِّي عَهِدْتُ رَسُولَ اللهِ صَلَّى اللهُ عَلَيْهِ وَسَلَّمَ وَأَصْحَابَهُ لَا يَفْعَلُونَ إِلَّا ذَلِكَ يَعْنِي لَا يَفْعَلُونَ إِلَّا ذَلِكَ الإِجْتِنَابَ.

(البخاري)

ʿAbdullāh ibn ʿAbbās instructed his disciple ʿIkrimah saying: "Avoid using rhymed prose as I have seen that the Prophet (peace be upon him) and his noble Companions did not use such language."

(Bukhārī)

Of course, if rhythmic and harmonious words do unintentionally flow from one's heart they have a literary quality and we see that many prayers of the Prophet (peace be upon him) are of that nature.

Finally, one should avoid what is termed as transgressing the bounds. The *ʿulamā'* have indicated some of the things that count as exceeding the bounds. Firstly, asking for things that are unlawful as this is the worst form of crossing limits. This is the antithesis of supplication. By such acts, one becomes liable to incur Allah's wrath. Suppose a Muslim is engaged in a business involving interest and then asks for increase in the profitability of his business, then this foolish person is inviting Allah's wrath, as taking interest is unlawful. One should only ask for things that one knows are lawful.

Secondly, we should avoid making *duʿā'* unnecessarily loudly, as we have seen that the verse from *Sūrah al-Aʿrāf* says: "Call upon your Lord with humility and in private." The prayer of the Prophet Zakarīyā (peace be upon him) as mentioned in *Sūrah Maryam* was: إِذْ نَادَىٰ رَبَّهُۥ نِدَآءً خَفِيًّا ﴿٣﴾ "*He cried to his Lord in secret.*" (Maryam 19: 3)

Thirdly, we should not use too many unnecessary words. The Prophet's (peace be upon him) supplications were very concise and compact. Thus, we should avoid verbosity and it is best to confine our supplications to those that are narrated in the Qur'ān and *aḥādīth*. Of course, one can always ask for one's specific needs in one's own words, which are particularly effective if heartfelt.

One further condition for acceptance of one's prayer is that one should not crave its quick fulfilment. As reported by Abū Hurayrah, the Prophet (peace be upon him) said:

عَنْ أَبِي هُرَيْرَةَ رَضِيَ اللهُ عَنْهُ، أَنَّ رَسُولَ اللهِ صَلَّى اللهُ عَلَيْهِ وَسَلَّمَ، قَالَ: يُسْتَجَابُ لِأَحَدِكُمْ مَالَمْ يَعْجَلْ يَقُولُ: دَعَوْتُ فَلَمْ يُسْتَجَبْ لِي.

(البخاري ومسلم)

A person's *du'ā'* is only accepted if he does not make haste and starts saying that he has prayed but that his prayers are unanswered.

(Bukhārī and Muslim)

One should always be patient and believe that Allah has listened to one's prayers and will accept them. It is narrated that 'Umar ibn Khaṭṭāb used to say: "I am not worried about the acceptance of my prayers. My only concern is about making prayers. If I have the *tawfīq* to make a prayer then surely its acceptance is assured."

Although *du'ā'* can be made any time during the day or night, there are nonetheless certain days and times that are indicated by authentic *aḥādīth* as being auspicious. They are *Laylat al-Qadr*, the day of *'Arafah*, the early morning before dawn, certain times on Fridays, at the time of breaking the fast, during *Ḥajj*, after completion of the Qur'ān and between the saying of the *Adhān* and the *Iqāmah*. Although *du'ā'* can be made in any language, if one chooses a *du'ā'* mentioned in the Qur'ān or *aḥādīth*, then it is hoped that this will be more effective.

O Lord! Your slaves are at Your door! Your beggars are at Your door! Your destitute servants are at Your door! Your helpless servants are at Your door! O Lord! You have said and whatever You have said is truth: "Call Me and I will respond." These are our prayers so please accept them.

... اللَّهُمَّ أَعُوذُ بِرِضَاكَ مِنْ سَخَطِكَ، وَبِمُعَافَاتِكَ مِنْ عُقُوبَتِكَ، وَأَعُوذُ بِكَ مِنْكَ، لَا أُحْصِي ثَنَاءً عَلَيْكَ أَنْتَ، كَمَا أَثْنَيْتَ عَلَى نَفْسِكَ.

(مسلم)

O Allah! We seek refuge in Your pleasure from Your displeasure. We seek refuge in Your forgiveness from Your punishment. We seek refuge in You from You. I am incapable of praising You as You have praised Yourself. (*Āmīn*)

(Muslim)

15

Humility in Prayers (*Khushūʿ fī al-Ṣalāh*)

قَدْ أَفْلَحَ ٱلْمُؤْمِنُونَ ﴿١﴾ ٱلَّذِينَ هُمْ فِى صَلَاتِهِمْ خَـٰشِعُونَ ﴿٢﴾

The believers have indeed attained true success. They [are the ones who] humble themselves in their Prayers.

(al-Mu'minūn 23: 1-2)

These verses from *Sūrah al-Mu'minūn* give the tidings from *Allāh Subḥānahu wa Taʿālā* that those who are humble in their prayers will attain eternal bliss and salvation – *falāḥ*. The word used is *khushūʿ* which comes from *khashaʿa*. It means to be submissive or humble. *Khushūʿ*, a noun from this root, means submissiveness, humility, lowliness, meekness or servility. This word is also used for a low and quiet voice and for downcast eyes.

Khushūʿ in *Ṣalāh* means bowing down before Allah with humility and submissiveness. As such, it affects both the inner feelings of the heart as well as the outward expression of the body. *Khushūʿ* of the heart means a state of being overpowered by glory and grandeur that creates awe, reverence and fear. The manifestation of *khushūʿ* on one's body results in the bowing down of one's head with downcast eyes in a state of humility and using the voice very quietly, all expressing a state of fright and timidity. This is the state of someone who is in the presence of a majestic and regal personality.

Khushūʿ is the soul of prayer. This fact is emphasized in several passages of the Qur'ān. The essential requirement of the *Ṣalāh* is humility of the heart and a submissive body posture. Hence, the glad tidings of success (*falāḥ*) is for those who pray with *Khushūʿ*.

So how can we achieve *khushūʿ* in our prayers? Firstly, we have to create the proper psychological atmosphere for prayer. This means that we should remove and avoid things that may distract us, such as praying in front of pictures and mirrors.

عَنْ أَنَسِ بْنِ مَالِكٍ، كَانَ قِرَامٌ لِعَائِشَةَ سَتَرَتْ بِهِ جَانِبَ بَيْتِهَا، فَقَالَ النَّبِيُّ صَلَّى اللهُ عَلَيْهِ وَسَلَّمَ: أَمِيطِي عَنَّا قِرَامَكِ هَذَا فَإِنَّهُ لَا تَزَالُ تَصَاوِيرُهُ تَعْرِضُ فِي صَلَاتِي.

(البخاري)

It is narrated by Anas ibn Mālik that *Umm al-Muʾminīn* ʿĀʾishah had a decorated and colourful curtain that used to cover the side of her room. The Prophet (peace be upon him) told her: "Take it off as its decorations keep distracting me when I pray."

(Bukhārī)

Secondly, one should, if possible, also avoid praying in places that are either very hot or too cold. For this reason, the Prophet (peace be upon him) instructed his Companions to delay praying *Ẓuhr* in the summer until the hottest part of the day was over. Ibn Qayyim commenting on this *ḥadīth* said: "Praying when it is intensely hot prevents a person from having proper *khushuʿ* and presence of mind and he does his worship reluctantly."

Thirdly, in *aḥādīth* it is recommended that one should not pray when food is ready and one is hungry or if one needs to answer a call of nature.

عَنْ أَنَسِ بْنِ مَالِكٍ، أَنَّ رَسُولَ اللهِ صَلَّى اللهُ عَلَيْهِ وَسَلَّمَ قَالَ: إِذَا قُدِّمَ الْعَشَاءُ فَابْدَءُوا بِهِ قَبْلَ أَنْ تُصَلُّوا صَلَاةَ الْمَغْرِبِ، وَلَا تَعْجَلُوا عَنْ عَشَائِكُمْ.

(البخاري)

As related by Anas ibn Mālik, the Prophet (peace be upon him) is reported to have said: "If dinner has been served and the *Iqāmah* has been said for prayers, eat first and do not rush to finish it."

(Bukhārī)

Similarly, the Prophet (peace be upon him) forbade praying when one is suppressing an urge to urinate or defecate (Ibn Mājah). If this happens, one should stop praying and go and answer the call of nature.

Fourthly, if one is feeling sleepy then it is preferable not to pray.

عَنْ أَنَسِ بْنِ مَالِك، عَنْ النَّبِيِّ صَلَّى اللهُ عَلَيْهِ وَسَلَّمَ قَالَ: إِذَا نَعَسَ أَحَدُكُمْ فِي الصَّلَاةِ فَلْيَنَمْ حَتَّى يَعْلَمَ مَايَقْرَأُ.

(البخاري)

It is narrated by Anas ibn Mālik that the Prophet (peace be upon him) said: "If any one of you feels sleepy when praying, he should sleep until he [has rested enough to] know what he is saying."

(Bukhārī)

This usually happens when one is praying optional prayers (*nawāfil*) during *Qiyām al-Layl.*

All these instructions mean that our external environment as well as our frame of mind is conducive to tranquility and peacefulness. They emphasize the fact that we should realize that we are about to perform an important task and that we are fully prepared to concentrate on what we will be doing.

Finally, during prayers, it is essential that we concentrate and listen attentively, thinking about the *āyāt* and *adhkār* that are being recited. When the Imām is not reciting loudly, we should remember Allah and the Hereafter (*Ākhirah*). If one especially and consciously reflects on the possibility that this may perhaps be one's last prayer, it will soften one's heart and create humility. One of the characteristics of those endowed with *khushūʿ* in their prayers is that they remember the Day of Judgement:

وَٱسْتَعِينُوا۟ بِٱلصَّبْرِ وَٱلصَّلَوٰةِ ۚ وَإِنَّهَا لَكَبِيرَةٌ إِلَّا عَلَى ٱلْخَٰشِعِينَ ﴿٤٥﴾
ٱلَّذِينَ يَظُنُّونَ أَنَّهُم مُّلَٰقُوا۟ رَبِّهِمْ وَأَنَّهُمْ إِلَيْهِ رَٰجِعُونَ ﴿٤٦﴾

And seek (Allah's) help with patience and Prayer. Truly Prayer is burdensome except for those who are humble. They realize that ultimately they will have to meet their Lord and to Him they are destined to return.

(al-Baqarah 2: 45-46)

If one is really concentrating one should avoid doing gratuitous acts like scratching, adjusting one's garment or doing anything that causes distraction.

عَنْ أَبَانَ قَالَ: رَأَى ابْنَ الْمُسَيَّبِ رَجُلاً يَعْبَثُ بِلِحْيَتِهِ فِي الصَّلَاةِ
فَقَالَ: إِنِّي لَأَرَى هَذَا لَوْ خَشَعَ قَلْبُهُ خَشَعَتْ جَوَارِحُهُ.

(مصنف عبد الرزاق)

It was related by Abān that Ibn al-Musayyab saw a man playing with his beard while he was praying. He said, "If this man had tranquility (*khushū*ʿ) in his heart, his limbs would be at rest (*khushū*ʿ)."

(*Muṣannaf ʿAbd al-Razzāq*)

It will help our concentration and *khushū*ʿ if we realize that we are standing in the presence of our Lord and we are seeing Him. It may be difficult for many to have such a vivid imagination but, at the very least, we should feel that our Lord is seeing us. This is the status of excellence (*iḥsān*) as mentioned in the famous *Ḥadīth Jibrīl*. The conscious realization that our Lord is observing us creates a feeling of humility, lowliness and extreme submissiveness before Him, our Lord and Creator.

If one is praying alone then one should recite slowly in a rhythmic tone (*tartīl*) while pausing at the end of each *āyah*. One should realize that Prayer is not a monologue as Allah responds to us as we recite the Qur'ān. The Prophet (peace be upon him) said:

Allah, the Blessed and Exalted has said: "I have divided the Prayer between Myself and My servant in two halves. When My servant says: '*Praise be to Allah, the Lord of the entire Universe*', Allah replies: 'My servant has praised Me.' When the servant says: '*The Most Merciful, the Most Compassionate*', Allah responds: 'My servant has extolled Me.' When the servant says: '*the Master of the Day of Judgement*', Allah says: 'My servant has glorified Me.' When the servant says: '*You alone do we worship and You alone do we turn for help*', Allah says; 'This is between Me and My servant and My servant shall have what he asked for.' When the servant says: '*Direct us on to the straight path, the path of those whom You have favoured, not those who incur Your wrath, nor those who have gone astray.*' Allah replies: 'All these are for My servant, and My Servant shall have what he asked for.'

(Muslim)

This is a significant *ḥadīth*, one we should keep in mind when we pray. If we do so, it will create an immense impact as we realise that our Lord responding to us.

We should also try to vary the *sūrah*s or passages of the Qur'ān we recite so that our recitation in the *Ṣalāh* does not become mechanical repetition. It will also help us enormously if we try to learn the meanings of all the *sūrah*s that we read in our *Ṣalāh*.

One other factor conducive to *khushūʿ* is that we should perform our *Ṣalāh* with complete composure. This means that our bowing down (*rukūʿ*) and prostration (*sujūd*) are properly done, without undue haste. It is narrated by Abū Qatādah that the Prophet (peace be upon him) said:

عَنْ أَبِي قَتَادَةَ: قَالَ: قَالَ رَسُولَ اللهِ صَلَّى اللهُ عَلَيْهِ وَسَلَّمَ: أَسْوَأُ النَّاسِ سَرَقَةً الَّذِيْ يَسْرِقُ مِنْ صَلَاتِهِ، قَالُوْا: يَارَسُولَ اللهِ، وَكَيْفَ يَسْرِقُ مِنْ صَلَاتِهِ؟ قَالَ: لَايُتِمُّ رُكُوعَهَا وَلَاسُجُودَهَا.

(أحمد)

The worst type of thief is the one who steals from his Prayers. When asked: "O Messenger of Allah, how can a person steal from his Prayers?" The Prophet (peace be upon him) replied: "By not doing *rukūʿ* and *sujūd* properly."

(Aḥmad)

Thus, to cultivate *khushūʿ* in our *Ṣalāh* we should make a start by first making a firm intention and having complete determination that we will try our best to perform our *Ṣalāh* properly. This will help us to concentrate our minds on what is being read instead of wandering and thinking about all manner of other things. Thus, when you raise your hands and say "*Allāhu Akbar*" and start the *Ṣalāh*, assume that you are cutting yourself off from this world and transposing yourself into another world. You should relinquish all your worries about worldly affairs and concentrate your mind solely upon your presence before your Lord. However, it is a natural weakness that one is often afflicted with distraction (*wasāwis*) and worldly thoughts, doubts and temptations. In prayer, we often suddenly remember things we have forgotten for a long time. This, according to a *ḥadīth*, is due to Satan who tries to distract us. The Prophet (peace be upon him) told us that Satan says to us while we are praying:

عَنْ أَبِي هُرَيْرَةَ رَضِيَ اللهُ عَنْهُ قَالَ: قَالَ رَسُولُ اللهِ صَلَّى اللهُ عَلَيْهِ وَسَلَّمَ: ... يَقُولُ اذْكُرْ كَذَا وَكَذَا مَالَمْ يَكُنْ يَذْكُرُ حَتَّى يَظَلَّ الرَّجُلُ لَا يَدْرِي كَمْ صَلَّى.

(البخاري)

He says: "Remember such and such" about something that he had forgotten until he misguides him to the extent that he does not know how much he has prayed.

(Narrated by Abū Hurayrah in Bukhārī)

To overcome this, the *ʿulamāʾ* recommend that you should consciously say: "I take refuge in Allah from the accursed Satan." You should not read silently but slightly aloud such that you can hear yourself. If you know what you are reading, then it will help to concentrate your mind. It is essential that you keep your thoughts clean. Thus, even if you are distracted, you will still be thinking about good things and not bad and evil things. If, after all these efforts, you are still distracted then try to counter feelings of self-doubt by positively thinking about prayer. And, finally, if you try to understand the purpose of prayer, that it is an act of submission to your Creator, surely Allah will help you.

Thus, we should try to generate a feeling of complete devotion, love and adoration for our Lord. It is essential that we should pledge earnestly to have *khushūʿ* in our prayers so that we may achieve success (*falāḥ*) and salvation. Let us pray:

اللَّهُمَّ إِنِّي أَعُوذُ بِكَ مِنْ عِلْمٍ لَا يَنْفَعُ، وَمِنْ قَلْبٍ لَا يَخْشَعُ، وَمِنْ نَفْسٍ لَا تَشْبَعُ، وَمِنْ دَعْوَةٍ لَا يُسْتَجَابُ لَهَا.

(مسلم)

O Allah! I seek refuge in You from knowledge that is not beneficial, the heart that has no *khushūʿ*, the soul that remains unsatisfied, and the supplication that is not accepted.

(Muslim)

May Allah make us among those who have *khushūʿ* and accept our prayers and grace them with His favour. (*Āmīn*)

16

Fear (*Khawf*)

إِنَّمَا ذَٰلِكُمُ ٱلشَّيۡطَٰنُ يُخَوِّفُ أَوۡلِيَآءَهُۥ فَلَا تَخَافُوهُمۡ وَخَافُونِ
إِن كُنتُم مُّؤۡمِنِينَ ﴿١٧٥﴾

It was Satan who urged you to have fear of his allies. But do not fear them; fear Me, if you truly believe.

(Āl ʿImrān 3: 175)

إِنَّمَا ٱلۡمُؤۡمِنُونَ ٱلَّذِينَ إِذَا ذُكِرَ ٱللَّهُ وَجِلَتۡ قُلُوبُهُمۡ ... ﴿٢﴾

True believers are those who, when Allah's name is mentioned, their hearts quake.

(al-Anfāl 8: 2)

This is how the Qur'ān depicts the inner feelings of believers whereby they always remain in constant reverence and awe of Allah. The verse I recited at the start of the *khuṭbah* instructs us to be fearful of Allah. The word used is *khawf*, which is derived from *khāfa* meaning to be frightened, scared or to be afraid.

Why should one be afraid of Allah, when the Qur'ān says:

... وَٱلَّذِينَ ءَامَنُوٓاْ أَشَدُّ حُبًّا لِّلَّهِ ... ﴿١٦٥﴾

Those who believe, they love Allah more than all else.

(al-Baqarah 2: 165)

As Allah's love is the part of our faith (*īmān*) then it should supersede all other affections. Similarly, our fear of Him should also overcome all our apprehensions. We fear Allah not because He is terrifying, but on the contrary is most satisfying and loveable and Whose remembrance provides satisfaction and succor to our hearts. Those who are acquainted with Allah's attributes know that He is the Most Merciful and the Most Kind despite being the Most Powerful and the Almighty as well.

نَبِّئْ عِبَادِىٓ أَنِّىٓ أَنَا ٱلْغَفُورُ ٱلرَّحِيمُ ﴿٤٩﴾ وَأَنَّ عَذَابِى هُوَ ٱلْعَذَابُ ٱلْأَلِيمُ ﴿٥٠﴾

(O Prophet!) Declare to My servants that I am indeed
Ever Forgiving, the Most Merciful. At the same time,
My chastisement is highly painful.

(al-Ḥijr 15: 49-50)

Those who are ignorant of the Qur'ān's teachings can spend their lives in complete disregard of the Day of Reckoning. However, those believers who are knowledgeable of Allah's attributes remain ever vigilant about their deeds and are apprehensive about their accountability before Allah on the Day of Judgement:

وَأَمَّا مَنْ خَافَ مَقَامَ رَبِّهِۦ وَنَهَى ٱلنَّفْسَ عَنِ ٱلْهَوَىٰ ﴿٤٠﴾ فَإِنَّ ٱلْجَنَّةَ
هِىَ ٱلْمَأْوَىٰ ﴿٤١﴾

And for such as had entertained the fear of standing before
their Lord and restrained (their) souls from lower
desires, their abode will be the Garden.

(al-Nāziʿāt 79: 40–41)

Their intense devotion and fervour is depicted as:

تَتَجَافَىٰ جُنُوبُهُمْ عَنِ ٱلْمَضَاجِعِ يَدْعُونَ رَبَّهُمْ خَوْفًا وَطَمَعًا ... ﴿١٦﴾

Their limbs forsake their beds and they call upon
their Lord in fear and hope.

(al-Sajdah 32: 16)

It is for this reason that it said in *Sūrah Fāṭir*:

... إِنَّمَا يَخْشَى ٱللَّهَ مِنْ عِبَادِهِ ٱلْعُلَمَٰٓؤُا۟ ... ﴿٢٨﴾

From among His servants, it is only those who know that fear Allah.

(Fāṭir 35: 28)

A couple of words used in this verse need some explanation. First, the word *yakhshā*, translated as fear, is derived from *khashiya*, although a synonym of *khawf*, it has a subtle difference in meaning. Whereas *khawf* is apprehension about the future as well as physical response when facing a terrifying situation, *khashyatun* is that fear that one feels rationally about one's superiors. Secondly, the word *ʿulamāʾ* used in this verse does not mean the conventional *ʿulamāʾ* commonly understood by this term. As Sayyid Mawdūdī explains, "that a truly knowledgeable person is not he who can read books, but he who fears God".[1]

Mawlānā Amīn Aḥsan Iṣlāḥī in his book *Tazkiyah-i-Nafs* similarly states:

> In this verse, by *ʿulamāʾ* it is not meant the traditional *ʿulamāʾ* but rather refers to those who are the real inheritors of the real knowledge of Allah and His Messenger. They are really knowledgeable about Allah's attributes, His laws and His ways of working, hence they fear Allah as He ought to be feared.[2]

It is not only human beings who are fearful of Allah for even angels, who are much closer to Him, are equally fearful because they are more knowledgeable of His attributes.

... وَيَرْجُونَ رَحْمَتَهُۥ وَيَخَافُونَ عَذَابَهُۥٓ ... ﴿٥٧﴾

---

1 *Towards Understanding the Qur'ān*, p.898.
2 *Tazkiyah-i-Nafs*, 1999, p. 251.

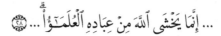

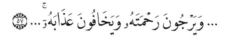

They hope for His mercy and fear His wrath.
(al-Isrāʾ 17: 57)

So what are the real reasons that should motivate one to fear Allah? Firstly, as explained above, Allah has created this world for a purpose and people should follow His guidance sent through His Messengers. One should lead a pious life and should act in accordance with Allah's guidance. On the Day of Judgement, everyone will be presented before Allah and his deeds will be scrutinized. His final destination depends on how he performed his duties in this world. This thought is the motivating force which should keep one in awe of Allah.

Secondly, it is only Allah Who can really punish people. It is quite possible to escape the wrath of a violent dictator. But, as mentioned in *Sūrah al-Raḥmān*, no one can escape Allah's domain.

... إِنِ ٱسْتَطَعْتُمْ أَن تَنفُذُوا۟ مِنْ أَقْطَارِ ٱلسَّمَٰوَٰتِ وَٱلْأَرْضِ فَٱنفُذُوا۟ ۚ
لَا تَنفُذُونَ إِلَّا بِسُلْطَٰنٍ ﴿٣٣﴾

If you have the power to go beyond the bounds of the heavens and earth, go beyond them. Yet you will be unable to go beyond them without authority.
(al-Raḥmān 55: 33)

Thirdly, the punishment in this world is only for the duration of one's life, while the punishment meted out by Allah is everlasting:

... وَمَن يَعْصِ ٱللَّهَ وَرَسُولَهُۥ فَإِنَّ لَهُۥ نَارَ جَهَنَّمَ خَٰلِدِينَ فِيهَآ أَبَدًا ﴿٢٣﴾

And whosoever disobeys Allah and His Messenger, surely the fire of hell awaits him; therein he will dwell forever.
(al-Jinn 72: 23)

Fourthly, it is quite possible to escape punishment for the crimes one commits if one has powerful and influential friends or one has the resources to bribe the authorities, thereby circumventing the wheels of justice. In the Hereafter, however, there will be nothing in one's possession to offer as ransom nor will anyone be able to intercede on one's behalf:

...أَن يَأْتِيَ يَوْمٌ لَّا بَيْعٌ فِيهِ وَلَا خُلَّةٌ وَلَا شَفَٰعَةٌ ... ﴿٢٥٤﴾

There comes a Day when there will be no buying and selling, neither friendship nor intercession will be of any avail.
(al-Baqarah 2: 254)

Indeed, it will be such a horrific day when no one will care for others, as everyone will be worried about his own fate.

يَوْمَ يَفِرُّ ٱلْمَرْءُ مِنْ أَخِيهِ ﴿٣٤﴾ وَأُمِّهِۦ وَأَبِيهِ ﴿٣٥﴾ وَصَٰحِبَتِهِۦ وَبَنِيهِ ﴿٣٦﴾
لِكُلِّ ٱمْرِئٍ مِّنْهُمْ يَوْمَئِذٍ شَأْنٌ يُغْنِيهِ ﴿٣٧﴾

On the Day when each man shall flee from his brother and his mother and his father and his consort and his children; on that Day, each will be occupied with his own business, making him oblivious to all save himself.
('Abasa 80: 34-37)

Finally, salvation in the Hereafter is solely dependent on one's own deeds and, of course, Allah's mercy. Nothing else will be of any benefit in achieving salvation:

فَمَن يَعْمَلْ مِثْقَالَ ذَرَّةٍ خَيْرًا يَرَهُۥ ﴿٧﴾ وَمَن يَعْمَلْ مِثْقَالَ ذَرَّةٍ شَرًّا يَرَهُۥ ﴿٨﴾

So whoever does an atom's weight of good shall see it; and whoever does an atom's worth of evil shall see it.
(al-Zilzāl 99: 7-8)

So how does the fear of Allah affect our lives? Firstly, on a personal level, it creates immense moral strength and courage. When one totally submits oneself to Allah, then one does not fear anyone or anything in this universe. One is endowed with satisfaction of heart and realizes that one is in the protection of a Mighty One Whose Will and Power no one can defy. He has no fear or regret and thus lives a life of contentment and tranquility.

Secondly, one remains concerned about one's family and is always aware that those in his charge should be on the right path:

قَالُوٓاْ إِنَّا كُنَّا قَبۡلُ فِيٓ أَهۡلِنَا مُشۡفِقِينَ ﴿٢٦﴾ فَمَنَّ ٱللَّهُ عَلَيۡنَا وَوَقَىٰنَا عَذَابَ ٱلسَّمُومِ ﴿٢٧﴾

They will say: "When we were living before among our kinsfolk we lived in constant fear (of Allah's displeasure). Then Allah graced us with His favour and saved us from the chastisement of the scorching wind."

(al-Ṭūr 52: 26-27)

Finally, on a social level, one assumes responsibility to see that society is kept free from the disobedience of Allah. This is a just and caring society and not a corrupt and careless one. One should feel responsible for good governance in social and political affairs. The reason being that, if the whole of society becomes corrupt and defiled, one cannot escape Allah's wrath. When Allah's punishment is meted out, even the pious and honest will be affected and they will not be able to save themselves:

وَٱتَّقُواْ فِتۡنَةٗ لَّا تُصِيبَنَّ ٱلَّذِينَ ظَلَمُواْ مِنكُمۡ خَآصَّةٗۖ ... ﴿٢٥﴾

And fear the tribulation that shall bring punishment not only the wrong-doers among you.

(al-Anfāl 8: 25)

However, a word of caution is necessary here. That is, one has to maintain a balance between fear and hope. If one is overwhelmed by fear, then it is likely that one will become despondent of Allah's mercy and thus one may become a target of despair created by Satan. So we see that in many verses fear and hope are mentioned together:

... وَٱدْعُوهُ خَوْفًا وَطَمَعًا ... ﴿٥٦﴾

Call upon Him with fear and longing.

(al-A'rāf 7: 56)

... وَيَرْجُونَ رَحْمَتَهُۥ وَيَخَافُونَ عَذَابَهُۥٓ ... ﴿٥٧﴾

They hope for His mercy and fear His wrath.

(al-Isrā' 17: 57)

... يَدْعُونَ رَبَّهُمْ خَوْفًا وَطَمَعًا ... ﴿١٦﴾

They call upon their Lord in fear and hope.

(al-Sajdah 32: 16)

All Islamic teachings are based on moderation and here as well we have to have fear of Allah but we should also remain hopeful of His Mercy.

Let me end with the *du'ā'* taught by our beloved Prophet (peace be upon him). It is narrated by 'Abdullāh ibn 'Umar as recorded in *Sunan Tirmidhī* that it was the practice of the Prophet (peace be upon him) that he used to make the following prayer for himself and his Companions when concluding any meeting:

... اللهُمَّ اقْسِمْ لَنَا مِنْ خَشْيَتِكَ مَا يَحُولُ بَيْنَنَا وَبَيْنَ مَعَاصِيكَ، وَمِنْ طَاعَتِكَ مَا تُبَلِّغُنَا بِهِ جَنَّتَكَ، وَمِنَ اليَقِينِ مَا تُهَوِّنُ بِهِ عَلَيْنَا مُصِيبَاتِ الدُّنْيَا، وَمَتِّعْنَا بِأَسْمَاعِنَا وَأَبْصَارِنَا وَقُوَّتِنَا مَا أَحْيَيْتَنَا، وَاجْعَلْهُ الوَارِثَ مِنَّا، وَاجْعَلْ ثَأْرَنَا عَلَى مَنْ ظَلَمَنَا، وَانْصُرْنَا عَلَى مَنْ عَادَانَا، وَلاَ تَجْعَلْ مُصِيبَتَنَا فِي دِينِنَا، وَلاَ تَجْعَلِ الدُّنْيَا أَكْبَرَ هَمِّنَا وَلاَ مَبْلَغَ عِلْمِنَا، وَلاَ تُسَلِّطْ عَلَيْنَا مَنْ لاَ يَرْحَمُنَا.

(الترمذي)

O Allah, apportion for us fear of You that prevents us from committing acts of disobedience against You, and obedience to You by which You will enter us into Your Garden, and certitude that makes the afflictions of this world easy for us; and allow us to enjoy our hearing and sight for as long as we live, and avenge us against him who wrongs us, and support us against him who declares enmity against us, and do not afflict us in our religion nor make this world our greatest concern or the only thing that we know, and do not set on us him who does not show mercy to us. (*Āmīn*)

(Tirmidhī)

17

Tranquility and Calmness (*Sakīnah wa Iṭmi'nān*)

هُوَ ٱلَّذِىٓ أَنزَلَ ٱلسَّكِينَةَ فِى قُلُوبِ ٱلْمُؤْمِنِينَ لِيَزْدَادُوٓا۟ إِيمَـٰنًا مَّعَ إِيمَـٰنِهِمْ ۗ ... ﴿٤﴾

He it is Who bestowed inner peace on the hearts of believers so that they may grow yet more in their faith.

(al-Fatḥ 48: 4)

... فَأَنزَلَ ٱللَّهُ سَكِينَتَهُۥ عَلَىٰ رَسُولِهِۦ وَعَلَى ٱلْمُؤْمِنِينَ وَأَلْزَمَهُمْ كَلِمَةَ ٱلتَّقْوَىٰ ... ﴿٢٦﴾

Then Allah bestowed inner peace upon His Messenger and upon the believers and imposed on them the word of self-restraint.

(al-Fatḥ 48: 26)

We live in turbulent times, facing so many pressures, problems and uncertainties. There is no peace of mind as we try to catch up with daily routines and working hard to satisfy the demands of family, work and wider society. It is not surprising that there is an increase in the number of nervous breakdowns and depression. We seem to have lost that precious gift of inner peace and tranquility that can only be gained by the grace of *Allah Subḥanahu wa Taʿālā*, as mentioned in the verses of *Sūrah al-Fatḥ* I have just recited. The word *sakīnah* is derived from *sukūn*, literary meaning calmness, serenity, silence, steadiness, solemnity, peace of mind and tranquility. It is opposed to restlessness, agitation, disturbance, noise and worry.

The word *sakīnah* is used six times in the Qur'ān and out of this it is mentioned thrice in *Sūrah al-Fatḥ*. As we know, this *sūrah* was revealed after the Treaty of Ḥudaybīyah, in which the Prophet and his Companions faced a very difficult situation. They were on their way to Makkah to perform *'Umrah* when they encountered opposition from the Makkans who would not allow them to enter and this was in violation of an age-old tribal tradition. In order to negotiate with the Makkans, the Prophet, (peace be upon him) sent 'Uthmān ibn 'Affān, as his envoy. It was rumoured that he was killed by the Makkans. Although the Muslims were unarmed and unprepared for armed conflict, a pledge (*bay'ah*) was made by the Companions, each placing a hand upon the Prophet's and pledging that they were ready to lay down their lives in any encounter with the Makkans. This oath, known as the *Bay'at al-Riḍwān* was, in fact, a pledge made to Allah, the Messenger being His representative. The Companions' act of loyalty and bravery was praised in *Sūrah al-Fatḥ*. It was Allah's mercy that He sent down tranquility and inner peace into the hearts of the believers throughout this period of conflict. As a result, they were able to overcome the Makkans' provocation and behave with a remarkable calmness and composure that represented Allah's favour and mercy.

It is this *sakīnah* that descended in the Cave of Thawr where the Prophet (peace be upon him) and Abū Bakr, his Companion, had taken refuge. They were pursued by the Quraysh while they were migrating to Madīnah. The Quraysh's agents were in hot pursuit to arrest them in order to gain a large ransom. They even reached the mouth of the cave and could have easily found the Prophet (peace be upon him) and Abū Bakr, who was very much agitated and said to the Prophet (peace be upon him) that even if the pursuers were to look at their own feet they would find them. The Prophet (peace be up on him), fully composed, consoled him saying: "Have no fear for Allah is with us." فَأَنزَلَ ٱللَّهُ سَكِينَتَهُۥ عَلَيْهِ *Then Allah sent down His peace* (*Sakīnah*) *on him*. (al-Tawbah 9: 40)

Similarly, in the Battle of Ḥunayn that took place after the Conquest of Makkah, the Muslim army was much larger and well-equipped against a much smaller army of unbelievers. Due to this, the Muslims became proud and thought they were bound to be victorious. However, the fight was tough and the Muslim army was routed with only the Prophet (peace be upon him) and a handful of the Companions standing their ground.

ثُمَّ أَنزَلَ ٱللَّهُ سَكِينَتَهُۥ عَلَىٰ رَسُولِهِۦ وَعَلَى ٱلْمُؤْمِنِينَ وَأَنزَلَ جُنُودًا لَّمْ تَرَوْهَا
وَعَذَّبَ ٱلَّذِينَ كَفَرُوا۟ ۚ وَذَٰلِكَ جَزَآءُ ٱلْكَٰفِرِينَ ﴿٢٦﴾

Then, Allah caused His tranquility (Sakīnah) to descend upon the Messenger and upon the believers, and He sent down forces whom you did not see and chastized those who disbelieved.

(al-Tawbah 9: 26)

The same was the case with the tribe of Israel. They were bestowed with *sakīnah* when the Ark of the Covenant containing the relics of the Prophets Mūsā and Hārūn (peace be upon them) was brought back on a bullock cart guided by angels. The Ark had earlier been captured by their enemies and its return boosted the tribe of Israel's morale. They believed that its return was a sign that they would dominate their enemies under their new King Ṭālūt. (*al-Baqarah* 2: 248)

This inner calm, peace and tranquilly is the result of complete reliance on Allah which strengthens hearts and lifts up morale when believers face difficult situations. A similar term used for this condition of the heart is called *iṭmi'nān*. Literally, this means something that is well-settled in its place and will not move to either side. For example, if pots are well-placed or the lamp's flame is straight and does not flicker on either side, these convey the meaning of *iṭmi'nān*. Similarly, if the heart is well set on faith and does not waver from the right path it is called *al-Nafs al-Muṭma'innah*. This word is derived from *ṭam'ana* and means to be quiet, to be calm or to soothe or to appease. Thus, *al-Nafs al-Muṭma'innah* represents the highest stage of *īmān* where one is absolutely at peace and, for those who attain this status, their reward is eternal bliss. The righteous soul will be addressed as *al-Nafs al-Muṭma'innah* with tidings of Allah's mercy and His reward:

يَـٰٓأَيَّتُهَا ٱلنَّفْسُ ٱلْمُطْمَئِنَّةُ ﴿٢٧﴾ ٱرْجِعِىٓ إِلَىٰ رَبِّكِ رَاضِيَةً مَّرْضِيَّةً ﴿٢٨﴾
فَٱدْخُلِى فِى عِبَـٰدِى ﴿٢٩﴾ وَٱدْخُلِى جَنَّتِى ﴿٣٠﴾

O Serene Soul! Return to your Lord well pleased (with your blissful destination), well-pleasing (to your Lord). So enter among My (righteous servants) and enter my Paradise.
(al-Fajr 89: 27–30)

Being well-pleased with our Lord comes from a total acceptance of whatever way Allah treats us – whether this seems agreeable or disagreeable. As this *ḥadīth* explains:

عَنْ الْعَبَّاس بْن عَبْدِ الْمُطَّلب، أَنَّهُ سَمِعَ رَسُولَ الله صَلَّى الله عَلَيْهِ وَسَلَّمَ، يَقُولُ: ذَاقَ طَعْمَ الإيمَانِ، مَنْ رَضيَ بِالله رَبًّا، وَبالإِسْلام دِينًا، وَبِمُحَمَّدٍ رَسُولًا.

(مسلم)

One who is pleased with Allah as the Lord and Islam as the religion and Muḥammad as the Prophet has tasted the delight of belief.
(Narrated by ʿAbbās ibn ʿAbd al-Muṭṭalib in Muslim)

This suggests that one should use one's free will to acquire Allah's pleasure, although ultimately it is a Divine gift. Thus, this reward is for:

إِنَّ ٱلَّذِينَ ءَامَنُوا۟ وَعَمِلُوا۟ ٱلصَّـٰلِحَـٰتِ أُو۟لَـٰٓئِكَ هُمْ خَيْرُ ٱلْبَرِيَّةِ ﴿٧﴾ جَزَآؤُهُمْ عِندَ رَبِّهِمْ جَنَّـٰتُ عَدْنٍ تَجْرِى مِن تَحْتِهَا ٱلْأَنْهَـٰرُ خَـٰلِدِينَ فِيهَآ أَبَدًا ۖ رَّضِىَ ٱللَّهُ عَنْهُمْ وَرَضُوا۟ عَنْهُ ۚ ذَٰلِكَ لِمَنْ خَشِىَ رَبَّهُۥ ﴿٨﴾

Those who believe and work righteous deeds, they are the best of creatures. Their recompense lies with their Lord: Gardens of eternity beneath which rivers flow; therein they shall dwell, forever and forever. Allah is well pleased with them, and they are well pleased with Him. All this is for him who fear his Lord.

(al-Bayyinah 98: 7-8)

Bliss and inner peace is something internal: it depends on one's inner spiritual experience. By turning to Allah, one is likely to achieve this enlightenment. This is the meaning of the verse in *Sūrah al-Ra'd*:

ٱلَّذِينَ ءَامَنُوا۟ وَتَطْمَئِنُّ قُلُوبُهُم بِذِكْرِ ٱللَّهِ ۗ أَلَا بِذِكْرِ ٱللَّهِ تَطْمَئِنُّ ٱلْقُلُوبُ ﴿٢٨﴾

Such are those who believe, and whose hearts find satisfaction in the remembrance of Allah. Surely in remembrance of Allah do hearts find satisfaction.

(al-Ra'd 13: 28)

It is said that 'Umar ibn al-Khaṭṭāb wrote to Mūsā al-Ash'arī: "All goodness is in satisfaction. If you are able to have it, then be satisfied; if not, then be patient."

However, there is shade of difference between the meanings of *sakīnah* and *iṭmi'nān*. The former is used to denote being calm in situations of worry, anxiety, fear and sorrow. The latter is used to describe the state of having freed oneself from doubts, uncertainty and perplexity.

For the satisfaction of the heart, another term is also used in the Qur'ān. It is referred to as *Sharḥ al-Ṣadr*, which literally means opening the breast or heart.

فَمَن يُرِدِ ٱللَّهُ أَن يَهْدِيَهُۥ يَشْرَحْ صَدْرَهُۥ لِلْإِسْلَٰمِ ۖ ... ﴿١٢٥﴾

So whomever Allah wants to guide – He opens his heart for Islam.

(al-An'ām 6: 125)

Similarly, in *Sūrah al-Zumar* (39: 22), it is mentioned that he whose heart Allah has opened for Islam moves along a path illuminated by a light from Him.

When prophethood was bestowed on the Prophet Mūsā (peace be upon him) his first prayer was:

قَالَ رَبِّ ٱشْرَحْ لِى صَدْرِى ﴿٢٥﴾

He (Moses) said: "O my Lord! Open my heart for me."
(Ṭā' Hā' 20: 25)

And the Prophet (peace be upon him) was told of Allah's blessings in these words:

أَلَمْ نَشْرَحْ لَكَ صَدْرَكَ ﴿١﴾

Have We not opened your heart?
(al-Sharḥ 94: 1)

If one reflects on the expression to open the heart used in the above verses, it is evident that it denotes a person who attains the conviction that Islam is the right way of life and who is willing to undergo all hardships faced in this way. This conviction and the satisfaction of the heart boosts one's morale such that one can face all difficulties and hardships without fear or apprehension. Let us pray:

O Lord! Guide us to what You love and are pleased with, and bestow on us the peace, the tranquility and the satisfaction of hearts and minds. Shower blessings and peace on our master, the Prophet (peace be upon him) and his family and Companions.

... اللهُمَّ اغْفِرْ لِي وَارْحَمْنِي وَاهْدِنِي وَعَافِنِي وَارْزُقْنِي.
(مسلم)

O Allah! Forgive us, have mercy upon us, guide us, provide us with Your blessings and nourish us.
(Muslim)

... اللَّهُـمَّ مَغْفِرَتَكَ أَوْسَـعُ مِـنْ ذُنُوبِي وَرَحْـمَتَكَ أَرْجَى
عِـنْدِي مِـنْ عَـمَلِي.

(الحاكم)

O Allah! Your forgiveness (*maghfirah*) far exceeds our sins. We all depend on Your mercy and not on our actions. (*Āmīn*)

(Ḥākim)

18

Humility (*Tawāḍu*ʿ)

وَعِبَادُ ٱلرَّحْمَـٰنِ ٱلَّذِينَ يَمْشُونَ عَلَى ٱلْأَرْضِ هَوْنًا ... ﴿٦٣﴾

The true servants of the Merciful One are those who walk on the earth in humility.

(al-Furqān 25: 63)

In the building up of human character, humility and modesty play a vital role. Their opposites are pride, arrogance and haughtiness, and an obvious manifestation of them is that people strut about arrogantly. As opposed to such arrogance, true believers walk gently and their gait is noble and modest. This is one of the judicious exhortations that the sage Luqmān made to his son:

وَلَا تُصَعِّرْ خَدَّكَ لِلنَّاسِ وَلَا تَمْشِ فِى ٱلْأَرْضِ مَرَحًا ۖ إِنَّ ٱللَّهَ لَا يُحِبُّ كُلَّ مُخْتَالٍ فَخُورٍ ﴿١٨﴾

Do not (contemptuously) turn your face away from people, nor tread haughtily upon the earth. Allah does not love the arrogant and vainglorious.

(Luqmān 31: 18)

The same message is also proclaimed more forcefully and graphically in one of the series of commandments given in *Sūrah al-Isrā*ʾ:

وَلَا تَمْشِ فِى ٱلْأَرْضِ مَرَحًا ۖ إِنَّكَ لَن تَخْرِقَ ٱلْأَرْضَ وَلَن تَبْلُغَ ٱلْجِبَالَ طُولًا ﴿٣٧﴾

Do not strut about in the land arrogantly. Surely you cannot cleave the earth, nor reach the heights of the mountains in stature.

(al-Isrā' 17: 37)

It is significant to note that the internal nature and condition of a person is reflected in his outer behaviour. Unless there is an inherent perception of Allah's graciousness and power, then there will be no humility and modesty in a person's life. However, a person's gait is only one of the signs that reveal whether they are is humble or arrogant. In fact, our entire lifestyle is a mirror of our internal personality. The renowned Turkish scholar Fethullah Gülen has made a very perceptive observation about humility. He writes:

> True humility is that a man must know what his worth really can be before God's infinite grandeur and make this an ingrained, essential part of his nature. Those who have been able to make this their second nature are humble and balanced in their relations with others. For those who have realized their nothingness before God Almighty are always balanced in both their religious lives and their relations with people.[1]

Islam teaches us humility and the way to acquire it to get rid of pride and arrogance from our hearts. On the authority of 'Abdullāh ibn Mas'ūd who said that the Prophet (peace be upon him) declared:

عَنْ عَبْدِ اللهِ بْنِ مَسْعُودٍ، عَنِ النَّبِيِّ صَلَّى اللهُ عَلَيْهِ وَسَلَّمَ، قَالَ:
لَا يَدْخُلُ الْجَنَّةَ مَنْ كَانَ فِي قَلْبِهِ مِثْقَالُ ذَرَّةٍ مِنْ كِبْرٍ، قَالَ رَجُلٌ: إِنَّ
الرَّجُلَ، يُحِبُّ أَنْ يَكُونَ ثَوْبُهُ حَسَنًا، وَنَعْلُهُ حَسَنَةً، قَالَ: إِنَّ اللهَ جَمِيلٌ
يُحِبُّ الْجَمَالَ، الْكِبْرُ بَطَرُ الْحَقِّ وَغَمْطُ النَّاسِ.

(مسلم)

---

1 *Emerald Hills of the Hearts: Key Concepts in the Practice of Sufism*. p. 98.

"Whoever has an atom's weight of pride in his heart will not enter Paradise." Then a man asked: "What if a person wishes to have nice garments and nice sandals?" So he replied: "Truly Allah is Beautiful and loves beauty. Pride is to be obstinate against truth and to be contemptuous of people."

(Muslim)

عَنْ إِبْرَاهِيمَ بْنِ رَبِيعَةَ ...أَيُّهَا النَّاسُ، تَوَاضَعُوا فَإِنِّي سَمِعْتُ رَسُولَ اللهِ صَلَّى اللهُ عَلَيْهِ وَسَلَّمَ يَقُولُ: مَنْ تَوَاضَعَ لِلهِ رَفَعَهُ اللهُ، فَهُوَ فِي نَفْسِهِ صَغِيرٌ، وَفِي أَعْيُنِ النَّاسِ عَظِيمٌ، وَمَنْ تَكَبَّرَ وَضَعَهُ اللهُ، فَهُوَ فِي أَعْيُنِ النَّاسِ صَغِيرٌ، وَفِي نَفْسِهِ كَبِيرٌ، حَتَّى لَهُوَ أَهْوَنُ عَلَيْهِمْ مِنْ كَلْبٍ أَوْ خِنْزِيرٍ.

(البيهقي)

While speaking from the pulpit ʿUmar ibn al-Khaṭṭāb said: "O people! Be humble, for I heard the Messenger of Allah saying: 'Whoever humbles himself for the sake of Allah, such that he feels small in himself, is great in the eyes of the people. Whoever is arrogant, Allah lowers him such that he becomes small in the eyes of the people, even though he feels great in himself, to the extent that he is worse than a dog or a pig in their view.

(Narrated by Ibrāhīm ibn Rabīʿā in Bayhaqī)

In the light of these *aḥādīth*, we should be on our guard. Pride (*takabbur*) is the prerogative of *Allāh Subḥānahu wa Taʿālā*. One of His names is the Proud (*al-Mutakabbir*). Hence, if one is proud, he is encroaching upon Allah's right, so Allah will debase him. However, if a person chooses a beautiful dress which is according to his means and status, this is not blameworthy. Arrogance means that one is immersed in worldly delights and does not care about others nor fulfils the rights of Allah.

There are many *aḥādīth* that exhort us to be humble, with ingrained humility as a part of our conduct so that it radiates from our personality. The Prophet (peace be upon him) said:

عَنْ عِيَاضِ بْنِ حِمَارٍ قَالَ: قَامَ فِينَا رَسُولُ اللهِ صَلَّى اللهُ عَلَيْهِ وَسَلَّمَ
فَقَالَ: وَإِنَّ اللهَ أَوْحَى إِلَيَّ أَنْ تَوَاضَعُوا حَتَّى لاَ يَفْخَرَ أَحَدٌ عَلَى أَحَدٍ.
(مسلم)

Allah has ordered me that you must be humble and that
no one must boast to others.
(Narrated by ʿIyāḍ ibn Ḥimār in Muslim)

عَنْ عَبْدِ اللهِ بْنِ مَسْعُودٍ، قَالَ: قَالَ رَسُولُ اللهِ صَلَّى اللهُ عَلَيْهِ وَسَلَّمَ:
أَلَا أُخْبِرُكُمْ بِمَنْ يَحْرُمُ عَلَى النَّارِ؟ أَوْ بِمَنْ تَحْرُمُ عَلَيْهِ النَّارُ؟
عَلَى كُلِّ قَرِيبٍ هَيِّنٍ سَهْلٍ.
(الترمذي)

Shall I inform you of one whom Hellfire will not touch?
It is one who is near to Allah, being amiable with people,
and being mild and easy to get along with.
(Narrated by ʿAbdullāh ibn Masʿūd in Tirmidhī)

The best example for us is the life of the Prophet (peace be upon him). We see how he led a very simple and humble life. He used to do his own household work and helped his wives with their daily chores. He used to mend his own clothes and shoes and would not allow his Companions to help him in these jobs. When he used to pass by children who were playing he would stop and say *Salām* and join in with them. He used to ride a donkey, visit the sick and accompany funeral processions. He even accepted invitations from slaves. Indeed, such was his humility that even in the company of his Companions a stranger would not be able to recognize him as the Prophet (peace be upon him).

Due to his life-example and teachings we see that eminent Companions followed this life of simplicity and modesty. ʿUrwah ibn

Zubayr related: "When I saw 'Umar ibn Khaṭṭāb with a full waterskin on his shoulder, I told him: 'O Commander of the Believers! This is not fitting for you.'" He responded: "When delegations came to me and they were listening obediently to what I was saying, a certain sense of arrogance was felt by me and so I wanted to kill it off." So, as an antidote, he carried a waterskin to the house of an Anṣār woman for her use.

It is reported by Abū Naṣr al-Sarrāj al-Ṭūsī that Abū Hurayrah was seen, while he was the Governor of Madīnah, with a bundle of firewood on his back saying: "Make way for the Governor." The reason being that he did not want to become proud of his high rank.

Such are the shining examples of our predecessors who, after achieving the highest ranks, remained humble by following the precept that all virtue destroys itself if it is not clothed in humility.

We find the same emphasis given to humility in the earlier Scriptures. In the Old Testament we find this reference:

> What the Lord requires of you is this: to do what is just, to show constant love, and to live in humble fellowship with our God. (Micah 6: 8)

In the New Testament, the Prophet 'Īsā (peace be upon him) is reported to have said:

> For whosoever exalts himself will be humbled; and whoever humbles himself will be exalted. (Matthew 23: 12)

And in the Sermon on the Mount he spoke about humility in these words:

> Blessed are the meek, for they shall inherit the earth. (Matthew 5: 5)

Imām Ghazālī drew attention to the fact that in all virtues there are gradations. In this respect, one should try to tread the path of moderation. Thus, at one end there is haughtiness and arrogance while at the other there is debasement and degradation. Hence, one should both avoid arrogance and being in a state of disgrace; humility is the path that Allah loves. The other pitfall that one should be aware of and must safeguard against is false modesty. This is a state in which one tries to appear humble in order to impress others. ʿUmar ibn Khaṭṭāb once saw a young man walking slowly and in a stooped position. He stopped him and said: "What is wrong with you? You are a young person and should walk upright."

عَنْ أَبِي الْأَحْوَص، عَنْ أَبِيه، قَالَ: أَتَيْتُ النَّبِيَّ صَلَّى اللهُ عَلَيْهِ وَسَلَّمَ فِي ثَوْب دُونٍ، فَقَالَ: أَلَكَ مَالٌ؟ قَالَ: نَعَمْ، قَالَ: مِنْ أَيِّ الْـمَـالِ؟ قَالَ: قَدْ آتَانِي اللهُ مِنَ الْإِبِلِ وَالْغَنَمِ وَالْـخَيْلِ وَالرَّقِيقِ، قَالَ: فَإِذَا آتَاكَ اللهُ مَالاً، فَلْيُرَ أَثَرُ نِعْمَةِ اللهِ عَلَيْكَ وَكَرَامَتِهِ.

(أبو داوود)

When the father of Abū al-Aḥwaṣ came to the Prophet (peace be upon him) wearing a simple dress, the Prophet asked him; "Do you have any wealth?" He replied: "Yes, Allah has bestowed upon me camels, cattle, horses and slaves." He said: "If Allah has bestowed upon you so much, the traces of His bounty and favour should be visible upon you."

(Abū Dāwūd)

Finally, one should realize that whatever we possess of wealth, prestige or nobility are the bounties bestowed upon us by Allah, the Most Merciful, and He has the ultimate power to honour us or to disgrace us:

... وَتُعِزُّ مَن تَشَآءُ وَتُذِلُّ مَن تَشَآءُ ۖ بِيَدِكَ ٱلْخَيْرُ ۖ إِنَّكَ عَلَىٰ كُلِّ شَىْءٍ قَدِيرٌ ﴿٢٦﴾

You exalt whom You please, and abase whom You please. In Your hands is all good. You are All-Powerful.

(Āl ʿImrān 3: 26)

One should never be proud of what one owns and never think of those who are less fortunate than oneself with contempt. One should always be thankful of whatever bounties one enjoys and remain truly humble and modest.

So let us pray as the Prophet (peace be upon him) has taught us:

... اللهُمَّ إنِّي عَبْدُكَ، ابْنُ عَبْدِكَ، ابْنُ أَمَتِكَ، نَاصِيَتِي بِيَدِكَ، مَاضٍ فِيَّ حُكْمُكَ، عَدْلٌ فِيَّ قَضَاؤُكَ، أَسْأَلُكَ بِكُلِّ اسْمٍ هُوَ لَكَ سَمَّيْتَ بِهِ نَفْسَكَ، أَوْ عَلَّمْتَهُ أَحَدًا مِنْ خَلْقِكَ، أَوْ أَنْزَلْتَهُ فِي كِتَابِكَ، أَوِ اسْتَأْثَرْتَ بِهِ فِي عِلْمِ الْغَيْبِ عِنْدَكَ، أَنْ تَجْعَلَ الْقُرْآنَ رَبِيعَ قَلْبِي، وَنُورَ صَدْرِي، وَجِلَاءَ حُزْنِي، وَذَهَابَ هَمِّي.

(أحمد)

O Allah! I am your slave, son of Your slave, son of Your maid. My forelock is in Your hands. I am under Your Judgement: Your judgement on me is just. I beseech You with all the Names by which You have described Yourself, or taught to Your creation, or revealed in Your Book, or kept to Your knowledge of the unseen. I implore You to make the Qur'ān the delight of my heart, the light of my chest, the remover of my sadness and the cure for all our troubles.

(Aḥmad)

O Allah! Make us insignificant and small in our own eyes but exalt us in Your sight. (*Āmīn*)

19

Morality (*Akhlāq*)

ظَهَرَ ٱلْفَسَادُ فِى ٱلْبَرِّ وَٱلْبَحْرِ بِمَا كَسَبَتْ أَيْدِى ٱلنَّاسِ لِيُذِيقَهُم بَعْضَ
ٱلَّذِى عَمِلُوا۟ لَعَلَّهُمْ يَرْجِعُونَ ﴿٤١﴾

Evil has become rife on the land and at sea because of men's deeds; this is in order that He may cause them to have a taste of some of their deeds; perhaps they will turn back (from evil).

(al-Rūm 30: 41)

From time to time, we experience many natural disasters in the form of hurricanes, floods, earthquakes and tsunamis as well as droughts and famines. We have to bear these misfortunes and also help those who are suffering. As we know, occurrences of these calamities are unpredictable and unavoidable, although we can take some measures to minimize their impact, thereby limiting the damage they may cause. However, there are far greater harms which human beings do that shake the very fabric of our society and cause far greater damage than natural disasters. These are corruption, deceit, dishonesty, fiddling and fraudulent transactions both at the personal as well as at the institutional level. Such criminal acts cause far greater upheaval that affect the whole of society.

Our society today is in chaos. Sub-prime mortgages, financial crisis, extravagant expense claims made by our elected representatives, and the greed of our financial institutions – these and other recurring scandals have shaken our faith in parliament, other elected bodies, the police, banks and financial institutions. These institutions were supposed to be the foundations of a free democratic society.

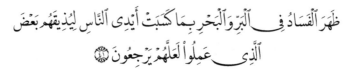

Then there is culture of blame that has developed. Nobody wants to take responsibility when things go wrong. Some sacrificial lambs are slaughtered to appease public opinion. Some efforts are being made to repair the cracks by plastering over them. But one should ask: "Is this going to solve the problems we face?"

Still, we have to think and assess what has gone wrong? One fundamental casualty in all these affairs is the loss of trust. We no longer easily believe what our Members of Parliament, bankers, police, newspapers media or even government ministers are saying is true.

I believe that we have lost our moral values. In this age when everything is relative, there is nothing which we can say is right or wrong. These are now themselves considered as relative terms. What suits me is right. Hence, we see that MPs and bankers when confronted say: "What we have done is legal. We were following the rules, therefore it is moral. Besides everyone else is doing it so why shouldn't I?" Hence it is not the failure of an individual but the failure of a whole culture. Thus, we all share the responsibility for this malaise.

If we look back, we see that our society was built upon faith, which teaches us the values of duty, obligation, responsibility and honour. All human beings have a conscience, that inner voice within us that admonishes us if we do something wrong. This what the Qur'ān calls: the reproaching self (*al-Nafs al-Lawwāmah*). This expresses itself in such emotions as guilt, remorse or feelings of shame when we do something wrong. However, now these concepts are considered outmoded and obsolete. If we constantly try to suppress the voice of our conscience, it becomes dead. This is what the Qur'ān terms as sealing the heart (*khatm al-qalb*):

خَتَمَ ٱللَّهُ عَلَىٰ قُلُوبِهِمْ وَعَلَىٰ سَمْعِهِمْ ۖ وَعَلَىٰٓ أَبْصَـٰرِهِمْ غِشَـٰوَةٌ ۖ ... ٧

Allah has sealed their hearts and their hearing and a cover has fallen over their eyes.

(al Baqarah 2: 7)

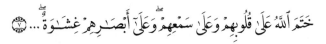

Once this happens, one loses all sense of right and wrong. Instead of this inner code of discipline that used to keep us on the right path, we have created regulatory authorities. Whereas before we had God-consciousness (*Taqwā*) in our hearts, which kept us alert, now we have to rely on CCTV and video surveillance. When our self-imposed restraint disappears we find ways and means of avoiding detection. All our regulations and systems fail without a necessary sense of responsibility, as people's ingenuity will always find ways to outwit our fail-safes no matter how sophisticated they are.

In order to rebuild trust and to regulate our society in the right way, we have to go back to a basic sense of morality. This is the inbuilt mechanism of all human societies. We all value truth, honesty, courage and modesty and hate deceit, dishonesty, cowardice and lying. Even a thief will not like to be labeled as such. However, our societies are more complex and, thus, we need Divine guidance as well to refine these virtues and build a just and caring society.

If we think we can bring about a change by parliamentary reform and financial regulations, then we are only treating the symptoms rather than the causes. It is not too late to recover our moral sense. But if we delay it further, we will be heading towards a far greater crisis. The key question is how to regain this moral sense? I have already mentioned the reproaching self (*al-Nafs al-Lawwāmah*). The Qur'ān has argued that this is clear proof of the Day of Accountability – a day when all human beings will be brought forth in the presence of their Lord and will be judged by their deeds in this world.

لَآ أُقْسِمُ بِيَوْمِ ٱلْقِيَٰمَةِ ﴿١﴾ وَلَآ أُقْسِمُ بِٱلنَّفْسِ ٱللَّوَّامَةِ ﴿٢﴾ أَيَحْسَبُ ٱلْإِنسَٰنُ
أَلَّن نَّجْمَعَ عِظَامَهُۥ ﴿٣﴾ بَلَىٰ قَٰدِرِينَ عَلَىٰٓ أَن نُّسَوِّىَ بَنَانَهُۥ ﴿٤﴾

Nay, I swear by the Day of Resurrection; and nay, I swear by the self-reproaching soul! Does man imagine that We will not be able to bring his bones together again? Yes indeed, We have the power to remould even his fingertips.

(al-Qiyāmah 75: 1-4)

So, if people realize that their deeds are recorded and will be shown to them on the Day of Judgement, then they usually will listen to their conscience and remain on the right path. Indeed, on that day, one's record will be presented to one to read so that one can judge oneself. In this respect, then, what is the point in seeking to avoid earthly detection by fraud or some other ingenuity, when it is all recorded for the Hereafter? Surely, then, this becomes the moral imperative by which we can all lead our lives according to the way of truth.

ٱقْرَأْ كِتَٰبَكَ كَفَىٰ بِنَفْسِكَ ٱلْيَوْمَ عَلَيْكَ حَسِيبًا ﴿١٤﴾

Read your scroll: this Day you suffice to take account of yourself.

(al-Isrā' 17: 14)

This record is persevered within each of us and this will be revealed to us on the Day of Judgement.

وَكُلَّ إِنسَٰنٍ أَلْزَمْنَٰهُ طَٰٓئِرَهُۥ فِى عُنُقِهِۦ ۖ وَنُخْرِجُ لَهُۥ يَوْمَ ٱلْقِيَٰمَةِ
كِتَٰبًا يَلْقَىٰهُ مَنشُورًا ﴿١٣﴾

We have fastened every man's actions to his neck. On the day of Resurrection We shall produce for him a scroll in the shape of an open book.

(al-Isrā' 17: 13)

This sense of being watched by the Supreme Being all the time and that one is accountable for one's deeds to one's Lord creates a sense of responsibility. This is illustrated by a small incident recorded during the time of the second Caliph 'Umar ibn al-Khaṭṭāb. When the mother of a young girl asked her daughter whether she had milked the goats and she replied in the affirmative, the mother then suggested to her that she pour some water into it. She replied that there was a decree by the Caliph against such practices. The mother said that as the Caliph was not there he would not find out. The honest girl briefly replied: "But Allah is here and watching us." If such a sense of God-consciousness is kept live in our lives, then one will always be deterred from committing dishonest acts even in the privacy of one's own home.

As for honesty in business dealings, we have the examples from the pious life of one of the great pioneers of jurisprudence (*fiqh*), Imām Abū Ḥanīfah. The *fiqh* that evolved from his style of reasoning became associated with his name. The Ḥanafī School is the most widely followed among Sunni Muslims. Besides being a jurist, Imām Abū Ḥanīfah was a very successful silk merchant, and the owner of a very well-known shop in the business quarter of Kūfah. He once sent some cloth to his partner with instructions to point out to the prospective buyers certain defects in some of the lengths. However, the partner forgot the instruction and sold off the cloth with defective lengths. When Abū Ḥanīfah learned about this he was very sorry and as it was not possible to trace the customer, so he gave away the entire proceeds from the sale to charity.

His honesty was demonstrated both in selling and buying. A woman brought a silk dress that she wanted to sell. She asked 100 dirhams for it, but Abū Ḥanīfah, being an expert in this field, realized that it was far more expensive and asked the women to increase the price. She kept on increasing the price, reaching 400 dirhams. Yet Abū Ḥanīfah said that it was worth much more. She got suspicious and said: "Are you making fun of me?" He suggested that she call an expert to evaluate it. The expert valued it at 500 dirhams and Abū Ḥanīfah bought it at that price.

These incidents now appear to us like fairy tales. But if one has a moral sense as well as concern about one's accountability on the Day of Judgement then one will not try to cheat others or take undue advantage of their ignorance.

... كَانَ النَّبِيُّ صَلَّى اللهُ عَلَيْهِ وَسَلَّمَ، يَقُولُ: اللَّهُمَّ إِنِّي أَعُوذُ بِكَ مِنَ الْهَمِّ، وَالْحَزَنِ، وَالْعَجْزِ، وَالْكَسَلِ، وَالْجُبْنِ، وَالْبُخْلِ، وَضَلَعِ الدَّيْنِ، وَغَلَبَةِ الرِّجَالِ.

(البخاري)

O Allah, I seek refuge in you from anxiety and grief,
from impotence and lassitude, from cowardice
and stinginess and from the burden of debt
and being overpowered by men.

(Bukhārī)

May Allah give us the wisdom to understand what is right and what is wrong. Instead of following the crowd, may we create a new path that leads to the welfare of all humanity. (*Āmīn*)

20

Good Manners (*Ḥusn al-Khulq*)

وَإِنَّكَ لَعَلَىٰ خُلُقٍ عَظِيمٍ ﴿٤﴾

And you are certainly on the most exalted standard of moral excellence.

(al-Qalam 68: 4)

We are social beings and live in this world along with other humans. It is vital that we live in peace and harmony with each other by helping and caring for one another. Most friction is caused by bad manners and rude behaviour. In Islam, there is a great emphasis on following the moral code of behaviour provided by the Qur'ān and examples from the life of our blessed Prophet (peace be upon him). The verse I have just recited extols the moral excellence of the Prophet (peace be upon him). Even so he was instructed by Allah:

خُذِ ٱلْعَفْوَ وَأْمُرْ بِٱلْعُرْفِ وَأَعْرِضْ عَنِ ٱلْجَـٰهِلِينَ ﴿١٩٩﴾

(*O Prophet!*) *Show forgiveness, enjoin what is good, and avoid the ignorant.*

(al-A'rāf 7: 199)

While praising the God-fearing folk for whom Allah has prepared the pleasures of *Jannah*, the Qur'ān mentions their virtues:

ٱلَّذِينَ يُنفِقُونَ فِى ٱلسَّرَّآءِ وَٱلضَّرَّآءِ وَٱلۡكَٰظِمِينَ ٱلۡغَيۡظَ وَٱلۡعَافِينَ عَنِ ٱلنَّاسِۗ وَٱللَّهُ يُحِبُّ ٱلۡمُحۡسِنِينَ ﴿١٣٤﴾

(The God-fearing) who spend in the way of Allah both in affluence and hardship, who restrain their anger and forgive others. Allah loves those who do good.

(Āl ʿImrān 3: 134)

The covenant Allah made with Banī Isrā'īl is recorded in *Sūrah al-Baqarah* and some of its terms include the following:

...لَا تَعۡبُدُونَ إِلَّا ٱللَّهَ وَبِٱلۡوَٰلِدَيۡنِ إِحۡسَانًا وَذِى ٱلۡقُرۡبَىٰ وَٱلۡيَتَٰمَىٰ وَٱلۡمَسَٰكِينِ وَقُولُواْ لِلنَّاسِ حُسۡنًا وَأَقِيمُواْ ٱلصَّلَوٰةَ وَءَاتُواْ ٱلزَّكَوٰةَ ... ﴿٨٣﴾

You shall serve none but Allah and treat with kindness your parents, kinsmen and orphans and the needy; you shall speak kindly to people and establish Prayers and give Zakāh.

(al-Baqarah 2: 83)

We know that the Prophet (peace be upon him) had many excellent qualities. His was a life full of praiseworthy virtues. However, from among them *Allāh Subḥānahu wa Taʿālā* selected his moral excellence for praise, as stated above. This is also testified to by *Umm al-Mu'minīn* ʿĀ'ishah, when she was asked by Saʿd ibn Hishām about the character of the Prophet (peace be upon him). She said:

... كَانَ خُلُقُهُ الْقُرْآنَ.

(أحمد)

His morals are the embodiment of the Qur'ān.

(Aḥmad)

It is narrated by Abū Hurayrah that the Prophet (peace be upon him) said:

... إِنَّمَا بُعِثْتُ لِأُتَمِّمَ صَالِحَ الْأَخْلَاقِ.

(أحمد والحاكم)

I have been sent to complete the best moral standards.

(Aḥmad and Ḥākim)

Who can be in closer contact with a husband than his wife? She shares in the secrets of his life and knows his character much more than anyone else. Look at the testimony of the Prophet's wife *Umm al Mu'minīn* Khadījah, when he returned home after receiving his call to Prophethood. He was trembling and asked her to cover him. Khadījah comforted him saying:

... قَالَتْ خَدِيجَةُ: كَلَّا وَاللهِ مَا يُخْزِيكَ اللهُ أَبَدًا، إِنَّكَ لَتَصِلُ الرَّحِمَ، وَتَحْمِلُ الكَلَّ، وَتَكْسِبُ الـمَعْدُومَ، وَتَقْرِي الضَّيْفَ، وَتُعِينُ عَلَى نَوَائِبِ الـحَقِّ.

(البخاري)

No, you have nothing to fear. God will never let you down, you are kind to your relatives, you are astute and patient, you give to the needy, you are generous to guests and you never fail to give people their due.

(Bukhārī)

We have already seen what *Umm al Mu'minīn* 'Ā'ishah said about his character. His life was the manifestation of the Qur'ān. She also told us extensively about his character and qualities. She said: "He did not scold anyone, nor did he take revenge on anyone. He used to forgive and pardon those who oppressed him. He never abused anyone. He never hit anyone, not even an animal. He never refused any request unless of course if it was illegal. Whenever he used to come home he was always cheerful and smiling."

When the brother of Abū Dharr al-Ghifārī returned to his tribe after visiting the Prophet (peace be upon him) in Makkah he told them:

... ثُمَّ رَجَعَ إِلَى أَبِي ذَرٍّ، فَقَالَ: رَأَيْتُهُ يَأْمُرُ بِمَكَارِمِ الْأَخْلَاقِ ...

(البخاري ومسلم)

He enjoins his people to have good moral character.
(Bukhārī and Muslim)

Even a sworn enemy, Abū Sufyān (before he accepted Islam), testified in the court of Caesar of Rome about the Prophet (peace be upon him) saying:

عَنْ عَبْدِ اللهِ بْنِ عَبَّاسٍ، أَنَّ أَبَا سُفْيَانَ بْنَ حَرْبٍ أَخْبَرَهُ، أَنَّ هِرَقْلَ أَرْسَلَ إِلَيْهِ فِي رَكْبٍ مِنْ قُرَيْشٍ وسَأَلَهُ عَنِ النَّبِيِّ صَلَّى اللهُ عَلَيْهِ وَسَلَّمَ، فَقَالَ: مَاذَا يَأْمُرُكُمْ؟ قُلْتُ: يَقُولُ اعْبُدُوا اللهَ وَحْدَهُ وَلَا تُشْرِكُوا بِهِ شَيْئًا، وَاتْرُكُوا مَا يَقُولُ آبَاؤُكُمْ، وَيَأْمُرُنَا بِالصَّلَاةِ وَالصِّدْقِ وَالْعَفَافِ وَالصِّلَةِ.

(البخاري)

He tells us to worship One God and not associate anyone with Him, abandon what was said by our forefathers, to establish the prayer, to be truthful and chaste, and to fulfill our obligations towards our relatives.
(Narrated by ʿAbdullāh ibn ʿAbbās in Bukhārī)

So we see how his close relations and friends as well as his enemies testified that the Prophet (peace be upon him) possessed superb character and always treated everyone with compassion and love.

The Prophet (peace be upon him) wanted to inculcate these high moral standards among the believers. There are many sayings of the Prophet (peace be upon him) in which he exhorted his followers to adopt good character:

عَنْ أَبِي هُرَيْرَةَ قَالَ: قَالَ رَسُولُ اللهِ صَلَّى اللهُ عَلَيْهِ وَسَلَّمَ: أَكْمَلُ الْمُؤْمِنِينَ إِيمَانًا أَحْسَنُهُمْ خُلُقًا

(أحمد)

It is related by Abū Hurayrah that someone asked: "O Messenger of Allah! Who among the believers has the greatest faith?" He replied: "The one who has the finest character."

(Aḥmad)

عَنْ أَبِي الدَّرْدَاءِ، أَنَّ النَّبِيَّ صَلَّى اللهُ عَلَيْهِ وَسَلَّمَ قَالَ: مَا شَيْءٌ أَثْقَلُ فِي مِيزَانِ الْمُؤْمِنِ يَوْمَ الْقِيَامَةِ مِنْ خُلُقٍ حَسَنٍ، وَإِنَّ اللهَ لَيُبْغِضُ الْفَاحِشَ الْبَذِيءَ.

(الترمذي)

It is reported by Abū Dardā' that the Prophet (peace be upon him) said: "There is nothing weightier than the good character of a believer on the Day of Judgement. Allah abhors those who indulge in obscene and frivolous talk."

(Tirmidhī)

Abū Hurayrah narrates that when the Prophet (peace be upon him) was asked:

عَنْ أَبِي هُرَيْرَةَ قَالَ: سُئِلَ رَسُولُ اللهِ صَلَّى اللهُ عَلَيْهِ وسَلَّمَ عَنْ أَكْثَرِ مَا يُدْخِلُ النَّاسَ الْجَنَّةَ؟ فَقَالَ: تَقْوَى اللهِ وحُسْنُ الخُلُقِ.

(الترمذي)

"Which acts will lead most people into *Jannah*?" He replied: "God-Consciousness (*Taqwā*) and good conduct."

(Tirmidhī)

... أَنَّ رَسُولَ اللهِ صَلَّى اللهُ عَلَيْهِ وَسَلَّمَ، خَرَجَ عَلَيْهِمْ وَعَلَيْهِ أَثَرُ غُسْلٍ، وَهُوَ طَيِّبُ النَّفْسِ، ... فَقُلْنَا: يَا رَسُولَ اللهِ، نَرَاكَ طَيِّبَ النَّفْسِ؟ قَالَ: ... وَطِيبُ النَّفْسِ مِنَ النِّعَمِ.

(الأدب المفرد)

It is narrated that "The Messenger of Allah (peace be upon him) came out to us with signs on him that he had had a bath. He was cheerful. We said, 'O Messenger of Allah! We see you are cheerful.' He said: 'Cheerfulness is a blessing.'"

(Bukhārī, *al-Adab al-Mufrad*)

عَنْ أَبِي ثَعْلَبَةَ الْخُشَنِيِّ، قَالَ: قَالَ رَسُولُ اللهِ صَلَّى اللهُ عَلَيْهِ وَسَلَّمَ: إِنَّ أَحَبَّكُمْ إِلَيَّ وَأَقْرَبَكُمْ مِنِّي يَوْمَ الْقِيَامَةِ أَحَاسِنُكُمْ أَخْلَاقًا.

(مصنف ابن أبي شيبة)

In a *ḥadīth* related by Abū Tha'labah al-Khushanī in which the Prophet (peace be upon him) said: "On the Day of Judgement the person with best moral conduct will be nearest and dearest to me."

(*Muṣṣanaf Ibn Abī Shaybah*)

The word *khulq* meaning nature which is used in the verse of *Sūrah al-Qalam* and *khalq* meaning creation are both derived from the same root *kh-l-q*. Whereas *khalq* relates to the outward appearance of a person that is readily visible, *khulq* refers to the inner dimension of one's personality, which only reveals itself in one's dealings with others. Thus, fine moral character is the most excellent virtue that one can possess. As it is rightly said, "Man is veiled by his body, revealed by his character."

We all know what is meant by good conduct and moral behaviour. All of us instinctively know what is good and what is bad. Thus, good moral behaviour includes: self-control, forgiveness and magnanimity, dignity, humility, contentment, simplicity, moderation, generosity, honesty and trustworthiness, good etiquette, treating people well and speaking politely, etc.

We also all know that selfishness, rudeness, miserliness, bad temper, foul language, greed, backbiting, arrogance, vulgarity, ridiculing others, spying, enmity, hatred, haughtiness, treachery, bribery, ingratitude, corruption, etc. are indications of bad and poor manners. So we know what constitutes good and bad manners. The question is, then, why do we not adopt good manners? If we reflect a little we will know the answer as well. It is our ego, our self-interest, our short-term gain that makes us indulge in bad behaviour. The other reason is that we know that the time of our accountability is far off and we also forget that all our actions are recorded and will eventually be presented to us and we will have to account for them. We ran the danger of deceiving ourselves that, as we pray, fast and spend in the way of Allah, these good deeds will save us on the Day of Judgement. But we should remember this *ḥadīth* of the Prophet:

> Once, the Prophet (peace be upon him) was told about two Muslim women. One used to pray voluntary prayers (*nawāfil*) at night and fast during the day as well as spend her wealth in Allah's way, but was abusive and impudent which distressed her neighbours and put them in a state of disquiet. Whereas there was another women who only used to pray and fast when it was obligatory. She used to help the poor whenever she could, and she did not harm anyone. The Prophet (peace be upon him) said about the first woman: "There is no goodness in her and she will be punished for her rude behaviour." And about the other woman he said: "She will be in *Jannah*."

Seeing that many devout and pious people do not possess polite and pleasant dispositions, a learned Sufi, al-Fuḍayl ibn ʿIyāḍ, commented:

> I would rather have a sinning rogue of good character as a friend than a religious person of bad character. The reason is that if the sinner is admonished he will bear it because of his good character and may perhaps be reformed. But the life of a devotee is nothing but prayers and fasting. As his behaviour and character is bad he will not accept any advice.[1]

[1] *Al-Risālah al-Qushayrīyah*, in the chapter on *Khulq*.

Let me conclude by praying that Allah grant us success from Him (*tawfīq*) to follow the guidance of the Prophet (peace be upon him). He used to pray:

... اللَّهُمَّ إِنِّي أَعُوذُ بِكَ مِنَ الشِّقَاقِ، وَالنِّفَاقِ، وَسُوءِ الأَخْلَاقِ.

(أبو داوود)

O Allah! I seek refuge in You from discord, hypocrisy and bad manners.

(Abū Dāwūd)

... اللَّهُمَّ إِنِّي أَسْأَلُكَ أَنْ تُبَارِكْ لِي فِي نَفْسِي، وَفِي سَمْعِي، وَفِي بَصَرِي، وَفِي رُوحِي، وَفِي خَلْقِي، وَفِي خُلُقِي، وَفِي أَهْلِي، وَفِي مَحْيَايَ، وَفِي مَمَاتِي، وَفِي عَمَلِي، فَتَقَبَّلْ حَسَنَاتِي، وَأَسْأَلُكَ الدَّرَجَاتِ الْعُلَى مِنَ الْجَنَّةِ

(الحاكم)

O Allah! I ask you to bless me in my body, my hearing, my sight, my soul, my appearance, my character, my family, my life and my death as well as in my deeds. Accept my good deeds and I seek an exalted status in Heaven.

(Ḥākim)

... اللَّهُمَّ كَمَا حَسَّنْتَ خَلْقِي، فَأَحْسِنْ خُلُقِي.

(الطبراني في الدعاء)

O Allah! As you have given me a goodly appearance, improve my character. (*Āmīn*)

(Ṭabarānī)

21

Modesty (*Ḥayā'*)

... وَهُوَ مَعَكُمْ أَيْنَ مَا كُنتُمْ ۚ وَٱللَّهُ بِمَا تَعْمَلُونَ بَصِيرٌ ﴿٤﴾

He is with you wherever you are. Allah sees all that you do.
(al-Ḥadīd: 57: 4)

We are living in age where we are surrounded and inundated by a flood of immodesty, shameful and evil deeds. To save society and oneself from this, *Allāh Subḥānahu wa Ta'ālā* has endowed human beings with natural modesty, shyness and bashfulness as a first line of defence. In Islamic terminology, this attribute is called *al-ḥayā'*. Literally, *ḥayā'* means shame, shyness, bashfulness and refraining from saying or doing something improper or indecent. The word *ḥayā'* is derived from the word *ḥayāt* which means life. Thus, it is said that a person without *ḥayā'* is like a corpse. In essence, it is a feeling in one's heart that keeps one away from indulging in immoral deeds that may cause embarrassment. It is very close to what is termed one's moral conscience in Western society. If one has no conscience, then one can do whatever one likes without any care for what society might think. Conversely, someone with a conscience will feel ashamed to do any immoral deed even if no one is watching.

The Qur'ān commands us to refrain from all immoral and indecent acts, whether done openly or in secret.

... وَلَا تَقْرَبُوا۟ ٱلْفَوَٰحِشَ مَا ظَهَرَ مِنْهَا وَمَا بَطَنَ ۖ ... ﴿١٥١﴾

And do not even draw near to shameful things –
be they open or secret.
(al-An'ām 6: 151)

Some shameful and immoral things also have legal and social sanctions as they are also offences against society and they are universally considered abominable. Then, there are certain acts that one may indulge in privately but will feel ashamed if they were to become public knowledge, for example watching pornography or looking at someone with lust, which the Qur'ān describes as the treachery of the eyes.

يَعۡلَمُ خَآئِنَةَ ٱلۡأَعۡيُنِ وَمَا تُخۡفِي ٱلصُّدُورُ ١٩

Allah knows the treachery of the eyes and all the secrets that hearts conceal.

(Ghāfir 40: 19)

And the verse that I recited at the beginning of the *khuṭbah* says:

...وَهُوَ مَعَكُمۡ أَيۡنَ مَا كُنتُمۡۚ وَٱللَّهُ بِمَا تَعۡمَلُونَ بَصِيرٞ ٤

He is with you wherever you are. Allah sees all that you do.

(al-Ḥadīd: 57: 4)

Both these verses remind us that Allah is watching over us wherever we might be and whatever we might be doing. He even knows the inner secrets of our hearts. This realization will surely prevent us from doing any shameful deed, either publicly or secretly.

The Prophet (peace be upon him) emphasized the importance of *ḥayā'* on many occasions. Once, as reported by Ibn 'Umar, he said:

... الْحَيَاءُ وَالْإِيمَانُ قُرِنَا جَمِيعًا، فَإِذَا رُفِعَ أَحَدُهُمَا رُفِعَ الْآخَرُ.

(الحاكم)

Modesty (*ḥayā'*) and faith (*īmān*) are companions of each other. If one of them is lifted, then so is the other.

(al-Ḥākim)

It is clear from this *ḥadīth* that a person who has no *ḥayā'* lacks faith as well. In another *ḥadīth* reported by Abū Hurayrah, the Prophet (peace be upon him) said:

... الْـحَيَاءُ شُعْبَةٌ مِنَ الإِيمَـانِ.

(مسلم)

Modesty (*al-ḥayā'*) is part of faith (*īmān*).

(Muslim)

This shows how important it is for us to be always vigilant and refrain from doing anything shameful, either intentionally or carelessly.

Al-Ḥayā' is a natural defence against obscenity. It safeguards one from committing indecent acts and our conscience always tries to stop us from indulging in vice. As the Prophet (peace be upon him) observed:

عن عُقْبَةَ بن عَمْرو، قَالَ: قَالَ النَّبِيُّ صَلَّى اللهُ عَلَيْهِ وَسَلَّمَ: إِنَّ مِـمَّـا أَدْرَكَ النَّاسُ مِنْ كَلَامِ النُّبُوَّةِ إِذَا لَمْ تَسْتَحْيِ فَافْعَلْ مَا شِئْتَ.

(البخاري)

From among the maxims of the previous prophets that the people still retain is: "If you feel no shame, then do as you wish."

(Narrated by ʿUqbah ibn ʿAmrū in Bukhārī.)

This *ḥadīth* indicates the importance of and emphasis upon modesty that has been passed on from the earlier prophets. This is the legacy that humanity has inherited from time immemorial. It also means that modesty or shame is the criterion by which one decides whether or not one should do something. If one is satisfied that there is no shame in doing something, only then should it be done. Conversely, if one feels ashamed of doing something, then one should refrain from it.

As we know, whilst in Paradise (*Jannah*), the Prophet Ādam and his wife (peace be upon them) were unaware of their private body parts or that they should keep them covered up. After their disobedience of Allah's command, they realized that they were naked. In desperation, they gathered leaves from the trees and patched them together to cover their nakedness (*al-Aʿrāf* 7: 21). This episode indicates that the covering of private parts is a natural human instinct. Modesty and feelings of shame are ingrained in human nature. Those who say that covering the private parts is the product of a custom developed later on are wrong. On the contrary, modesty and bashfulness have been an integral part of human nature right from the first human beings. The first target of *Shayṭān* is to undermine man's sense of modesty, as his sexual instincts are the most vulnerable aspects of his nature. Hence, we should be careful not to succumb to Satan's temptations as he was responsible for pulling off our ultimate parents' clothing to reveal to them their shame. But, according to the Qur'ān, it is not enough to cover up one's private parts and dress to protect one from climatic conditions or for adornment. Rather, a person's dress should be the dress of piety (*libās al-taqwā*). This means that one's dress should be modest and serve the purpose of clothing oneself respectfully, neither too extravagantly nor too shabbily (*al-A'rāf* 7: 26).

It should also be noted that *ḥayā'* is also one of the attributes of Allah.

عَنْ يَعْلَى، أَنَّ رَسُولَ اللهِ صَلَّى اللهُ عَلَيْهِ وَسَلَّمَ قَالَ: إِنَّ اللهَ عَزَّ وَجَلَّ حَيِيٌّ سِتِّيرٌ يُحِبُّ الْحَيَاءَ وَالسَّتْرَ.

(أبو داوود)

The Prophet (peace be upon him) said: "Verily, Allah has the attributes of great modesty and concealment. And He loves modesty and concealment."

(Narrated by Ya'lā in Abū Dāwūd)

The example of Allah's modesty is that He feels shy to refuse someone who raises his hands to Him in supplication. And one of His attributes is also *al-Sattār*, meaning that He loves His servants' sins to remain concealed and not be made public. In our society, both the print and electronic media indulge in disseminating the private affairs of people by publishing and broadcasting the same in tantalizing and salacious detail. Huge amounts of money are paid to bribe people to spy upon and reveal the secret lives of public figures. In this way, their irresponsible actions promote the creation of a shameless society.

Once, the Prophet (peace be upon him) asked his Companions to have proper *ḥayā'* towards Allah. The Companions said: "O Messenger of Allah, we observe modesty towards Allah and we praise Allah." The Prophet (peace be upon him) then told them, "This is not what is meant. True *ḥayā'* towards Allah is for a person to be mindful of his head (i.e. senses and manners), what it contains, as well as his stomach and what is close to it (i.e. the private parts) and to remember death and distress. One who desires the Hereafter abandons the luxuries of this world. The one who lives in this manner has proper *ḥayā'* towards Allah." (Tirmidhī and Aḥmad)

This *ḥadīth* explains that to have proper *ḥayā'* towards Allah one should be ashamed of doing anything that displeases Him. One tries to remain alert and control one's senses and avoid temptation. Muḥammad al-Muqaddam narrates that a sage once said:

> "If a person's behaviour is better in private than his behaviour in public, then this is true virtuousness." Once Ḥumayd al-Ṭawīl asked Sulaymān ibn 'Alī to advise him and was told: "If you disobey Allah in private, knowing that Allah sees you, then you have taken a bold step about a serious matter. If you thought that He does not see you, then you have committed an act of disbelief (*kufr*)."[1]

So far, we have seen the virtues of praiseworthy *ḥayā'*. Yet there is another kind of *ḥayā'* that prevents one from speaking out against injustice and oppression. Such behaviour is not *ḥayā'* but instead is human weakness, fear and cowardice. As stated by Imām al-Qurṭubī: The Prophet (peace be upon him) followed the path of *ḥayā'* and commanded and encouraged others to do the same. However, *ḥayā'* did not prevent him from speaking the truth or following a command of the religion. He was, in this way, obeying Allah's words:

...وَٱللَّهُ لَا يَسْتَحْيِۦ مِنَ ٱلْحَقِّ... ﴿٥٣﴾

And Allah is not ashamed of speaking out the truth.
(al-Aḥzāb 33: 53)

---

1 Quoted in Muḥammad al-Muqaddam, *Al-Ḥayā': Khuluq al-Islām*, 1993.

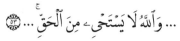

Thus, if a person's modesty and shyness stops him from speaking the truth then this is not considered *ḥayā'*.

Another area where *ḥayā'* should not become an obstacle is in acquiring knowledge. It is reported that ʿAlī ibn Abī Ṭālib said that if one does not know something then one should always ask about it. And if one is asked about something which one does not know, then one should not be shy of saying: "I don't know." *Umm al-Mu'minīn* ʿĀ'ishah, while praising the virtues of the women of the Anṣār, said that shyness did not stop them from acquiring an understanding of the religion. (Bukhārī)

Thus, for all matters in our lives we should tread the middle path and lead a balanced life. Finally, I will end with this *ḥadīth* recorded in *Kanz al-ʿUmmāl*. When the Archangel Jibrīl conveyed a message to Allah's Messenger (peace be upon him), the Prophet, his eyes filled with tears, said:

> God Almighty feels ashamed to punish those of my community whose beards have turned white but those of my community with white beards do not feel ashamed to commit sin.

Let us pray:

اللَّهُمَّ إِنِّي أَسْأَلُكَ الْعَافِيَةَ فِي الدُّنْيَا وَالآخِرَةِ، اللَّهُمَّ إِنِّي أَسْأَلُكَ الْعَفْوَ وَالْعَافِيَةَ فِي دِينِي وَدُنْيَايَ، وَأَهْلِي وَمَالِي، اللَّهُمَّ اسْتُرْ عَوْرَاتِي، وَآمِنْ رَوْعَاتِي، اللَّهُمَّ احْفَظْنِي مِنْ بَيْنِ يَدَيَّ وَمِنْ خَلْفِي، وَعَنْ يَمِينِي وَعَنْ شِمَالِي، وَمِنْ فَوْقِي، وَأَعُوذُ بِعَظَمَتِكَ مِنْ أَنْ أُغْتَالَ مِنْ تَحْتِي.

(الأدب المفرد)

O Allah! We ask for success and well-being in this world and in the Hereafter. O Allah! We ask for Your forgiveness and well-being in our religious and worldly affairs, for our families and our wealth. O Allah! Cover us from shameful exposure and replace our anxieties with tranquility. O Allah! Preserve me from what is in front of me and

behind me, and on my right and on my left, and above
me and I seek refuge in Your Majesty from any
harm beneath me.

(Bukhārī, *al-Adab al-Mufrad*)

O Allah! Give us the *tawfīq* to observe proper *ḥayā'* in our lives and to be always vigilant about our behaviour and to live a life of piety and modesty. (*Āmīn*)

22

Steadfastness (*Istiqāmah*)

إِنَّ ٱلَّذِينَ قَالُوا۟ رَبُّنَا ٱللَّهُ ثُمَّ ٱسْتَقَـٰمُوا۟ تَتَنَزَّلُ عَلَيْهِمُ ٱلْمَلَـٰٓئِكَةُ أَلَّا تَخَافُوا۟
وَلَا تَحْزَنُوا۟ وَأَبْشِرُوا۟ بِٱلْجَنَّةِ ٱلَّتِى كُنتُمْ تُوعَدُونَ ﴿٣٠﴾ نَحْنُ أَوْلِيَآؤُكُمْ فِى
ٱلْحَيَوٰةِ ٱلدُّنْيَا وَفِى ٱلْـَٔاخِرَةِ ۖ وَلَكُمْ فِيهَا مَا تَشْتَهِىٓ أَنفُسُكُمْ وَلَكُمْ
فِيهَا مَا تَدَّعُونَ ﴿٣١﴾ نُزُلًا مِّنْ غَفُورٍ رَّحِيمٍ ﴿٣٢﴾

Those who say "Allah is our Lord" and then remain steadfast, upon them descend angels (and say): "Do not fear or grieve, and receive the good tidings of Paradise, which you were promised. We are your companions in this world and in the Hereafter. There you shall have all that you desire and all that you will ask for. This is by way of hospitality from Him Who is Most Forgiving, Most Merciful."

(Fuṣṣilat 41: 30-2)

The great tidings conveyed in these verses are for those who persevere, being resolute and firm in their faith. The word *istiqāmah* that is used here means uprightness, sincerity, integrity, steadfastness or firmness. This is a desirable quality in believers. It means that that they remain steadfast in their faith (*īmān*).

The key to *istiqāmah* is to remain upright and steadfast facing all difficulties and hardships. This can only be achieved if one's heart is full of firm *īmān* and is devoid of any doubt. Imām Ghazālī stated that the importance and need for *istiqāmah* is so great that Allah has ordered the recitation of *Sūrah al-Fātiḥah* in every *rakʿah* of prayer in which there is a supplication of *istiqāmah* or continuous guidance on the straight path.

Istiqāmah is the essential requirement to accomplish one's affairs properly. This enables one to achieve the desired result in a steady and proper manner. The efforts of those who are not steadfast are really all wasted pursuits. As Allah Almighty has warned us:

وَلَا تَكُونُوا۟ كَٱلَّتِى نَقَضَتْ غَزْلَهَا مِنۢ بَعْدِ قُوَّةٍ أَنكَـٰثًا ... ﴿٩٢﴾

And do not become like the woman who, after having painstakinglys pun her yarn, unravels the thread.

(al-Naḥl 16: 92)

One who is not steadfast in his commitments will never achieve anything. The reasons why people slip away from the path of steadfastness are many. Some are temperamentally fickle and they cannot be firm on anything; instead, they follow their own whims. The other reason is lassitude. People become lazy and do not want to stick to a set routine. These weaknesses can be overcome by determination and will power. But the main reason why people forsake steadfastness is because of the trials and difficulties that they have to face in the path of *īmān*. It is Allah's Practice (*Sunnah*) to test the commitment and authenticity of those who proclaim that they are believers.

This trial is an essential requirement to test the sincerity of one's *īmān*. The path of Islam is the path of struggle. People will not be left alone just by saying that they believe. They will be tested so as to establish whether their belief is superficial or rooted firmly in their hearts and manifested in their actions. The Qur'ān mentions this fact in several places so that one should not be perturbed when these trials come but instead remain steadfast in one's resolve:

أَحَسِبَ ٱلنَّاسُ أَن يُتْرَكُوٓا۟ أَن يَقُولُوٓا۟ ءَامَنَّا وَهُمْ لَا يُفْتَنُونَ ﴿٢﴾ وَلَقَدْ فَتَنَّا ٱلَّذِينَ
مِن قَبْلِهِمْ ۖ فَلَيَعْلَمَنَّ ٱللَّهُ ٱلَّذِينَ صَدَقُوا۟ وَلَيَعْلَمَنَّ ٱلْكَـٰذِبِينَ ﴿٣﴾

Do people think that they will be left alone on saying, "We believe", and that they will not be tested? We did test those before them, and Allah will certainly distinguish between those who are true from those who are false.

(al-'Ankabūt 29: 2–3)

There are similar verses in *sūrahs al-Baqarah* 2: 214 and *Āl 'Imrān* 3: 142.

The verse that I recited at the beginning of this *khuṭbah* is also repeated with a slight variation in *Sūrah al-Aḥqāf*:

إِنَّ ٱلَّذِينَ قَالُوا۟ رَبُّنَا ٱللَّهُ ثُمَّ ٱسْتَقَـٰمُوا۟ فَلَا خَوْفٌ عَلَيْهِمْ وَلَا هُمْ يَحْزَنُونَ ۝١٣

Surely those who say: "Our Lord is Allah", and then remain steadfast have nothing to fear nor shall they grieve.

(al-Aḥqāf 46: 13)

The import of the two verses is that the reward of *istiqāmah* is given to one attains the status of being a friend of Allah (*walī Allāh*). The friend of Allah neither experiences fear nor suffers grief over any loss. This is also stated in *Sūrah Yūnus*:

أَلَآ إِنَّ أَوْلِيَآءَ ٱللَّهِ لَا خَوْفٌ عَلَيْهِمْ وَلَا هُمْ يَحْزَنُونَ ۝٦٢ ٱلَّذِينَ ءَامَنُوا۟
وَكَانُوا۟ يَتَّقُونَ ۝٦٣ لَهُمُ ٱلْبُشْرَىٰ فِى ٱلْحَيَوٰةِ ٱلدُّنْيَا وَفِى ٱلْـَٔاخِرَةِ ۚ لَا تَبْدِيلَ
لِكَلِمَـٰتِ ٱللَّهِ ۚ ذَٰلِكَ هُوَ ٱلْفَوْزُ ٱلْعَظِيمُ ۝٦٤

Surely the friends of Allah have nothing to fear, nor shall they grieve – the ones who believe and are God-fearing. For them are glad tidings in this world and in the Hereafter. The words of Allah shall not change. That is the supreme triumph.

(Yūnus 10: 62-4)

Mawlānā Mawdūdī explaining the meaning of the verse from *Sūrah Fuṣṣilat* writes in *Tafhīm al-Qur'ān*:

> This is a major characteristic of those who have true faith in God. When they committed themselves to God, declaring Him to be their Lord, such a declaration was not an accidental utterance. Such people were under no misperception that they could commit themselves to God as their Lord, and then combine this with accepting others as their Lord. On the contrary, once they had made up their minds to accept God as their One True God, they steadfastly stood by that commitment. Such people neither adopted any creed repugnant to their exclusive commitment to the One True God, nor allowed their belief to be adulterated by mixing it with elements drawn from false creeds. Moreover, they also strove hard to translate their belief in the One True God into practice.[1]

In both verses, the reward of remaining steadfast is achieving closeness to Allah and His angels and becoming His friend. Apart from the rewards in the Hereafter (*Ākhirāh*), Allah has also promised continued sustenance for those who follow the path of steadfastness. As stated in *Sūrah al-Jinn*:

وَأَلَّوِ ٱسْتَقَٰمُوا۟ عَلَى ٱلطَّرِيقَةِ لَأَسْقَيْنَٰهُم مَّآءً غَدَقًا ﴿١٦﴾

If people were to keep firmly on the Right Path, We would have bestowed on them abundant rain.

(al-Jinn 72: 16)

The verses I have cited so far about *istiqāmah* mention that its rewards are given both in this world and the Hereafter. However, in *Sūrah Hūd*, to remain steadfast is given in the form of a command to the Prophet (peace be upon him) and his Companions:

فَٱسْتَقِمْ كَمَآ أُمِرْتَ وَمَن تَابَ مَعَكَ وَلَا تَطْغَوْا۟ ... ﴿١١٢﴾

---

[1] *Towards Understanding the Qur'ān*, abridged version, 2006, p. 979.

So remain steadfast (in following the Right Way) as you are commanded – you and those who repented with you, do not transgress (from the Right Way).

(Hūd 11: 112)

This means that to remain firm and steadfast is a specific requirement of *īmān*. This is further reinforced by many *aḥādīth* as well. When Sufyān ibn ʿAbdullāh al-Thaqafī came to the Prophet (peace be upon him) requesting that he teach him a short and simple thing about Islam to remember, the Prophet said:

عَنْ سُفْيَانَ بْنِ عَبْدِ اللهِ الثَّقَفِيِّ، قَالَ: قُلْتُ: يَا رَسُولَ اللهِ، قُلْ لِي فِي الْإِسْلَامِ قَوْلًا لَا أَسْأَلُ عَنْهُ أَحَدًا بَعْدَكَ، قَالَ: قُلْ: آمَنْتُ بِاللهِ، فَاسْتَقِمْ.

(مسلم)

Say: I believe in Allah and thereafter remain steadfast.

(Muslim)

عَنْ أَنَسِ بْنِ مَالِكٍ، أَنَّ رَسُولَ اللهِ صَلَّى اللهُ عَلَيْهِ وَسَلَّمَ قَالَ: قَدْ قَالَ النَّاسُ ثُمَّ كَفَرَ أَكْثَرُهُمْ، فَمَنْ مَاتَ عَلَيْهَا فَهُوَ مِمَّنْ اسْتَقَامَ.

(الترمذي)

It is related by Anas ibn Mālik that the Prophet (peace be upon him) said: "Many people have said that Allah is their Lord yet lost their faith. The steadfast one is he who remains firm in his belief."

(Tirmidhī)

It is said: "Only the great man can remain steadfast because it entails leaving behind what is familiar and abandoning conventions and habits. It means that one should stand before God firm in the inner reality of truthfulness, and for this reason the Prophet (peace be upon him) commanded: 'Be steadfast, although you will never be able to achieve it completely.'" Similarly, the same thing is said about *taqwā*:

فَٱتَّقُوا۟ ٱللَّهَ مَا ٱسۡتَطَعۡتُمۡ ... ﴿١٦﴾

So have Taqwā of Allah as much as you can.
(al-Taghābun 64: 16)

It is reassuring that Allah has not burdened us with commands that we cannot fulfil. We are only obliged to do what we can possibly do with sincerity. Allah, Who is Most Merciful and the Most Kind, will overlook any of our shortcomings, *Inshā' Allāh.*

Those who follow the right path of the *Sharīʿah* say that the most miraculous deed is to control one's carnal self and the temptations of Satan and this cannot be achieved without *istiqāmah.* It is narrated that someone came and stayed with al-Junayd al-Baghdādī (may Allah have mercy on him) for a few months. He neither tried to learn anything from the Shaykh nor did he ask for anything from him. When he decided to leave, the Shaykh asked him why he had come and why he was now departing even though he had never explained the purpose of his visit. The person said: "I heard that you were a great, pious person but I did not observe you performing any miraculous deeds. Hence, I am dismayed and want to leave." Al-Junayd asked him: "Have you ever seen anything that I have done against the *Sunnah*?" He admitted that he had not seen the Shaykh doing anything against the *Sharīʿah*. Then al-Junaid remarked: "O Brother! What can be a more miraculous deed than this?"

Thus, constancy and commitment to remain on the straight path is the greatest miracle one can perform. This is the prayer that the Prophet (peace be upon him) taught to one of his Companions saying: "O Shaddād! When you see people getting busy in accumulating gold and silver, then recall and remember these words:

... اللَّهُمَّ إِنِّي أَسْأَلُكَ الثَّبَاتَ فِي الْأَمْرِ، وَالْعَزِيمَةَ عَلَى الرُّشْدِ، وَأَسْأَلُكَ شُكْرَ نِعْمَتِكَ، وَأَسْأَلُكَ حُسْنَ عِبَادَتِكَ، وَأَسْأَلُكَ قَلْبًا سَلِيمًا، وَأَسْأَلُكَ لِسَانًا صَادِقًا، وَأَسْأَلُكَ مِنْ خَيْرِ مَا تَعْلَمُ، وَأَعُوذُ بِكَ مِنْ شَرِّ مَا تَعْلَمُ، وَأَسْتَغْفِرُكَ لِمَا تَعْلَمُ، إِنَّكَ أَنْتَ عَلَّامُ الْغُيُوبِ.

(أحمد)

O Lord! I seek steadfastness in affairs of Religion (*Dīn*), and constancy in being truthful. I ask You to make me thankful for Your bounties, and to worship You in the best way. I ask you for a heart that is sound and for a truthful tongue. I ask You for the good that in Your knowledge, and I seek refuge in You from the evil that You are aware of. I seek forgiveness for all my sins that are in Your knowledge, as You have knowledge of all that is beyond human perception.

(Aḥmad)

May Allah give us the success (*tawfīq*) to remain firm on the Straight Path which we regularly pray for in *Sūrah al-Fātiḥah*. (*Āmīn*)

23

Self-Scrutiny (*Muḥāsabah*)

يَٰٓأَيُّهَا ٱلَّذِينَ ءَامَنُوا۟ ٱتَّقُوا۟ ٱللَّهَ وَلْتَنظُرْ نَفْسٌ مَّا قَدَّمَتْ لِغَدٍ ۖ وَٱتَّقُوا۟ ٱللَّهَ ۚ
إِنَّ ٱللَّهَ خَبِيرٌۢ بِمَا تَعْمَلُونَ ١٨

O you who believe! Fear Allah and let every person look to what he sends forward for the morrow. Fear Allah, for surely Allah is well aware of all that you do.

(al-Ḥashr 59: 18)

This verse from *Sūrah al-Ḥashr* exhorts us to scrutinize our deeds and actions and to always remain conscious of Allah. Repetition of the word *taqwā* (God-consciousness) emphasizes that it is a vital duty that consciousness of Allah's presence should always be with us as this will help us to remain on the right path. The other command is that we should be mindful of our accountability on the Day of Judgement. In religious terminology this scrutiny and taking account of one's deeds is called *muḥāsabah*. The word *muḥāsabah* comes from *ḥ-s-b* which means to reckon, to calculate, to consider and to take to task. Basically it is self-criticism and self-analysis, which one should undertake diligently without giving oneself any latitude.

Our carnal self is extremely clever and cunning in concocting ingenious excuses in order to try to satisfy us. Thus, one should always be on guard against the deceptions of the carnal self and Satan's promptings.

إِنَّ ٱلَّذِينَ ٱتَّقَوْا۟ إِذَا مَسَّهُمْ طَٰٓئِفٌ مِّنَ ٱلشَّيْطَٰنِ تَذَكَّرُوا۟
فَإِذَا هُم مُّبْصِرُونَ ﴿٢٠١﴾

If the God-fearing are prompted by any suggestion of Satan, they instantly become alert, whereafter they clearly perceive the right way.

(al-Aʿrāf 7: 201)

Self-criticism should take account of both the quantity and the quality of the tasks we have performed. Thus, one should take account of the number of duties one is required to perform and whether one has fulfilled them all. By quality is meant how well one has performed them. Were these fulfilled as required or were they merely a completion of formalities? Were there any shortcomings in their performance and, if so, then how were these compensated for? After completing *muḥāsabah* one should thank Allah for the good deeds one has done and if there are any shortcomings then one should try to erase them with repentance (*tawbah*), seeking forgiveness (*istighfār*) and by giving charity (*ṣadaqah*) as well. We find many instances from the lives of the Companions, narrated in *ṣaḥīḥ aḥādīth* about their vigilant conduct in cases of any negligence or shortcoming on their part. They either used to perform extra voluntary prayers (*nawāfil*) or give money in charity. In this, they were following the advice that the Prophet (peace be upon him) gave them, as narrated by Shaddād ibn Aws:

عَنْ شَدَّادِ بْنِ أَوْسٍ، قَالَ: قَالَ رَسُولُ اللهِ صَلَّى اللهُ عَلَيْهِ وَسَلَّمَ الْكَيِّسُ مَنْ دَانَ نَفْسَهُ وَعَمِلَ لِمَا بَعْدَ الْمَوْتِ، وَالْعَاجِزُ مَنْ أَتْبَعَ نَفْسَهُ هَوَاهَا وَتَمَنَّى عَلَى اللهِ عَزَّ وَجَلَّ.

(أحمد والترمذي)

A wise person is he who makes the self obedient and does (good) deeds for the life after death while the incompetent

> one is he who follows the desires of his carnal self and pins his hopes upon Allah (that he might be forgiven).
> (Aḥmad and Tirmidhī)

This *ḥadīth* reminds us that wishful thinking and going through one's life carelessly is living in a fool's paradise. One has to be vigilant and make serious efforts for the life in the Hereafter.

Shāh Walīullāh has quoted a saying of 'Umar ibn al-Khaṭṭāb regarding *muḥāsabah* in *Izālat al-Khifā'* that is pertinent and insightful:

> You should scrutinize your affairs before your account is taken on the Day of Judgement. Before your actions are weighed in the scale in the Hereafter you should weigh them here in this world and be prepared for your appearance before Allah where nothing will be concealed.[1]

Imām Ghazālī explained the process of *muḥāsabah* with the example of a person in a business partnership. He has to keep an account of whether the business is profitable or making a loss. As in any business account is taken to the last penny, similarly one should scrutinize all acts however small and insignificant.[2]

The best time to make *muḥāsabah* is when one retires at night. Then, one should devote a few minutes to scrutinize what one has done during the day. If there are any shortcomings, one should seek Allah's forgiveness and promise that one will try not to repeat them. It is narrated in a *ḥadīth* that a believer's tomorrow should be better than his yesterday.

At times it may be that scrutinizing our conduct regularly we see that we are committing the same sins again and again, although we keep promising *Allāh Subḥānahu wa Ta'ālā* that we will not repeat them. There is a danger that one becomes depressed and loses hope. This is the trick of our arch enemy Satan who wants us to abandon the process of

---

1 Quoted by Sayyid 'Urūj Qādirī in his book, *Islāmī Taṣawwuf*, 1980, p. 256.
2 *Iḥyā' 'Ulūm al-Dīn*, Vol. 4, Chapter 8.

self-criticism. The other name of Satan is *Iblīs*, which comes from *b-l-s*, meaning to lose hope. Unlike the Prophet Ādam (peace be upon him) who repented when he transgressed Allah's command, *Iblīs* lost hope, became arrogant and rebelled. Allah always reassures us that even if we make mistakes repeatedly we should seek His forgiveness. As a Persian poet has very aptly said:

> My domain is not where there is hopelessness
> Even if you have lapsed a hundred times still turn back

We see that the Glorious Qur'ān keeps reminding us to turn to our Lord and to seek His forgiveness. In *Sūrah al-Nūr* it says:

... وَتُوبُوٓاْ إِلَى ٱللَّهِ جَمِيعًا أَيُّهَ ٱلۡمُؤۡمِنُونَ لَعَلَّكُمۡ تُفۡلِحُونَ ٣١

Believers! Turn together, all of you, to Allah in repentance so that you may achieve success.

(al-Nūr 24: 31)

Alongside such exhortations, there is also reassurance for the believers not to get depressed with their struggle and, despite constant failings, to live up to the ideal they have set for themselves. One of the most reassuring and heart-warming verses of the Majestic Qur'an is:

قُلۡ يَٰعِبَادِيَ ٱلَّذِينَ أَسۡرَفُواْ عَلَىٰٓ أَنفُسِهِمۡ لَا تَقۡنَطُواْ مِن رَّحۡمَةِ ٱللَّهِۚ إِنَّ ٱللَّهَ
يَغۡفِرُ ٱلذُّنُوبَ جَمِيعًاۚ إِنَّهُۥ هُوَ ٱلۡغَفُورُ ٱلرَّحِيمُ ٥٣

Tell them (O Prophet): "My servants, who have committed excesses against themselves, do not despair of Allah's mercy. Surely Allah forgives all sins. He is Most Forgiving, Most Merciful."

(al-Zumar 39: 53)

Abū Hurayrah narrates that the Prophet (peace be upon him) warned his Companions:

... لَوْ تَعْلَمُونَ مَا أَعْلَمُ لَضَحِكْتُمْ قَلِيلًا، وَلَبَكَيْتُمْ كَثِيرًا.

(البخاري ومسلم)

If you knew what I know, you would laugh little and weep much.

(Bukhārī and Muslim)

We can see from the lives of the Companions that they were always worried about accountability on the Day of Judgement. It is reported that Abū Bakr Ṣiddīq used to say: "If only I had been a tree and been cut into pieces that animals might eat." (Tirmidhī) Once, when he saw a bird sitting in a tree and singing, he said: "How lucky she is that she sits where she likes and eats and drinks as she pleases without having any fear of accountability." 'Umar ibn al-Khaṭṭāb also remained fearful of the account he would have to give on the Day of Judgement. Once, he took hold of a straw and said: "I wish I were a straw (to be saved from the accountability)." Once the Prophet (peace be upon him) saw *Umm al-Mu'minīn* 'Ā'ishah crying. He asked her: "Why are you crying?" She said: "I am worried about the Day of Judgement. Will you remember us on that Day?" The Prophet (peace be upon him) replied: "I will remember you all except on three occasions: at the *Ṣirāṭ*,[3] at the time when each person will be handed his register of deeds, and at the *Mīzān*.[4] On these three occasions, everyone will only think of himself." Then she asked: "Where will we find you?" He replied: "I will be waiting for you at the Fountain of Kawthar."

Fethullah Gülen, a Turkish scholar, has described the importance and value of *muḥāsabah* beautifully:

> Self-criticism is like a lamp in the heart of a believer and a warner and well-wishing adviser in his conscience. Every believing man distinguishes through it between what is good

[3] The Bridge over which everyone will have to pass in pitch darkness. The only light will be that of the person's *īmān* and righteous deeds (*al-Ḥadīd* 57: 12).

[4] The Balance in which our deeds will be weighed.

> and evil and what is beautiful and ugly and what is pleasing to God and what is displeasing to Him, and by the guidance of that well-wishing adviser, he surmounts all obstacles, however seemingly insurmountable, and reaches his destination.
>
> Self-criticism attracts divine mercy and favor, enabling one to go deeper in belief and servanthood, to succeed in practising Islam, and to gain nearness to God and eternal happiness. Self-criticism opens for man the door to spiritual peace and tranquility, it also causes him to fear God and His punishment and remain in awe of Him.[5]

We see that *muḥāsabah* is such an important part of Islamic teachings and it permeates all levels of a believer's life. The whole purpose is that one should lead a pious life adhering to the duties one is required to fulfil. One's private life as well as one's public behaviour should reflect the values lay down by the *Sharīʿah*. Let us pray:

... اللَّهُمَّ بَاعِدْ بَيْنِي وَبَيْنَ خَطَايَايَ كَمَا بَاعَدْتَ بَيْنَ الْمَشْرِقِ
وَالْمَغْرِبِ، وَنَقِّ قَلْبِي مِنَ الْخَطَايَا كَمَا يُنَقَّى الثَّوْبُ
الْأَبْيَضُ مِنَ الدَّنَسِ.

(البخاري ومسلم)

O Allah, put a distance between me and my sins as You put a distance between east and west. O Allah, cleanse me of sins just as a white robe is cleansed of dirt. O Allah, wash away my sins with water, snow and hail.

(Bukhārī and Muslim)

اللَّهُمَّ إِنِّي أَسْأَلُكَ حُبَّكَ وَحُبَّ مَنْ يُحِبُّكَ وَالْعَمَلَ الَّذِي
يُبَلِّغُنِي حُبَّكَ، ....

(الترمذي)

---

5 *Emerald Hills of the Heart: Key Concepts in the Practice of Sufism*, pp. 23-24.

O Allah! We ask for Your love, the love of those
who love You and the love of those actions
that take us to Your love.

(Tirmidhī)

O Allah! We pray that we should always remain alert and take account of our deeds and also look after those who are our friends and neighbours and together we embark on the path of righteousness self-correcting and self-monitoring. May Allah be Merciful when calling us to account on the Day of Judgement. (*Āmīn*)

24

Asceticism (*Zuhd*)

ٱلْمَالُ وَٱلْبَنُونَ زِينَةُ ٱلْحَيَوٰةِ ٱلدُّنْيَا ۖ وَٱلْبَـٰقِيَـٰتُ ٱلصَّـٰلِحَـٰتُ
خَيْرٌ عِندَ رَبِّكَ ثَوَابًا وَخَيْرٌ أَمَلًا ﴿٤٦﴾

Wealth and children are an adornment of the life of the world. But deeds of lasting righteousness are best in the sight of your Lord in reward, and far better a source of hope.
(al-Kahf 18: 46)

In today's rat race, people are obsessed with acquiring wealth and material goods so that they can enjoy a luxurious life. In their pursuit, they become ruthless and even trample upon the lives of others, often not caring whether their actions are lawful or ethical. Often there is a competition with one's colleagues and neighbours to best them by having more expensive cars or other gadgets. Whereas the Qur'ān tells us that the luxuries of this world are transitory, while good deeds are everlasting. There are many Qur'ānic verses that draw the attention of believers to the fact that they should not be lured and dazzled by worldly glitter. The verse I recited draws our attention to this fact, as so does the following verse from *Sūrah Āl 'Imrān*:

زُيِّنَ لِلنَّاسِ حُبُّ ٱلشَّهَوَٰتِ مِنَ ٱلنِّسَآءِ وَٱلْبَنِينَ وَٱلْقَنَـٰطِيرِ ٱلْمُقَنطَرَةِ مِنَ
ٱلذَّهَبِ وَٱلْفِضَّةِ وَٱلْخَيْلِ ٱلْمُسَوَّمَةِ وَٱلْأَنْعَـٰمِ وَٱلْحَرْثِ ۗ ذَٰلِكَ مَتَـٰعُ
ٱلْحَيَوٰةِ ٱلدُّنْيَا ۖ وَٱللَّهُ عِندَهُۥ حُسْنُ ٱلْمَـَٔابِ ﴿١٤﴾

People are naturally tempted by the lure of women, children, treasures of gold and silver, horses of mark, cattle and plantations. These are the enjoyments in the life of this world; but with Allah lies the goodly abode to return to.

(Āl 'Imrān 3: 14)

In *Sūrah al-Ḥadīd* the worthlessness of this world is even more explicitly explained:

ٱعْلَمُوٓا۟ أَنَّمَا ٱلْحَيَوٰةُ ٱلدُّنْيَا لَعِبٌ وَلَهْوٌ وَزِينَةٌ وَتَفَاخُرٌۢ بَيْنَكُمْ وَتَكَاثُرٌ فِى ٱلْأَمْوَٰلِ
وَٱلْأَوْلَـٰدِ ۖ كَمَثَلِ غَيْثٍ أَعْجَبَ ٱلْكُفَّارَ نَبَاتُهُۥ ثُمَّ يَهِيجُ فَتَرَىٰهُ مُصْفَرًّا ثُمَّ
يَكُونُ حُطَـٰمًا ۖ وَفِى ٱلْـَٔاخِرَةِ عَذَابٌ شَدِيدٌ وَمَغْفِرَةٌ مِّنَ ٱللَّهِ وَرِضْوَٰنٌ ۚ
وَمَا ٱلْحَيَوٰةُ ٱلدُّنْيَآ إِلَّا مَتَـٰعُ ٱلْغُرُورِ ﴿٢٠﴾

Know well that the life of this world is merely sport and diversion and adornment and an object of your boasting with one another, and a rivalry in the multiplication of riches and children. Its likeness is that of rain: when it produces vegetation it delights the tillers. But then it withers and you see it turn yellow, and then it crumbles away. In the Hereafter there is (either) grievous chastisement (or) forgiveness from Allah and (His) good pleasure. The life of this world is nothing but delusion.

(al-Ḥadīd 57: 20)

Following the Qur'ān's exhortation, the renunciation of worldly pleasures and resistance to one's carnal desires is called *zuhd*. This amounts to renouncing temporary worldly ease and comfort for the sake of eternal bliss and happiness in the Hereafter. The word *zuhd* is used only once in the Qur'ān to convey the meaning of being undesirable, indifferent or of low estimation. When a passing caravan found the Prophet Yūsuf (peace be upon him) in a well:

وَشَرَوْهُ بِثَمَنٍ بَخْسٍ دَرَاهِمَ مَعْدُودَةٍ وَكَانُوا۟ فِيهِ مِنَ ٱلزَّٰهِدِينَ ۝

He was bought for a miserable price just for a few dirhams as they were indifferent to him.

(Yūsuf 12: 20)

Many *aḥādīth* also remind believers that they should remain on their guard and not be tempted by the pleasures of this world. When sending Mu ʿādh ibn Jabal to the Yemen the Prophet (peace be upon him) advised him: "O Mu ʿādh! Beware of indolence and a life of pleasure as the special servants of Allah avoid such an attitude." (Aḥmad)

It is narrated by Anas Ibn Mālik that the Prophet (peace be upon him) used to say:

اللَّهُمَّ لَا عَيْشَ الَّا عَيْشَ الأَخِرَة

(البخاري ومسلم)

There is no pleasure except the pleasure in the Hereafter (*Ākhirah*).

(Bukhārī and Muslim)

There is a *ḥadīth* in which the importance of *zuhd* is beautifully explained by the Prophet (peace be upon him). It is related by Sahl ibn Sa ʿd al-Sā ʿidī that a person came to the Prophet (peace be upon him) and asked him: "O Messenger of Allah! Direct me to an act which, if I do it, [will cause] Allah to love me and people to love me." The Prophet said: "Shun and ignore the world and Allah will love you and shun and ignore what people possess (of wealth and fame) and they will love you." (Ibn Mājah) The fact is that it is usually love of this world which holds one back from devotion to Allah. Once we ignore this worldly attachment our hearts will fill with the love of Allah. When people realize that one is not competing with them in acquiring wealth, high position and fame, it is part of human nature that they will respect and love him.

Once the Prophet (peace be upon him) recited this verse from *Sūrah al-Anʿām:*

فَمَن يُرِدِ ٱللَّهُ أَن يَهْدِيَهُۥ يَشْرَحْ صَدْرَهُۥ لِلْإِسْلَٰمِ ... ﴿١٢٥﴾

So whomsoever Allah wills to guide, He opens his heart for Islam.

(al-Anʿām 6: 125)

He explained this verse by saying: "When light is received by the heart it widens the heart." He was asked what the sign is so that one can recognize it. The Prophet (peace be upon him) said: "Yes, one avoids and ignores this world which is the abode of fraud and deceit and turns towards the Hereafter (*Ākhirah*) and prepares for it before one's death. (Bayhaqī)

The essence of the teachings of the Qur'ān and *Sunnah* is that one should not get too attached to worldly goods and engross one's whole life and energy in their acquisition. What Islam wants is change of attitude regarding the importance of this world. It is not required that one should completely abandon this world but one should not have a longing for it. It is the inclination of the heart that should always point to Allah and the *Ākhirah*. We come across many *āyāt* and *aḥādīth* that show the absolute worthlessness of the world and worldly possessions. Yet the word *khayr*, which means goodness and benevolence, is used for wealth in the Qur'ān. Similarly, there are many *aḥādīth* that emphasize the importance of wealth and property.

عَنْ أَبِي هُرَيْرَةَ، قَالَ: قَالَ رَسُولُ اللهِ صَلَّى اللهُ عَلَيْهِ وَسَلَّمَ: مَا نَفَعَنِي مَالٌ قَطُّ، مَا نَفَعَنِي مَالُ أَبِي بَكْرٍ ....

(أحمد)

The Prophet (peace be upon him) used to say: "No one's wealth has benefited me so much as that of Abū Bakr's."

(Narrated by Abū Hurayrah in Aḥmad)

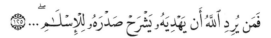

عَنْ سَعْدِ بْنِ أَبِي وَقَّاصٍ رَضِيَ اللهُ عَنْهُ، قَالَ النَّبِيُّ صَلَّى اللهُ عَلَيْهِ وَسَلَّمَ: إِنَّكَ أَنْ تَدَعَ وَرَثَتَكَ أَغْنِيَاءَ خَيْرٌ مِنْ أَنْ تَدَعَهُمْ عَالَةً يَتَكَفَّفُونَ النَّاسَ فِي أَيْدِيهِمْ. . . .

(البخاري)

The Prophet (peace be upon him) told Sa'd ibn Abī Waqqāṣ that, "You should leave your inheritors prosperous rather than in poverty so they do not have to resort to begging."

(Bukhārī)

عَنْ أَنَسٍ أَنَّ النَّبِيَّ صَلَّى اللهُ عَلَيْهِ وَسَلَّمَ دَعا لَهُ فَقَالَ: اللَّهُمَّ ارْزُقْه مَالًا وَوَلَدًا، وَبَارِكْ لَهُ فِيهِمْ.

(أحمد)

It is reported by Anas ibn Mālik that the Prophet (peace be upon him) prayed for his prosperity and finished it by saying: "O Allah! Provide and bless him with wealth and children."

(Aḥmad)

عَنْ كَعْبِ بْنِ مَالِكٍ، أَنَّهُ قَالَ لِرَسُولِ اللهِ صَلَّى اللهُ عَلَيْهِ وَسَلَّمَ حِينَ تَابَ اللهُ تَبَارَكَ وَتَعَالَى عَلَيْهِ: يَا رَسُولَ اللهِ، أَنْخَلِعُ مِنْ مَالِي صَدَقَةً إِلَى اللهِ وَرَسُولِهِ أَفَقَالَ لَهُ رَسُولُ اللهِ صَلَّى اللهُ عَلَيْهِ وَسَلَّمَ: أَمْسِكْ عَلَيْكَ بَعْضَ مَالِكَ، فَإِنَّهُ خَيْرٌ لَكَ.

(أحمد)

It is narrated by Ka'b ibn Mālik that when his repentance was accepted by Allah, he came to the Prophet (peace be upon him) and said: "Shall I give all my wealth in charity (*ṣadaqah*) for the sake of Allah and His Messenger. The Prophet advised him: "Keep some of your wealth, it is better for you."[1]

(Aḥmad)

---

1 Imām Ibn al-Jawzī: *Talbīs Iblīs*. Chapter 10, Section on *The Misunderstanding of Sufis about Wealth*.

The Prophet (peace be upon him) used to wear very simple clothes but in some cases he wore quite expensive and elegant clothes as well. Thus, one aspect of his life was that of simplicity and plainness, yet he also wanted to repel the tendency of monasticism. This is apparent in his saying: "Allah loves that His bounties should be reflected in His servants' lives." (Tirmidhī) Sometimes he wore expensive Roman cloaks with silken borders and once he bought a very expensive outfit costing 27 camels, which he wore and prayed in. He also worn distinctive and gorgeous clothes sent as gifts by different rulers and kings. (Tirmidhī and Abū Dāwūd)

The Prophet's *Sunnah* and *aḥādīth* quoted above explain the real nature of *zuhd*. It does not mean the abandonment of wealth and worldly goods, but rather that one should not crave them by making their acquisition the sole purpose of one's life. Sufyān al-Thawrī, an eminent Successor of the Companions (Tābiʿī), said: "*Zuhd* is not wearing coarse clothes and eating tasteless food but it is to annihilate those desires and expectations that makes one forgetful of death and the *Ākhirah*." (*Mishkāt*) The same message is given by Imām Mālik, when he was asked about *zuhd*. He told the enquirer: "*Zuhd* is lawful and pure earnings and the curtailment of hope of worldly gain."

Jalāl al-Dīn al-Rūmī expresses this in some very apt couplets:

What is the world? It is the forgetfulness of God.
The world is not clothes, nor silver, nor children, nor women.
If you have worldly possessions in the name of God,
Then the Messenger said: "How fine is the property a righteous one has."
The water in a ship causes it to sink,
While the water under it causes it to float.

Thus, the correct attitude is that one should never show any inclination toward worldly allurements. However, wealth and possessions are to be acquired for Allah's sake and for the service of oneself, one's family and humanity.

Allah praises the generosity of the Helpers (*Anṣār*) who accommodated the migrants from Makkah (*Muhājirūn*) in *Sūrah al-Ḥashr*:

... يُحِبُّونَ مَنْ هَاجَرَ إِلَيْهِمْ وَلَا يَجِدُونَ فِي صُدُورِهِمْ حَاجَةً مِّمَّآ أُوتُوا۟
وَيُؤْثِرُونَ عَلَىٰٓ أَنفُسِهِمْ وَلَوْ كَانَ بِهِمْ خَصَاصَةٌ ۚ وَمَن يُوقَ شُحَّ
نَفْسِهِۦ فَأُو۟لَـٰٓئِكَ هُمُ ٱلْمُفْلِحُونَ ۝

They love those who migrated to them and entertain no desire in their hearts for what has been given them; they even prefer them above themselves though poverty be their own lot. And whosoever are saved from their own greed, such are the ones that will prosper.

(al-Ḥashr 59: 9)

It is evident from the life of the Prophet (peace be upon him) and his Companions that they did not abandon wealth but, rather, they used it to acquire Allah's pleasure and reward in the *Ākhirah*, as there is a famous *ḥadīth* that this world is a plantation in which one reaps for the Hereafter.

Let me end with this very profound and comprehensive *du'ā'* that was taught to us by the Prophet (peace be upon him):

عَنْ أَبِي هُرَيْرَةَ، قَالَ: كَانَ رَسُولُ اللهِ صَلَّى اللهُ عَلَيْهِ وَسَلَّمَ، يَقُولُ:
اللَّهُمَّ أَصْلِحْ لِي دِينِي الَّذِي هُوَ عِصْمَةُ أَمْرِي، وَأَصْلِحْ لِي دُنْيَايَ
الَّتِي فِيهَا مَعَاشِي، وَأَصْلِحْ لِي آخِرَتِي الَّتِي فِيهَا مَعَادِي وَاجْعَلِ
الْحَيَاةَ زِيَادَةً لِي فِي كُلِّ خَيْرٍ، وَاجْعَلِ الْمَوْتَ رَاحَةً لِي
مِنْ كُلِّ شَرٍّ.

(مسلم)

O Allah! Make my religious life sound as my well-being and welfare depends upon it, and make my worldly life sound as my livelihood depends upon it, and make the

Next Life where I must return increase in all goodness
and make my death a repose from all evil.
(Narrated by Abū Hurayrah in Muslim)

There is also the *du'ā'* that Allah has asked us to make:

رَبَّنَآ ءَاتِنَا فِى ٱلدُّنْيَا حَسَنَةً وَفِى ٱلْءَاخِرَةِ حَسَنَةً وَقِنَا عَذَابَ ٱلنَّارِ ﴿٢٠١﴾

Our Lord, grant us what is good in this world and what is good in the World to come, and protect us from the chastisement of fire. (*Āmīn*)

(al-Baqarah 2: 201)

25

Commanding Good and Forbidding Evil (*al-Amr bi al-Maʿrūf wa al-Nahy ʿan al-Munkar*)

كُنتُمْ خَيْرَ أُمَّةٍ أُخْرِجَتْ لِلنَّاسِ تَأْمُرُونَ بِٱلْمَعْرُوفِ وَتَنْهَوْنَ
عَنِ ٱلْمُنكَرِ وَتُؤْمِنُونَ بِٱللَّهِ ... ﴿١١٠﴾

You are now the best nation that has been brought forth for mankind. You command what is right and forbid what is wrong and believe in Allah.

(Āl ʿImrān 3: 110)

Islam has laid down a basic principle and a fundamental code of conduct for the establishment and sustenance of the Muslim *ummah*. This is what is enunciated in the verse of *Sūrah Āl ʿImrān* which I have recited, instructing us to command right conduct and to forbid all evil deeds. It is the same duty that is the mark of distinction for this *ummah* as it is chosen to be a witness unto mankind as mentioned in *Sūrah al-Baqarah*:

وَكَذَٰلِكَ جَعَلْنَٰكُمْ أُمَّةً وَسَطًا لِّتَكُونُوا۟ شُهَدَآءَ عَلَى ٱلنَّاسِ
وَيَكُونَ ٱلرَّسُولُ عَلَيْكُمْ شَهِيدًا ... ﴿١٤٣﴾

And it is thus that we have appointed you a community of the middle way so that you might be witness to all mankind and the Messenger might be a witness unto you.

(al-Baqarah 2: 143)

These verses explicitly define the real mission and purpose, the essential characteristic and place of honour that has been awarded to this *ummah*. It is raised to call mankind towards good and wherever they see any evil they have to make all the necessary efforts to correct it. As this *ummah* follows the path of justice and equity, of balance and moderation, it is distinguished as the middle community. Just as the Prophet (peace be upon him) has conveyed the message of Islam to the *ummah*, now it is the duty of the *ummah* to communicate it to the rest of mankind until the end of time. Although this is the responsibility of the entire *ummah*, Allah, in His Mercy, has given this allowance whereby there must be at least a group of people who are exclusively devoted to this task as mentioned in this verse:

وَلْتَكُن مِّنكُمْ أُمَّةٌ يَدْعُونَ إِلَى ٱلْخَيْرِ وَيَأْمُرُونَ بِٱلْمَعْرُوفِ وَيَنْهَوْنَ
عَنِ ٱلْمُنكَرِ ۚ وَأُو۟لَـٰٓئِكَ هُمُ ٱلْمُفْلِحُونَ ﴿١٠٤﴾

And from amongst you there must be a party who will call people to all that is good and will command the doing of all that is right and will forbid the doing of all that is wrong. It is they who will attain true success.

(Āl ʿImrān 3: 104)

In the language of jurisprudence (*fiqh*), *al-amr bi al-maʿrūf wa al-nahy ʿan al-munkar* is not obligatory (*farḍ al-ʿayn*) but *farḍ al-kifāyah*, which means that if some people carry out this duty then the rest of the *ummah* will not be held accountable for this. But, if none undertake this task, then all are equally responsible. However, the success (*falāḥ*) promised in this verse is only for those who engage in this task. Being the hallmark of the entire Muslim *ummah*, it is the duty shared by both men and women:

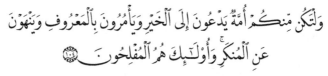

وَٱلْمُؤْمِنُونَ وَٱلْمُؤْمِنَٰتُ بَعْضُهُمْ أَوْلِيَآءُ بَعْضٍ يَأْمُرُونَ بِٱلْمَعْرُوفِ
وَيَنْهَوْنَ عَنِ ٱلْمُنكَرِ... ﴿٧١﴾

The believers, both men and women, are allies of one another.
They command good and forbid evil.

(al-Tawbah 9: 71)

Commanding good and forbidding evil is one of the most important injunctions imposed upon an individual Muslim as well as upon the *ummah* as a whole. Its importance can be gauged by the fact that it is mentioned at least nine times in the Qur'ān.

The word *maʿrūf* is used for good in these verses. Its root is *ʿarafa*, to know, to recognize, to perceive. Hence *maʿrūf* is something that is well known, universally recognized and generally accepted. In Qur'ānic terminology, it means all good deeds that human beings recognize as wholesome and desirable: for example, helping the poor and destitute, widows and orphans, the sick and infirm, or establishing peace and harmony in society. Muslims are duty bound to get actively involved in working for the social betterment of the society in which they live.

The opposite of *maʿrūf* is *munkar*. Its root is *nakira* which means not to know, to have no knowledge, to deny. Hence *munkar* means disagreeable, objectionable and detestable acts that human beings abhor. Such acts include abusing others, wrongful acts, pride, misappropriation, miserliness and shameful and lewd acts. Such acts and behaviour should be checked and stopped. The following *ḥadīth* makes it clear how necessary this task is:

It is narrated by Abī Saʿīd al-Khudrī that the Prophet (peace be upon him) said:

عَنْ أَبِي سَعِيدِ الْـخُدْرِيِّ قَالَ: سَمِعْتُ رَسُولَ اللهِ صَلَّى اللهُ عَلَيْهِ
وَسَلَّمَ، يَقُولُ: مَنْ رَأَى مِنْكُمْ مُنْكَرًا فَلْيُغَيِّرْهُ بِيَدِهِ، فَإِنْ لَمْ يَسْتَطِعْ
فَبِلِسَانِهِ، فَإِنْ لَمْ يَسْتَطِعْ فَبِقَلْبِهِ، وَذَلِكَ أَضْعَفُ الإِيمَانِ.

(مسلم)

If someone sees an evil act being done, he should stop it with his hands. If one is not in a position to stop such an act physically then one should verbally condemn it and if even this is not possible then one should at least feel abhorrence in one's heart. This is the lowest degree of *īmān*.

(Muslim)

It is the mercy of Allah that He has given us the basic instincts to differentiate between good and evil. But human affairs are much more complex and need more precise guidance. Thus, Allah Who has provided for the fulfilment of our physical needs on earth has also provided detailed guidance through His Prophets – Ādam, Ibrāhīm, Mūsā, ʿĪsā and Muḥammad (peace be upon them all). He gave them Scriptures that laid down the law like the Ten Commandments. It is God who made these laws just as He made physical laws that govern the universe. Thus, the criterion for *maʿrūf* and *munkar* is provided by the *Sharīʿah*.

We should note that the neglect of performing this duty incurs severe reproach as well as punishment. The Qur'ān records the censure and condemnation directed at the tribe of Israel as follows:

لُعِنَ ٱلَّذِينَ كَفَرُوا۟ مِنۢ بَنِىٓ إِسْرَٰٓءِيلَ عَلَىٰ لِسَانِ دَاوُۥدَ وَعِيسَى ٱبْنِ مَرْيَمَ ۚ ذَٰلِكَ
بِمَا عَصَوا۟ وَّكَانُوا۟ يَعْتَدُونَ ﴿٧٨﴾ كَانُوا۟ لَا يَتَنَاهَوْنَ عَن مُّنكَرٍ فَعَلُوهُ ۚ
لَبِئْسَ مَا كَانُوا۟ يَفْعَلُونَ ﴿٧٩﴾

Those of the tribe of Israel who took to unbelief have been cursed by the tongue of Dāwūd and ʿĪsā, the son of Maryam, for they rebelled and exceeded the bounds of right. They did not forbid each other from committing the evil deeds they did. Evil indeed was what they did.

(al-Mā'idah 5: 78-79)

One incident of such rebellion on the part of tribe of Israel is narrated in *Sūrah al-Aʿrāf.* The Israelites were required to observe the sanctity of the Sabbath by giving it over to rest and total devotion. To test their commitment, the people of a town situated alongside the sea (probably today's Elat) faced a challenge. They could not restrain their temptation when fish appeared at the water's surface. Thus, by fishing, they profaned the Sabbath. Some of the God-fearing admonished them for their sin so that they could proffer the excuse before their Lord that they had performed their duty. But the others said it was no use admonishing them for they would not listen. Hence, God afflicted the wrong-doers with a grievous chastisement but saved those who forbade them from committing an evil deed. (al-Aʿrāf 7: 163-166)

There are also many *aḥādīth* that emphasize the importance of stopping injustice and corruption in the society where one lives.

It is reported by Jābir ibn ʿAbdullāh that the Prophet (peace be upon him) said:

عَنْ جَابِر، قَالَ: قَالَ رَسُولُ اللهِ صَلَّى اللهُ عَلَيْهِ وَسَلَّمَ: أَوْحَى اللهُ إِلَى مَلَكٍ مِنَ الْـمَلائِكَةِ أَنِ اقْلِبْ مَدِينَةَ كَذَا وَكَذَا عَلَى أَهْلِهَا، قَالَ: إِنَّ فِيهِ عَبْدَكَ فُلانًا لَمْ يَعْصِكَ طَرْفَةَ عَيْنٍ، قَالَ: اقْلِبْهَا عَلَيْهِ وَعَلَيْهِمْ، فَإِنَّ وَجْهَهُ لَمْ يَتَمَعَّرْ لِي سَاعَةً قَطُّ.

(الطبراني)

Allah sent an angel to a city and ordered it to be destroyed. The angel said: "O Lord! There is a person in that city who never disobeyed any of Your commands." Allah said: "Yes destroy them all as that person was never perturbed by the evil committed around him."

(Ṭabarānī)

عَنْ حُذَيْفَةَ بْنِ الْيَمَانِ، عَنِ النَّبِيِّ صَلَّى اللهُ عَلَيْهِ وَسَلَّمَ قَالَ: وَالَّذِي نَفْسِي بِيَدِهِ لَتَأْمُرُنَّ بِالْـمَعْرُوفِ، وَلَتَنْهَوُنَّ عَنِ الْـمُنْكَرِ، أَوْ لَيُوشِكَنَّ اللهُ أَنْ يَبْعَثَ عَلَيْكُمْ عِقَابًا مِنْهُ، ثُمَّ تَدْعُونَهُ فَلَا يُسْتَجَابُ لَكُمْ.

(الترمذي)

It is narrated by Ḥudhayfah that the Prophet (peace be upon him) said; "By the One in Whose Hands is my life!

You must command good and forbid evil. Otherwise Allah will certainly send down a punishment upon you and then you will pray but your prayers will not be accepted.
(Tirmidhī)

عَنْ أَبِي سَعِيدِ الْخُدْرِيِّ، قَالَ: قَالَ رَسُولُ اللهِ صَلَّى اللهُ عَلَيْهِ وَسَلَّمَ: أَفْضَلُ الْجِهَادِ كَلِمَةُ عَدْلٍ عِنْدَ سُلْطَانٍ جَائِرٍ.
(أبو داوود)

It is reported by Abī Sa'īd al-Khudrī that the Prophet (peace be upon him) said: "The most excellent Jihād is saying a righteous thing in the court of a tyrannical ruler."
(Abū Dāwūd)

Of course, it is important for us to censure those who are indulging in evil acts. But it is also vitally important that one should take stock of one's own life and scrutinize it to see if one is not involved in the same misdeed. As the Qur'ān rebukes such people:

أَتَأْمُرُونَ ٱلنَّاسَ بِٱلْبِرِّ وَتَنسَوْنَ أَنفُسَكُمْ وَأَنتُمْ تَتْلُونَ ٱلْكِتَٰبَ ۚ أَفَلَا تَعْقِلُونَ ﴿٤٤﴾

Do you command righteousness upon people and forget your own selves even though you recite the Scripture.
(al-Baqarah 2: 44)

And in *Sūrah al-Ṣaff* the rebuke is even more critical:

يَٰٓأَيُّهَا ٱلَّذِينَ ءَامَنُوا۟ لِمَ تَقُولُونَ مَا لَا تَفْعَلُونَ ﴿٢﴾ كَبُرَ مَقْتًا عِندَ ٱللَّهِ أَن تَقُولُوا۟ مَا لَا تَفْعَلُونَ ﴿٣﴾

O you who believe! Why do you say that which you do not practise? It is most loathsome in the sight of Allah that you should say what you do not practise.
(al-Ṣaff 61: 2-3)

Due to the importance accorded to *al-amr bi al-maʿrūf wa al-nahy ʿan al-munkar*, it is also one of the duties that an Islamic State is required to enforce.

ٱلَّذِينَ إِن مَّكَّنَّٰهُمْ فِى ٱلْأَرْضِ أَقَامُوا۟ ٱلصَّلَوٰةَ وَءَاتَوُا۟ ٱلزَّكَوٰةَ
وَأَمَرُوا۟ بِٱلْمَعْرُوفِ وَنَهَوْا۟ عَنِ ٱلْمُنكَرِ ... ﴿٤١﴾

(They are) those whom if We were to bestow authority on them in the land will establish prayers, render Zakāh, command good and forbid evil.

(al- Ḥajj 22: 41)

Hence, the Islamic state is duty-bound to see that its citizens are adhering to the code of life and behaviour required by Islam. The institution of inspection (*ḥisbah*) and the appointment of a inspector (*muḥtasib*) was set up during the time of the Rightly-guided Caliphs (*al-Khulfāʾ al-Rāshidūn*). ʿUmar ibn al-Khaṭṭāb laid the foundation of this institution. By the mid-eight century under ʿAbbasid rule, *ḥisbah* had become a full-fledged institution. It remained part of the government machinery in other Muslim states.

This duty of commanding good and forbidding evil is such an important part of Islamic teachings that it permeates all the affairs of a Muslim's life. The real purpose is that one should lead a pious life both in private affairs as well as in public behaviour. Let us pray:

... اللَّهُمَّ أَنْتَ رَبِّي لا إِلَهَ إِلا أَنْتَ عَلَيْكَ تَوَكَّلْتُ، وَأَنْتَ رَبُّ الْعَرْشِ
الْكَرِيمِ، مَا شَاءَ اللهُ كَانَ وَمَا لَمْ يَشَأْ لَمْ يَكُنْ، لاحَوْلَ وَلاقُوَّةَ إِلا بِاللهِ،
أَعْلَمُ أَنَّ اللهَ عَلَى كُلِّ شَيْءٍ قَدِيرٌ، وَأَنَّ اللهَ قَدْ أَحَاطَ بِكُلِّ شَيْءٍ
عِلْمًا، اللَّهُمَّ إِنِّي أَعُوذُ بِكَ مِنْ شَرِّ نَفْسِي، وَمِنْ شَرِّ كُلِّ دَابَّةٍ
أَنْتَ آخِذٌ بِنَاصِيَتِهَا إِنَّ رَبِّي عَلَى صِرَاطٍ مُسْتَقِيمٍ.

(الطبراني)

O Allah! You are my Lord, there is no god save Him, I put my trust in Allah, and He is the Lord of the Mighty Throne. What Allah wills takes place, and what Allah does not will does not take place. I know that Allah has power over all things and that He encompasses all things with His knowledge. O Allah! I seek refuge in You from the mischief of my carnal self and I seek refuge in You from the mischief of all creatures whose reins are in Your Hand. No doubt My Lord is on the Straight Path.

(Ṭabrānī)

We pray O Allah that we should always remain alert and take account of our deeds and also look after those who are our friends and neighbours and together we embark on the path of righteousness, self-correcting and self-monitoring. (*Āmīn*)

APPENDIX

First *Khuṭbah*

الحَمْدُ للهِ نَحْمَدُهُ وَنَسْتَعِينُهُ وَنَسْتَغْفِرُهُ وَنُؤْمِنُ بِهِ وَنَتَوَكَّلُ عَلَيْهِ - وَنَعُوذُ بِاللهِ مِنْ شُرُورِ أَنْفُسِنَا وَمِنْ سَيِّئَاتِ أَعْمَالِنَا - مَنْ يَهْدِهِ اللهُ فَلاَ مُضِلَّ لَهُ وَمَنْ يُضْلِلْهُ فَلاَ هَادِيَ لَهُ - وَنَشْهَدُ أَنْ لاَ إِلَهَ إِلاَّ اللهُ وَحْدَهُ لاَ شَرِيكَ لَهُ - وَنَشْهَدُ أَنَّ مُحَمَّدًا عَبْدُهُ وَرَسُولُهُ - أَرْسَلَهُ بَشِيْرًا وَنَذِيرًا بَيْنَ يَدَيِ السَّاعَةِ - مَنْ يُطِعِ اللهَ وَرَسُولَهُ فَقَدْ رَشَدَ وَاهْتَدَىٰ، وَمَنْ يَعْصِهِمَا فَإِنَّهُ قَدْ غَوَىٰ - وَإِنَّهُ لاَ يَضُرُّ إِلاَّ نَفْسَهُ وَلاَ يَضُرُّ اللهَ شَيْئًا - إِنَّ خَيْرَ الحَدِيثِ كِتَابُ اللهِ وَخَيْرَ الهَدْيِ هَدْيُ مُحَمَّدٍ صَلَّى اللهُ عَلَيْهِ وَسَلَّمَ، وَإِنَّ خَيْرَ الأُمُورِ عَوَازِمُهَا وَشَرَّ الأُمُورِ مُحْدَثَاتُهَا، وَكُلُّ مُحْدَثَةٍ بِدْعَةٌ وَكُلُّ بِدْعَةٍ ضَلاَلَةٌ وَكُلُّ ضَلاَلَةٍ فِي النَّارِ.

أَمَّا بَعْدُ، فَأَعُوذُ بِاللهِ مِنَ الشَّيْطَانِ الرَّجِيمِ - بِسْمِ اللهِ الرَّحْمَٰنِ الرَّحِيمِ - قَالَ اللهُ تَعَالَى فِي كِتَابِهِ الْمَجِيدِ ...*

All thankful praise be to Allah (*swt*). We thank and praise Allah seeking His help and His Forgiveness. We believe in Him and we place our trust in Him. We seek refuge in Him from the evil of our carnal selves and from our sinful actions. Whomsoever Allah has guided no one can lead

* Please recite the *āyah* from the *Khuṭbah* you have chosen to deliver.

astray and whomsoever Allah leaves to his own misguidance no one can guide him. We bear witness that there is no deity except Allah and He is One and has no equal. We bear witness that Muḥammad is His servant and Messenger (peace be upon him). He was sent as a Bearer of glad tidings and as a Warner before the coming of the Hour. He who obeys Allah and His Messenger is guided and achieves righteousness and he who disobeys them has transgressed. He does not harm anyone but himself and he does not harm Allah in the least. Certainly the best discourse is the Book of Allah and the best of guidance is the guidance of Muḥammad. The peace and blessings of Allah be on him. The best deeds are firm and balanced acts and evil deeds are novel acts and new things introduced in the *dīn*. All novel acts are innovations and all innovations are spurious and misguided and all those who are misguided are in the Fire.

I seek refuge with Allah from the accursed Satan. I begin in the Name of Allah, the Merciful, the Beneficent. *Allah Taʿālā* says in His Glorious Book...**

** Please read the translation of the *āyah*.

Second *Khuṭbah*

الـحَمْدُ لِلهِ رَبِّ العَالَـمِينَ، وَالصَّلاَةُ وَالسَّـلاَمُ عَلَى رَسُولِهِ الأَمِينِ، أَمَّا بَعْدُ: فَيَامَعْشَرَ الـمُسْلِمِينَ! أَعُوذُ بِاللهِ مِنَ الشَّيْطَانِ الرَّجِيمِ، بِسْمِ اللهِ الرَّحْمَـٰنِ الرَّحِيمِ، قَالَ اللهُ تَعَالَىٰ فِي كِتَابِهِ الكَرِيمِ: «إِنَّ اللهَ وَمَلاَئِكَتَهُ يُصَلُّونَ عَلَىٰ النَّبِيِّ. يَاأَيُّهَا الَّذِينَ آمَنُوا صَلُّوا عَلَيْهِ وَسَلِّمُوا تَسْلِيمًـا». اللَّهُمَّ صَـلِّ عَلَىٰ سَـيِّدِنَا وَمَوْلاَنَا مُحَمَّدٍ بِعَدَدِ مَنْ صَلَّىٰ وَصَامَ. اللَّهُمَّ صَلِّ عَلَىٰ سَيِّدِنَا وَمَوْلاَنَا مُحَمَّدٍ بِعَدَدِ مَنْ قَعَدَ وَقَـامَ. اللَّهُمَّ صَلِّ عَلَىٰ جَمِيعِ الأَنْبِيَاءِ وَالـمُرْسَلِينَ، وَعَلَىٰ سَائِرِ الصَّحَابَةِ وَالتَّابِعِيْنَ، وَعَلَىٰ عِبَادِكَ الصَّالِحِينَ. اللَّهُمَّ أَيِّدِ الإِسْلاَمَ وَالـمُسْلِمِينَ. اللَّهُمَّ انْصُرْ مَنْ نَصَرَ دِينَ مُحَمَّدٍ صَلَّى اللهُ عَلَيْهِ وَسَلَّمَ وَاجْعَلْنَا مِنْهُمْ، وَاخْذُلْ مَنْ خَذَلَ دِينَ مُحَمَّدٍ صَلَّى اللهُ عَلَيْهِ وَسَلَّمَ وَلاَتَجْعَلْنَا مِنْهُمْ. اللَّهُمَّ أَرِنَا الْحَقَّ حَقًّا وَارْزُقْنَا اتِّبَاعَهُ، وَأَرِنَا البَاطِلَ بَاطِلاً وَارْزُقْنَا اجْتِنَابَهُ. اللَّهُمَّ ثَبِّتْنَا عَلَىٰ الإِسْلاَمِ. اللَّهُمَّ نَوِّرْ قُلُوبَنَا بِنُـورِ الإِيـمَـانِ. اللَّهُمَّ اغْفِرْ لِلْمُؤْمِنِيْنَ وَالـمُؤْمِنَاتِ، الأَحْيَاءِ مِنْهُمْ وَالأَمْوَاتِ.

عِبَادَ اللهِ، رَحِمَكُمُ اللهُ، إِنَّ اللهَ يَأْمُرُ بِالعَدْلِ وَالإِحْسَانِ وَإِيتَاءِ ذِي القُرْبَى وَيَنْهَى عَنِ الفَحْشَاءِ وَالـمُنْكَرِ وَالبَغْيِ، يَعِظُكُمْ لَعَلَّكُم تَذَكَّرُونَ. اُذْكُرُوا اللهَ

يَذْكُرْكُمْ، وَادْعُوهُ يَسْتَجِبْ لَكُمْ، وَلَذِكْرُ اللهِ تَعَالَىٰ أَعْلَىٰ وَأَوْلَىٰ وَأَعَزُّ وَأَجَلُّ وَأَتَمُّ وَأَهَمُّ وَأَكْبَرُ.

Praise be to Allah the Cherisher and Sustainer of the Worlds. Peace, blessings and salutations be upon His Trustworthy Messenger. O assembly of Muslims! I seek refuge with Allah from the accursed Satan. I begin in the name of Allah, the Merciful, the Beneficent. *Allāh Taʿālā* has said in His Exalted Book: "Allah and His Angels send blessings on the Prophet: O you who believe send your blessings on him and salute him with respect." O Allah! Bless Our Master and Our Leader Prophet Muḥammad equal in number to those who pray and fast. O Allah! Bless Our Master and Our Leader Prophet Muḥammad equal in number to those who sit and stand. O Allah! Bless all Prophets and Messengers and bless all Companions and their successors and bless all Your pious servants. O Allah! Help those who help Islam and make us amongst them and forsake those who fail to help Islam and do not make us amongst them. O Allah! Show us the Truth as Truth and make us obey it and show us the Falsehood as Falsehood and save us from it. O Allah! Keep us steadfast in Islam. O Allah! Brighten our hearts with the light of *īmān*. O Allah! Forgive all believing men and women whether alive or dead.

Servants of Allah! May Allah have His Mercy on you. Allah commands justice, the doing of good, and liberality to kith and kin, and He forbids all shameful deeds, and injustice and rebellion: He instructs you that you may receive admonition. Remember Allah and He will remember you and pray to Him and He will respond. Remembrance of *Allāh Taʿālā* is the highest, the foremost, the most honourable, the everlasting, the most important and the greatest (act).

CPSIA information can be obtained
at www.ICGtesting.com
Printed in the USA
LVHW090734131118
596892LV00006B/8/P

9 780860 375760